ALASKA

THE CRUISE-LOVER'S GUIDE

GREYSTONE BOOKS
Douglas & McIntyre Publishing Group
Vancouver/Toronto

ALASKA NORTHWEST BOOKS™
Anchorage · Portland

To our sisters, Karen, Lorraine, Eleanor, and Donna.

Greystone Books | A division of Douglas & McIntyre Ltd. | 2323 Quebec Street, Suite 201 Vancouver, British Columbia | Canada v5T 4S7 | www.greystonebooks.com

National Library of Canada Cataloguing in Publication Data

Grescoe, Paul, 1939–
  Alaska
  Includes bibliographical references and index.
  ISBN 1–55054–911–1
  1. Cruise Ships—Alaska—Guidebooks.   2. Cruise Ships—Inside Passage—Guidebooks.
3. Alaska—Guidebooks   4. Inside Passage—Guidebooks.   I. Grescoe, Audrey.   II. Title.
F902.3.G74 2002   917.9804'52   C2002–910297–9

Library of Congress Cataloging-in-Publication Data

Grescoe Paul, 1939-
  Alaska : the cruise lover's guide / Paul and Audrey Grescoe.—3rd ed.
    p. cm.
  Includes bibliographical references (p.) and index.
  ISBN 0-88240-567-5
  1. Alaska—Guidebooks.   2. Northwest Coast of North America—Guidebooks.   3. Cruise ships—
  Alaska—Guidebooks.   4. Cruise ships—Northwest Coast of North America—Guidebooks.
  I. Grescoe, Audrey.   II. Title.
    F902.3 .G74 2002   917.9804'52—dc21   2002018679

Originated by Greystone Books and published simultaneously in the United States by Alaska Northwest Books™ | An imprint of Graphic Arts Center Publishing Company P.O. Box 10306 | Portland, Oregon 97296-0306 | 503-226-2402 | www.gacpc.com

PERMISSIONS

The quote on page 95 is from *A Guide to the Birds of Alaska* (1991) by Robert H. Armstrong. Reprinted with permission of Alaska Northwest Books, Seattle.
  The quotes on pages 120 and 123 are from *Bashful No Longer: An Alaskan Eskimo Ethnohistory,* 1778–1988 by Wendell H. Oswalt. © 1990 by the University of Oklahoma Press. Reprinted with permission.
  The quote on page 148 is © 1989 by Art Davidson, from *Alakshak: The Great Country* by Art Wolfe and Art Davidson. Reprinted with permission of Sierra Club Books.
  The quote on page 178 is © 1988 by Bridget A. Smith, from the book *Death of an Alaskan Princess* by Bridget A. Smith. Reprinted with permission from St. Martin's Press, Inc.
  The section on Yukon, Canada, contains material by Paul Grescoe adapted from Heritage of Canada, © 1978, 1984 Reader's Digest Association (Canada) Ltd., Montreal. Adapted with permission.

Copyediting by Maja Grip
Cover design by Peter Cocking
Cover photo: RO-MA Stock/Máxx Images
Text design by Sigrid Albert
Maps by Dennis & Struthers Visual Communications Inc.
Printed and bound in Hong Kong by C&C Offset Ltd.
Printed on acid-free paper ∞

We gratefully acknowledge the financial support of the Canada Council for the Arts, the British Columbia Ministry of Tourism, Small Business and Culture, and the Government of Canada through the Book Publishing Industry Development Program (BPIDP) for our publishing activities.

ACKNOWLEDGEMENTS

We would like to thank the management and staff of the many cruise lines that have assisted us over the years. Our thanks as well to Jack Walsh of Alaska Airlines, who so generously arranged our air travel from Alaska. In a project like this, there are so many people who participate in so many ways. Among them: Dennis C. Trabant of the U.S. Geological Survey, Alaska; Taras Grescoe, who researched and wrote the section Stalking the Land as well as generally researching for the entire book; Danny Lehman, whose in-the-field knowledge enhanced the section on photography; Roy Corral, former photo editor of *Alaska*, for his kind help in locating photographers; R. Roy Forster, former curator of the VanDusen Botanical Garden in Vancouver, for identifying Alaska wildflowers; Dr. Richard Morlan of the Museum of Civilization, Hull, Quebec; Robert Sheldon of Friends Church in Kotzebue; Nelson Angapak of the Alaska Federation of Natives; the people of the U.S. Fish and Wildlife Service in Anchorage and the Enforcement Division, Pacific and Yukon Region, of the Canadian Wildlife Service; Fred and Sandra Tremblay for their contributions to the Alaska Highway section; Joyce Tiplady for her treasure trove of Alaskana; and Bob and Rennie Ducich for their personal knowledge of Alaska (and countless cappuccinos). Most of all, our gratitude to the people of Alaska who have always been unfailingly helpful as we ask even the most basic questions about the Great Land they love so deeply.

Contents

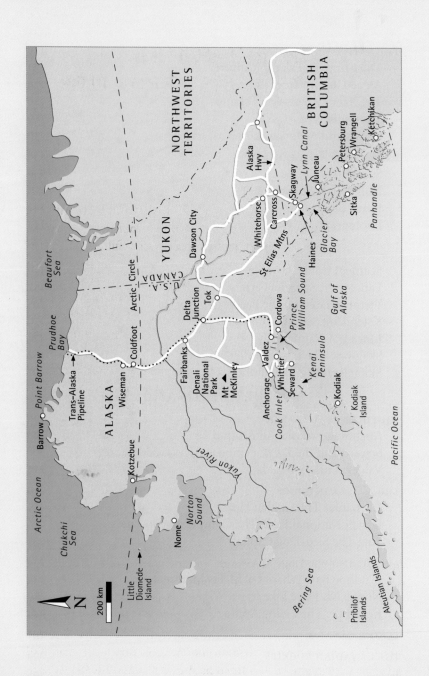

INTRODUCTION:
THE LAST, VAST FRONTIER

The small open skiff had taken a half-dozen of us forty minutes out of Ketchikan that early September morning before we dropped our fishing lines 500 feet into a mercifully calm north Pacific. The pewter-clouded port was the first stop in southeastern Alaska on our northbound cruise from Vancouver aboard an elegant cruise ship. And this guided fishing and wilderness trek was among the first of scores of adventurous shore excursions the ship's passengers could experience on land, lake, and sea and in the air aboard helicopters and floatplanes.

Along the way to our angling ground, we'd paused for a photo op of totem poles in a Tlingit village, lingered to watch a pod of white-sided dolphins breaching like synchronized swimmers, and had close encounters with a lone Dall's porpoise and a scattering of marbled murrelets, a threatened species of seabird anywhere but here in Alaska. Now our guide and helmsman, A.J. Slagle, Jr., hawk-nosed, red-bearded, and grizzled beyond his three decades, was warning us in a gravelly voice, "We mainly target rockfish, but let me land them—they've got venomous spines on them. They're sharp and unpleasant."

Within minutes, Doug, a veteran angler from the Gulf of Mexico, landed the first beautifully ugly rockfish with an artificial lure. Paul, the rookie from British Columbia, hooked the next two. Then twenty minutes into it, A.J. quietly told all of us but Ken, the firefighter from Chicago, to reel in our lines. "That's a halibut," our skipper said, watching Ken's sharply bent rod. "If he's really big, one of us is going to have to swim home." It took Ken more than half an hour to bring in a determined halibut that was quite big enough at 70 pounds. The rest of us, including two fly-fisherwomen, were happy with our haul of four silver-gray, two rosethorn, and one each of dusky, quillback, and yellowtail rockfish.

Not that this was the end of the adventure. Stopping at Lucky Cove, our guide packed his old rifle along as we walked up a creek to observe bald eagles lunching on spawning salmon. And there, a city block away, a 200-pound black bear was slapping the red-skinned fish into its mouth. We edged gingerly away from the pre-occupied young creature and, hungry now ourselves, left for a little island where A.J. skinned and cleaned our catch and cooked it over an open fire. He served us halibut steaks and all the rock-fish—enhanced with caramelized shallots and lemon thyme and accompanied by terrific potato salad and honey-sweet cornbread prepared by his wife, a professional chef.

Feasting outdoors on the seafood we'd just caught, having witnessed a profusion of wildlife, helped crystallize the Alaska cruise experience for us. We were suddenly aware that we were blissfully perched in the evergreen wilderness of the 17-million-acre Tongass National Forest. America's largest federal forestland, larger than

Luxury cruising, 1895 style: tourists from the *City of Topeka* ashore at Glacier Bay.

West Virginia, Tongass encompasses most of the southeastern Alaska Panhandle.

There was another defining moment, again well away from our cruise ship. A group of us had slipped into slickers and tall rubber-soled boots and clambered into a helicopter at the Juneau airport. The chopper took off across the city and climbed over a lake and mountains before landing on the moonscape of Mendenhall Glacier, with its monolithic columns forming a cliff and its frigid meltwater whirlpooling down deep crevasses. Here at its terminus the glacier is more than 200 feet thick, and though we were already a mile onto its expanse, Mendenhall wound sinuously up the Coast Mountains for another 11 miles. Touching down at an altitude of 1,600 feet, we stepped off onto an eerie surface. Some of the glacial ice looked like smooth Italian marble, some of it was a series of jagged spires streaked with blue. Above us loomed Suicide Falls, where ice avalanched down a few times a day. Yet, alien as the environment was, we realized the face of the glacier was only a brief bus ride away from the busy downtown of the Alaska capital.

Most glaciers in Alaska are much less approachable by land and are best beheld from the water. Which is how we came to experience yet another moment of revelation. From the Russian-influenced town of Sitka, we cruised to Yakutat Bay along one of the most dramatic approaches to any Alaska glacier. The mountains flanking the entrance were furred with green but those in the background were frosted with snow and ice. Mount Logan, Canada's tallest peak, soared off the port side. A black bear was wandering the shore to starboard. Small bergs of pale blue and black ice were now pocking the lead-gray water. At eight in the morning, as the sun pierced the clouds, our ship advanced slowly into Disenchantment Bay to reveal the grandeur of Hubbard, that old mother of an ice flow, at 76 miles the state's longest valley glacier and North America's second-largest glacier in overall size. Suddenly a limousine-sized chunk of ice sheared off Hubbard's six-mile-wide face and plopped

**A field of buttercups borders the stunning
sea- and mountainscape of Sitka's harbor. ▸**

into the bay with a sound that Native people described as white thunder. We had our own word for Nature's noisy, splashy creation of instant icebergs: astounding.

Alaska is abrim with such moments, and today's cruise-ship passengers can savor them firsthand, up close, both onboard and off the luxurious vessels that have opened up the vast wilds to everyone. The 49th state offers some of the world's most sublime adventure holidays to satisfy virtually any taste, any level of fitness, any age. Henry Gannett, who sailed with the 1899 Harriman Expedition, which named many of the glaciers of Prince William Sound, had his tongue slightly in cheek when he wrote: "There is one word of advice and caution to be given those intending to visit Alaska for pleasure, or for sight-seeing. If you are old, go by all means, but if you are young, wait. The scenery of Alaska is much grander than anything else of its kind in the world, and it is not well to dull one's capacity for enjoyment by seeing the finest first."

The fact is, there is *so much* scenery and there are so few people. Alaska is 99 percent uninhabited; the population is only about 630,000, with more than 40 percent of residents living in the Anchorage area. At 571,951 square miles, this is the largest state in the Union—one-fifth the size of the entire Lower 48. It spreads across two time zones, Alaska and Hawaii-Aleutian. If superimposed on a map of the contiguous states, it would cover an area from California to Georgia and from Mexico to Canada. Or, to put it another way, it's almost double the size of California, Oregon, and Washington combined. Alaska is America's northernmost, westernmost, and—because the Aleutian chain extends into the eastern hemisphere—easternmost state.

More than 20,000 square miles of its area is water. Its convoluted coast, 6,640 miles measured point to point, has 47,300 miles of tidal shoreline, more than all the other continental states combined. The state has more than three million lakes of 20 acres or larger and thirty-nine mountain ranges, including seventeen of America's highest twenty peaks. Its landforms range from 25,000 feet below sea level in the Pacific Ocean's Aleutian Trench to the 20,306-foot summit of Mount McKinley.

The list of Alaska natural splendors seems endless. All the thousand or so glaciers in the western United States would not equal the area of one of Alaska's big valley glacier systems. One of its glaciers, Malaspina, is larger than Rhode Island. The largest federal park in the U.S. is Wrangell–Saint Elias National Park and Preserve, bordering on Canada's Yukon: its 8.1 million acres and 4.1-million-acre preserve make it four times the size of Yellowstone.

There is so much more, including wildlife roaming freely in staggering numbers. The state has 600,000 barren ground caribou, for instance, and one estimate suggested an average of more than seventy collisions a year between moose and car in Anchorage alone. Animals that are rare or nonexistent down south flourish here, among them grizzlies, polar bears, and the primitive-looking musk oxen. The landscapes they live on differ dramatically, from the icy desert of the Arctic tundra to the rich green rain forests of Southeast— which is how Alaskans refer to the panhandle-like mainland and hundreds of islands that parallel the British Columbia coastline for about 500 miles between Dixon Entrance in the south and Skagway in the north.

The land is considered a creature of plate tectonics, a theory that says the planet's crust "floats" on a mobile upper layer of the mantle that rings Earth's molten outer core. When magma oozes out from enormous fissures in the ocean basins, the ruptured pieces of the crust, called plates, drift and slowly reassemble themselves. The plates beneath the northeastern Pacific Ocean collided with those of continental North America millions of years ago, moving north along such fault lines in the Earth as the San Andreas. Simultaneously, land in the far north of North America drifted westward into the Pacific and perhaps eighty million years ago created a bridge between North America and Asia—the origin of northern Alaska and northeastern Siberia. When the plate sliding to the north along the Pacific struck this land bridge, it squeezed under the continental plate, unleashing tremendous geologic forces—earthquakes, volcanoes—that continue to this day. One effect of this process, called subduction, may have been the relatively sudden uprising of the central Alaska Range, including mighty Mount McKinley.

The major mountain ranges help define Alaska while influencing its weather systems. (*See* And Now, the Weather, *page 71.*) The Coast Range in the lush Southeast winds northwest toward Anchorage. The Alaska Range stretches westward for 600 miles to the Alaska Peninsula, creating a rainy and reasonably mild climate, to link with the storm-battered, 1,600-mile-long Aleutian Range, whose forty-seven active volcanoes are part of what is called the Pacific Ring of Fire. The impressive bulk of the Brooks Range, 150 miles wide and 600 long, separates the dry, cold, open Interior from the petroleum-rich, permafrosted North Slope running into the Arctic Ocean.

A land as diverse and theatrical as Alaska is bound to produce a people just as distinctive. As the stories in this book reveal, the state has had (and continues to have) larger-than-life good guys and bad. Like Jimmy Doolittle, a newspaper delivery boy in Nome who grew up to lead Doolittle's Raiders, the U.S. Army pilots who launched their bomb-laden B-25s off navy carriers to pound Japan and change the course of World War II. Or Linious (Mac) McGee of Indiana, who stowed away on a steamship to Alaska and found work as a dishwasher, truck driver, miner, and eventually fur buyer, an occupation that led him and a partner to acquire a couple of three-seat Stinson aircraft in the early 1930s. McGee soon decided to take paying passengers along on his business trips. McGee Airways survived numerous crashes and forced landings as its fleet of seven black-and-white Stinsons battled the state's harsh terrain and weather. And it was the genesis of what in 1944, under subsequent owners, became Alaska Airlines—which six decades later is routinely hailed by travel-magazine readers' polls as America's best domestic airline (which cruise passengers rely on when taking one-way sea voyages to and from Anchorage or extending their stay with visits to other parts of the state).

Life on the frontier has always given an idiosyncratic edge to the inhabitants here. Remember that Alaskans as a whole tolerated legalized marijuana for fifteen years, until the nation's most liberal pot law was overturned in 1990. At the same time, the state's gun-control laws have been among the weakest in the U.S. Such social

Eliza, Alaska's Intrepid Tourist

Today, more than a million visitors come to Alaska in a year, helping to make the tourist industry the second-largest primary employer. But the state's most ardent tourist may well have been one of its first.

Writer Eliza Ruhamah Scidmore was a passenger on the Pacific Coast Steamship Company vessel *Idaho* on its maiden glacier-seeking voyage in July 1883. Only four years earlier, naturalist John Muir found and explored a bay of glaciers that Native seal hunters had described to him. Capt. James Carroll, following Muir's verbal instructions, eased the *Idaho* up the eastern shores of this bay looking for a large inlet. There, Muir assured him, he could safely anchor and see bergs breaking away from one of the largest glaciers. So it was, writes Scidmore, that Alaska's first cruise-ship passengers sailed into an unnamed and uncharted inlet and viewed for the first time the massive glacier at its head.

The next year, 1,650 people cruised the Inside Passage and Glacier Bay. Within a few years, Muir Glacier was world-famous and by 1890, the number of visitors had reached 25,000. Eliza was frequently among them. She spent four summers in Alaska, once camping for several weeks in a cabin at the side of Muir Glacier.

In a *National Geographic* article, she described 19th-century cruising in the bay. Because of the floating ice, boats had to stop, back up, and proceed at half speed. There was the uncomfortable sound of paddle wheels crunching the ice. In a more positive vein, in her 1896 *Appleton's Guide to Alaska*, she writes that the shipboard accommodations of the two major lines "are first class . . . catering to an expensive style of pleasure travel, offering most luxuries and comforts."

Tourists of the 1880s and 1890s experienced Glacier Bay's marvels firsthand and at some risk. Steamers anchored about a quarter-mile below the east end of Muir Glacier and remained for six to eight hours. Once ashore, passengers followed a trail and boardwalk onto the surface of the ice, which they freely explored with the help of rented alpenstocks. Scidmore tells her readers of an easy walk up the east beach to the base of the ice cliffs, but warns of the danger of being swept away at high tide when falling bergs could send great waves across the inlet.

anomalies reflect the individuality of the people. Today's crop of characters includes men like our fishing guide in Ketchikan, A.J. Slagle, Jr., who was born in Juneau and has spent most of his young life hunting, fishing, trapping, logging, and big-game guiding in Southeast. As co-owner of Baranof Skiff Excursions, he told us, "I wanted to show this country the way I've seen it, show folks what it's like to play here. The wilderness has been pretty good to me." The women here can be just as singular. Consider Illinois native Senator Drue Pearce, whom the *Alaskan Journal of Commerce* ranked as one of the Top 25 Most Powerful Alaskans after she shaped legislation to widen the oil-spill safety response while continuing to work on behalf of abused women. Before going into politics, the former bank manager in the far-north community of Kotzebue earned her master's degree in public administration at Harvard.

The governor who took the state into the twenty-first century had his own intriguing mix of ivory-tower education and ground-level experience. Tony Knowles left Tulsa, Oklahoma, to study economics at Yale and serve with the army in Vietnam. Moving to Alaska, he toiled as a roughneck on the North Slope drilling rigs before opening a couple of struggling burger joints and then a successful restaurant in Anchorage. As the city's two-term mayor in the 1980s, he oversaw the building of major public projects such as the Alaska Center for the Performing Arts and the Egan Civic & Convention Center. As governor, Knowles soon built his reputation on encouraging job creation, which is why he became a booster of the controversial concept of drilling in the Arctic National Wildlife Refuge.

One of his predecessors as governor had an even more checkered history. Jay Hammond was a bearded homesteader, bush pilot, commercial fisherman, guide, and a self-reliant trapper who lived in a log cabin he built himself. He governed the state from 1974 to 1982. One of his accomplishments was the creation of the Alaska Permanent Fund, which has since given residents annual dividend checks from the state's savings-account earnings. Early in the new century, each eligible resident was receiving about $1,850 from a fund dependent on petroleum revenues, the source of 85 percent of the state income. At this writing, Alaska was not only giving its taxpayers that yearly bonus but also still refusing to levy any state income tax or sales tax.

Alaskans are optimists, as any breed of people must be to settle in a land that for so long was so isolated and could impose such stern living conditions. All that has changed, of course, with modern transportation, communications, and comforts. Today's ease of travel has helped make tourism the state's primary employer, vying with fishing as the second-largest industry, behind petroleum, and generating more than $1 billion a year in revenue. The total of annual visitors is almost double the number of residents.

And the most convenient, dramatic—and popular—way to visit Alaska is by cruise vessel. Which is why we have written this book. Aimed at a specialized audience, *Alaska: The Cruise-Lover's Guide* combines all the functions of pre-trip planner, onboard and land-tour guidebook, and post-trip souvenir for the Alaska cruise-ship passenger. Because cruise passengers by definition have all their food and lodging needs accommodated automatically, we haven't included distracting, ever-changing listings of restaurants and hotels. This has left us more room to describe the glories of Alaska in full detail, focusing on those destinations where cruise tours are most likely to take you. It's also one of the few guides to the state that deals almost entirely with spring, summer, and autumn—making mention of its harsh winter features only when they are relevant and interesting.

Luxury vessels have been cruising regularly to Alaska since 1884, following on the heels of American naturalist and travel writer John Muir, whose summing-up of the Inside Passage voyage to Skagway still stands as an accurate description of the Alaska cruise experience today: "No other excursion that I know of can be made into any of the wild portions of America where so much fine and grand and novel scenery is brought to view at so cheap and easy a price."

Another hearing today before the Com.
on Territories on the Alaska bill to repeal
that clause in the Organic Act giving
the Legislature power to lay additional
license tax — Senators trying to make the
hearing general, exactly got in my ...

March 30th 1916.
The High Commissioner of the ...
of the ... of the Currency of the ...
from Canada.
Introduced the first Act
Mcleod Bill today.
H.R. 13951

A LITTLE ALASKA HISTORY

The events that formed Alaska as a modern political and economic entity took place during the lifetime of most of today's cruise-ship passengers. We remember when Alaska joined the United States of America, when the Alcan Highway was built, when oil was discovered in the north. Fundamental steps accomplished long ago by other states, such as the disposition of land, continue to be taken in Alaska. The 49th state of the Union is creating itself before our very eyes.

The First People

Over the last couple of decades, crossing the Bering Strait has become something of a fad. People have walked, swum, kayaked, dog-sledded, and even Sea-Dooed across it. In 1987, an English-woman swam the 56 miles of icy water that separate Asia and North America. In 1992, a Russian crew sailed from Cape Dezhneva, the easternmost point of Siberia, in a replica of the small wooden schooners Russian fur hunters sailed to North America. And in 1998, a Russian father and son skied 150 miles from Siberia to Cape Thompson, Alaska, over the frozen Chukchi Sea, falling through the ice and warding off polar bears as they completed the first such crossing of the strait ever recorded.

Another intriguing adventure occurred five years earlier, when members of an Alaska church expedition were airlifted from the port of Wales to Little Diomede Island, an American possession in

Pages from the diary of James Wickersham—judge, politician, mountaineer—bring Alaska's history to life.

the middle of the strait. They snowmobiled across 3 miles of ice to Russian-owned Big Diomede Island and then were flown to Chukchi Peninsula in Siberia, where they distributed gifts and clothing to Eskimos in several villages. In Russia, the Alaska missionaries met a group of Japanese adventurers who were planning to cross the strait on foot, like the prehistoric people who might have entered North America from Asia in this manner eons ago.

In doing so, the ancient ancestors of the Native peoples of North America would not have got their feet wet when they made the crossing. One prominent theory suggests they followed the animals they hunted onto a dry, broad plain—the Bering land bridge (the other hypothesis is that they could have crossed by boat). The so-called bridge, exposed because ocean water had been absorbed by the growing continental glaciers, was 1,200 miles wide from north to south. It remained passable until 10,000 years ago.

Beringia, as this land mass is known today, has been considered the most likely route prehistoric peoples took to Alaska. Some of them drifted south as the ice sheets melted. Others stayed. The ancestors of the Athabascan Indians spread into the Interior of Alaska and across northwest Canada; the ancestors of the Eskimo-Aleut occupied the coastal regions of Alaska and migrated through the Arctic to Greenland.

When these peoples first arrived is harder to pin down. Archeologists have found artifacts indicating that Eskimo hunters were on St. Lawrence Island in the Bering Sea 40,000 years ago. A Canadian archeologist has dated a bone-flake tool from a cave above the Blue Fish River in the Canadian Yukon at 25,000 years. In a cave on Prince of Wales Island in the Alaska Panhandle, American scientists have found human bones that are between 9,200 and 9,800 years old, the oldest ever discovered in Alaska or Canada. And in 1993, an American archeologist announced that while surveying on the northern slopes of Alaska's Brooks Range south of Point Barrow, he found paleo-Indian stone lance points that have been precisely carbon dated at 11,700 years. The imagination is stirred by this discovery—that in a distant time hunters stood on a 200-foot-high mesa surveying the Alaska plains for herds of bison and mammoth, and that their finely carved tools have endured many thousands of years longer than our own cultures.

The Russians Arrive

Traditional history awards the first Alaska sighting in historic times to Vitus Bering, the persevering Dane who undertook two monumental expeditions on behalf of Russia. Instructed by Peter the Great to locate the place where Russia joins North America, Bering set off from St. Petersburg in 1725, traveling arduously overland for three years before reaching the Pacific. In the summer of 1728, having built a small boat he named *Saint Gabriel*, he sailed north, passing through the strait that would bear his name. Had it been a clear day, he might have seen Alaska. As it was, he continued north until he was certain the continents were separate. Sailing east the following spring, he again failed to find the North American continent when he was blown off course in a gale.

Back in St. Petersburg in 1730, Bering convinced the Admiralty College that North America lay close to Kamchatka and that a second expedition should be financed. In 1733 he was appointed head of an overly ambitious endeavor mandated to explore and chart the Arctic and Siberian coasts, find America and explore its coast to Mexico, establish trade relations with Japan, study natural history and ethnography, build lighthouses, Christianize the Natives of Siberia, and establish a postal system east of the Urals so that he could mail reports every couple of days.

Once again he trekked across the country, this time burdened by tons of equipment and 900 people, including scores of quarrelsome scientists. At last, on June 4, 1741, the sixty-year-old Bering sailed from Avacha Bay. His two ships, which he had had to build, were soon separated. On July 15, Aleksey Chirikov, who was in charge of the *Saint Paul*, sighted what is believed to be Prince of Wales Island (west of Ketchikan). A couple of days later, those aboard the *Saint Peter* saw a vast mountain range extending inland. Georg Wilhelm Steller, the German naturalist who was part of the expedition, reports that in this historical moment of discovery Bering gazed at the land and shrugged his shoulders.

On July 20, Bering anchored off present-day Kayak Island (southeast of Cordova) and bestowed the name Cape St. Elias in honor of the prophet whose day it was. Steller had to plead with his incurious commander to be allowed to go ashore, and in ten hours he accomplished what he could, gathering plant and animal specimens and taking souvenirs from a dugout cellar stocked with arrows, seaweed straps, grass rope, and containers filled with smoked fish, which he said tasted better than the Kamchatkan version.

In quick order, Bering had the ship's casks filled with fresh water and headed home. It looked to Steller as though the sole result of the great expedition would be to carry water from America to Asia, but he was wrong. About 150 miles off the Russian mainland, Bering sought shelter from a storm on an island now named for him. The *Saint Peter* was wrecked, and the scurvy-weakened explorer and several of his crew died. The other men, having survived the winter on the meat of the abundant seals and otters, reached Russia in a makeshift boat bearing an unexpected cargo of furs.

Although official Russia showed no initial interest, individuals were quick to see the potential for profit, particularly in trade with China where one sea-otter fur was worth a Russian clerk's annual income. Within a year, the first merchant had built a *shitik*, a bargelike boat held together with leather thongs, and sent thirty hunters to Bering Island. On their second voyage, these *promyshlenniki* brought back the skins of 1,600 otter, 2,000 fur seal, and 2,000 blue fox, worth 200,000 rubles—a figure equal to the entire cost of the Bering expedition.

These lawless men hunted unhindered and unrestrained for several decades. They worked for shares of a voyage's profits, which in the early years would have made them rich had they not generally spent the winter back in Okhotsk, drinking and gambling and acquiring debts that forced them to hunt again. Unscientific as well as illiterate, they sailed into stormy and unpredictable waters, knowing nothing of marine navigation, a shortcoming shared by their navigators, who relied on acquired knowledge. One of these hapless men has given his name to a group of Alaska islands—the Pribilofs—which he discovered while steering a drunken course. In 1745, the *promyshlenniki* found the outermost of the Aleutian Islands. They enslaved the Aleuts, forcing them to work until they dropped of exhaustion. As they depleted the animal stocks on each island, they moved eastward, within twenty years reaching the Gulf of Alaska.

For thirty years after Bering's discovery, Russians dominated these northern waters. But three European countries had been taking notice. In 1773 and several times thereafter, Spain sent expeditions to Alaska to check on the Russians' activities, possess land, and search for a passage through the continent. Although it had a strong claim to north Pacific territories, Spain withdrew from the region in 1795 when it surrendered a plot of land at Nootka Sound on Vancouver Island to the British. Alaska place-names such as Valdez, Cordova, Revillagigedo, and Malaspina testify to the Spanish presence.

It was the English who were to leave an indelible mark on the north Pacific coast. They, too, believed in a northern passage through the continent and had offered a prize of £10,000 to the person who found it. On his third voyage in 1778, navigator James Cook, sailing north along the North American coast, sighted and named Capes Perpetua and Foulweather in Oregon and Cape Flattery at the entrance to the Strait of Juan de Fuca. After spending a month in Nootka Sound on Vancouver Island, he sailed on through the Gulf of Alaska to Prince William Sound, where he went ashore on Kayak, the same island Bering had first sighted. Here, he left a bottle and two silver tuppenny pieces, evidence of his presence that has never been recovered. After sailing partway up Cook Inlet and concluding that it was a river, he followed the south shore of the Aleutians, passing into the Bering Sea and through Bering Strait. At 70°44' north, he was turned back by ice.

With him on that voyage, and a witness to his death in Hawaii on February 14, 1779, was a young midshipman, George Vancouver. In the summers of 1792, 1793, and 1794 as captain of his own ship, Vancouver completed a meticulous and arduous survey of the north Pacific coast, a survey that laid to rest the pipe dream of an easy passage through the continent, peppered the Canadian and Alaska coasts with English names, and opened the area to commercial ventures. (*See* The Pacific Coast of George Vancouver, *page 51.*)

The Baranov Era

By the 1790s, the cost of outfitting longer and longer voyages was putting many Russian fur merchants out of business. Among the surviving larger companies, one established a permanent Russian settlement in Alaska at Three Saints Bay on Kodiak Island. Grigorii Shelikov, a partner in the venture, lived there from 1784 to 1786 with his wife, Natalya, the first white woman in Alaska. Returning to Russia, Shelikov hired the man who was to dominate Russian America for the next twenty-seven years.

Aleksandr Baranov came to Alaska in 1791 and stayed until 1818, managing the Russian-American Company from the time it was formed in 1798. As the chief employee of the company that by royal charter had a monopoly on Russian trade in North America, Baranov was the virtual governor of Alaska. He disciplined and punished his ruffian laborers but gave them ample reason to party with the aid of a home-brewed fruit and berry beverage. He established trade arrangements with British and American ships, buying their goods and selling his furs through them in China. Reaching far afield in an attempt to obtain secure supplies, he sent agents to King Kamehameha of Hawaii and established a fort in California 60 miles north of San Francisco Bay, which was to grow food for his ill-supplied colony. Fort Ross—from the old name Rossiia or Russia—remained in Russian hands until 1841 when it was bought by a Swiss rancher.

Baranov's dealings with the Natives were contradictory. He learned their languages, made his men treat their Native wives fairly, and took as his own wife the daughter of an Indian chief whom he described as a "Prince of Kenai." Even though he regarded the Aleuts with affection, he forced them to go on long hunting trips.

He feared the Tlingit, who sometimes blocked the fur hunt and who destroyed the settlement of Mikhailovsk (Fort St. Michael), north of Sitka. In retaliation, he waged war on a Tlingit clan, the Kiks.adi, in 1804, pounding their sapling fort with fire from the Russian ship *Neva*. Tlingit history says the battle reached a standoff and that the Russians displayed a white flag. A Kiks.adi woman, who was acting as mediator, told her people that the flag meant they would be wiped out clean as snow. And so they fled. (The site of that battle can be visited in Sitka National Historic Park.)

With Baranof Island cleared of Tlingit, Baranov began to build New Archangel on the site of present-day Sitka. When it was finished, the settlement had solid fortifications with sixty guns, streets with wooden sidewalks, cabins with flower gardens, a shipyard managed by an American named Lincoln, an orchestra, and on a prominent height a two-story wooden *kremlin*, or citadel. "Baranov's Castle" was both residence and administrative center. Here Baranov maintained a 1,200-book library, hung with paintings, and a banquet hall where amazed travelers, whose ships had been welcomed in the harbor with gun salutes, attended brilliant balls.

Baranov had agreed to come to Alaska for only five years and frequently asked to be relieved of his duties. Two of the men who were to replace him died on the journey out. Finally, after surviving an assassination attempt and periods of drunken despair, the seventy-two-year-old ruler of Russian America was retired. He died in the Dutch East Indies in 1819 without seeing Russia again.

The Sale

Under its second and third charters, the Russian-American Company was governed by naval officers who were good at creating a bureaucracy but not as skilled at business as the encroaching Americans and British. They began their rule hampered by a czarist decree that kept foreign ships from coming within 100 miles of the Russian coast in America. Intended to curtail foreign trading in Alaska, the ukase starved the colony of provisions. Clearly unable to maintain

this isolationist stance, Russia signed treaties with the United States and Britain that reopened trade and defined the Russian territory. In 1824, an agreement with the U.S. set 54°40′ as the southern Russian boundary. The next year, Britain and Russia signed the treaty that would later define the border between the U.S. and Canada.

Although official relations between Russia and the United States were extremely friendly, in Alaska itself the two nations were in conflict. In the mid-1850s, the Russian-American Company continued to ban foreigners from Alaska ports, an unenforceable law that American ships challenged by smuggling guns and liquor to trade for Native furs. The Russian czar's advisors wanted to sell the territory for a number of reasons. It would end the threat to the two countries' relations posed by these trade conflicts. It would avert a takeover of the territory by the United States, which seemed the likely consequence of American expansionism. And it would free Russia to deal with its Crimean War debts, its internal disorder, and its newly acquired territory in the Amur Valley in Siberia. The U.S. was eager to forestall a British takeover and to acquire a huge territory that Smithsonian scientists said held great natural resources.

The sale was negotiated in March 1867 by U.S. Secretary of State William H. Seward, an ardent proponent of Manifest Destiny, and the Russian ambassador Edouard de Stoeckel, who had helped convince the czar to sell. Seward offered $5 million, but Stoeckel got the price up to $7.2 million. Although some newspapers blew frigid wind on the deal—coining labels such as Seward's Icebox and Icebergia or Seward's Folly—most public comment approved the acquisition. The Senate ratified the treaty in 1867, but Seward had to entice the House of Representatives to agree to pay the bill, which was done in July 1868.

The Russians handed over their well-organized territory to the American army on October 18, 1867, in a ceremony on the windy knoll in front of Baranov's Castle in New Archangel. With poignant stubbornness, the Russian flag entangled itself in its ropes and had

Sitka's New Archangel Dancers are a legacy of Alaska's Russian past.

The Russian Orthodox Bishop's house in Sitka: Father Ivan
Veniaminov ministered to Natives during his 16 years there.

to be cut down—causing Princess Maksutova, the wife of the chief
manager of the Russian-American Company, to faint.

The event presaged seventeen years of military misrule and
neglect that drove away the Russian families, who had been invited
to remain. American settlers and speculators, who had hurried
north, departed as quickly, discouraged by their inability to obtain
title to land and by the rowdiness of the soldiers. These men con-
tributed to the lawlessness of the period by teaching Hoochinoo
Indians to distill a mind-blowing liquor, the kind we continue to
call *hooch*.

The U.S. Army ruled for a decade. When it left in 1877, the pretty
little town of New Archangel—with its teahouses, theater, public
library, two scientific institutes, and hospitals—had become Sitka, a
ghost town inhabited by only twenty families and stripped of public services. For the next two years, the law was a customs collector
with a few deputies, who were unable to patrol hundreds of miles
of coast. They watched helplessly as smugglers' boats brought in
liquor, guns, and opium. In 1879, as violence between whites and

Natives increased, Sitkans petitioned the British navy in Victoria, British Columbia: "We, the citizens of Sitka, Alaska, are now threatened with Massacre by Indians of this place." With the approval of Washington, Britain's Royal Navy sent a ship, and the predicted "entire demolition" of Sitka was averted. The U.S. navy took over then, ruling with only slightly more approbation than the army.

Years after the sale, Russian influence continued among those Natives who had been converted to the Orthodox faith. Early Russian priests had been chided for their neglect of missionary work, but those who came later Christianized the Natives and tried to improve their lives. One—Father Ivan Veniaminov—learned the Fox Aleut dialect, devised an alphabet, wrote an Aleut grammar, and translated religious books. In his Sitka seminar, he trained Natives for the priesthood. Back in Russia, he raised more money to support schools in Alaska than came from the American government.

Alaska was largely unexplored territory when it became an American possession. Private enterprise had instigated some exploration before the U.S. purchase: Western Union attempted and failed to connect America and Russia by telegraph cable in 1865–66, but the expedition mapped the entire 2,000 miles of the Yukon River and brought William Healy Dall to Alaska, where he stayed, chief among its naturalists. In the last decades of the nineteenth century, Alaska was explored largely by federal government agencies—the army, the navy, the Revenue Marine (predecessor of the Coast Guard), and, in the final years, the United States Geological Survey. In the 1880s, the army sent expeditions to the Yukon and Copper Rivers. The most successful was Lt. Henry Trueman Allen's remarkable exploration of the Copper, Chitina, Tanana, and Koyukon Rivers. In five months in 1885, this twenty-six-year-old accurately mapped 1,500 square miles of wilderness between the sixty-first parallel and the Arctic Circle. At the same time, the navy and Revenue Marine competed in exploring rivers in the northwest, following the Kobuk from its mouth near Kotzebue, linking with the Colville, and ultimately reaching the Arctic Ocean.

The 1880 census found 430 white men in Alaska. Some fished for salmon, the first canneries having been built in 1878. Some worked for the Alaska Commercial Company (owned by a San Franciscan), which had a monopoly on the seal hunt in the Pribilof Islands and extended its influence to the Aleutians, Kodiak Island, and the Yukon River valley. And some were miners drawn by discoveries of gold as early as 1869. Then in 1880, two prospectors found placer gold in a stream near Juneau. This was followed by the discovery of a lode on Douglas Island, across the Gastineau Channel from Juneau, and the opening of the Treadwell Mine, which attracted hundreds of newcomers who found employment as shift workers.

This growing white population created a demand for self-government. In 1881, Juneau miners sent a representative to lobby in Washington; although there was opposition to territorial government, Congress agreed to end military rule and patched together the Organic Act of 1884, which made Alaska a district operating under the legal code of Oregon. The advance was minimal: Alaskans were denied a legislature, were governed by appointed officials, and still could not own land. In 1890, a Juneau representative in Washington demonstrated Alaska disaffection by offering, with predictable futility, to buy the territory back for twice what it had

In April 1917, Juneau's Treadwell Mine was virtually destroyed when seawater swamped it during a cave-in.

cost. In the next ten years, a code of laws was adopted and a court system was set up, each steps toward statehood, but gold played a more significant role at this time in Alaska's development.

The Gold Rushes

In 1896, gold was discovered in Canada's Klondike. Ignoring newspaper warnings about hunger, hardship, and disappointment, 40,000 prospectors rushed there in 1897 and 1898, many of them passing through Skagway or Dyea and dropping money in these lawless boom towns before climbing over the White or Chilkoot Passes into Canada. Finding the best stakes claimed, some of these stampeders returned to Alaska to prospect and joined the rushes that followed strikes in Nome in 1899 and Fairbanks in 1902.

With all this human traffic into its territory, Canada sought control of the heads of some fjords, such as the Lynn Canal where Skagway and Dyea sat. The Canadians cited ambiguities in the 1825 treaty between Russia and Britain that had defined the border the U.S. inherited in 1867. The Alaska-Canada boundary dispute was settled by an American-Canadian-British tribunal, which voted four to two in favor of the American position, the deciding vote being cast by the Briton.

Because the influx of argonauts doubled Alaska's population in ten years, Congress saw the need in the last four years of the century to enact laws dealing with the economy and leading to self-government. The criminal code was altered to suit the state's needs. Settlers were allowed to have title to land, and railway companies could obtain a right-of-way to build. Nome and Fairbanks became the seats of new judicial districts, and the capital was moved from Sitka to Juneau. Towns were allowed to incorporate and elect councils. Business taxes were collected to pay the cost of governing the district, and business-license fees were either turned over to the new towns or used to build roads, pay for education, and care for the insane. By 1906, the district had elected a non-voting delegate to the U.S. House of Representatives.

Alaska for Alaskans

Although Alaskans were infuriated by federal government interference in their affairs—notably the creation of the Tongass and Chugach National Forests in southeastern Alaska, and President Theodore Roosevelt's closing of public lands to coal mining—they were by no means united in their desire for self-government. Conservationists feared the power it would give businessmen, and businessmen, notably the salmon packers, feared higher taxes.

James Wickersham—judge, politician, mountaineer—led the campaign for self-government. He had been appointed U.S. district judge for Alaska in 1900; in 1908, he left the bench and became the unenfranchised delegate to Congress during the presidency of William H. Taft, who thought Alaska should be administered by the Department of War. Coincidentally, Taft lost the next election over an Alaska issue—the Ballinger-Pinchot incident. (Secretary of the Interior Richard Ballinger was accused of having halted an investigation into the legality of some private coal-land claims in Alaska. Gifford Pinchot, chief U.S. forester, led a group of conservationists in demanding an investigation. Ballinger was exonerated, but Taft's support of Ballinger turned the 1912 election against him.)

In this climate, Wickersham succeeded in getting a territorial legislature approved by Congress. The Second Organic Act (1912) made the district of Alaska into a territory with a presidential appointee as governor and a legislature with limited powers. Its acts were subject to Congressional review, and it could not change existing laws on fish and game, which gave outsiders control of Alaska's natural resources. The first act of Alaska legislators was to enfranchise women—six years before the other states did. Another early law allowed wives to dispose of property without their husband's permission.

During World War I, as men entered the military or left to work in southern armaments factories, Alaska's population declined. (By 1930, it had not returned to the 1910 level.) In the 1920s, the economy fed on the territory's natural resources, such as copper, gold, and timber. Salmon fishing was the uncertain mainstay. With the

Alaska's Lively Railroads

They called it "the toughest 110 miles of track in the world," a right-of-way hacked out of a mountainside and laid through gorges on topography that was "too steep for a billy goat and too cold for a polar bear." But by July 1899, the first steam train of the WHITE PASS & YUKON ROUTE—the northernmost line in the western hemisphere, with one of the steepest grades on the continent—chugged into Skagway carrying a payload of half a million dollars in Klondike gold. Railway workers, braving deep snows and up to 60 degrees below Fahrenheit, had dangled by rope from sheer cliffs as they positioned blasting powder to dynamite their path through the Coast Mountains between Skagway and Whitehorse in the gold-rich Yukon Territory. Cruise passengers can take the Scenic Railway of the World to the top of the pass and back, on mountain flanks through a box canyon and a tunnel, past the nearly two dozen glacier-fed cataracts of Bridal Veil Falls, and along the Deadhorse Trail of '98. And those taking land cruises from Whitehorse, Yukon, can get aboard the railway at Fraser, British Columbia, and journey to the historic frontier town of Skagway.

The tale of the WP&Y is typical of Alaska's lively rail history, which cruise-ship passengers and others can revisit in trips through flabbergasting scenery and fascinating heritage sites. The state-owned ALASKA RAILROAD grew out of the financial failure of the Alaska Central Railway, a 70-mile line that a Seattle consortium built to the port of Seward in 1903. It was taken over by the Alaskan Northern Railway Company, which the Alaska Railroad bought in 1915 as it began construction of nearly 500 miles of track from Seward on the Kenai Peninsula, through the new rail town of Anchorage, to Fairbanks. The Loop District through the Kenai Mountains demanded a series of tunnels and cloverleafs over weblike wooden trestles—some of the most complicated engineering in railway history.

Today, the Anchorage–Fairbanks line passes through Denali National Park and Preserve and affords superb views of Mount McKinley and a variety of wildlife. On this route during the summer, major cruise lines offer luxe accommodations on special double-decker domed rail cars pulled by the railway's regular diesel engines.

Anchorage was born in 1915 with
the U.S. government land auction.

U.S. military as a major purchaser during the war, the industry had
expanded but stocks had been depleted. Attempts by the Bureau of
Fisheries to regulate the industry after the war were blocked by the
outside-owned corporations that operated 143 canneries in Alaska.
The many Alaskans who earned their living fishing resented federal
control of their livelihood. Federal government conservationists
prevailed in 1924 with the passing of the White Act, which required
the industry to allow half the fish in most streams to escape.

The widely promoted potential for farming and ranching in
Alaska's many fertile valleys brought only a few farmers to the territory. By 1929, there were about 4,000 acres under cultivation. Part
of President Franklin D. Roosevelt's New Deal was a settlement program for the Matanuska Valley, which installed about 200 farming
families in this beautiful area north of Anchorage. In the end, the
hard work of farming in the valley's unpredictable climate and the
high cost of shipping to an outside market defeated the colonists.

Cattle and sheep ranching also failed, but a reindeer industry, operated by white people and employing Natives, succeeded for a time
and still exists as a cottage industry. The small number of animals
introduced in 1891 increased to 700,000 in forty years. Exports
began in 1915, and in 1930 Seattle suppliers were buying the meat of
30,000 animals a year.

Transportation was the key to the development of Alaska. A road-
building program, begun in 1905, required every man to contribute
two days' labor a year. Nearly 5,000 miles of roads and trails were
built. There were privately owned railways, such as the Copper River
and Northwestern Railroad, and a federal government-financed
railroad from Seward to Fairbanks, finished in 1923. The truly effective means of linking the vast territory came with the arrival of the
airplane in the 1920s. By 1937, Alaska had ninety-seven civilian air-
ports and a regular airmail service, and distant communities could
finally be reached year-round.

World War II

As Europe edged toward war in 1939, Alaska's vulnerability to Japanese attack was apparent. Thousands of troops and construction
workers were brought north. They built bases at Sitka, Fairbanks,
Anchorage, Kodiak, and Unalaska, and in eight remarkable months
in 1942 constructed the 1,422-mile-long Alaska-Canada Military
Highway from Dawson Creek, B.C., to Delta Junction, 98 miles
before Fairbanks. (See The Alcan—or the Canal?—Highway, *page
41*.) In June 1942, the Japanese bombed Dutch Harbor and occupied two of the outer Aleutian islands. A year later, American
troops retook Attu Island—an exercise that cost 6,000 American
and Japanese lives—and reoccupied Kiska, which the Japanese had
evacuated.

The war transformed Alaska. A billion dollars had been spent
on roads, airfields, docks, wharves, and breakwaters. With the rec-
ognition of Alaska's strategic importance in the Cold War, military
spending continued on projects such as the Distant Early Warning

System. To accommodate a growing population, construction in the civilian sector kept pace. Soldiers who had served in Alaska during the war returned to settle, as did professional people. By 1960, the population was triple what it had been at the beginning of the war.

Statehood

With patience and not a little ingenuity, Alaskans worked their way through the long process of achieving statehood. Early ill-fated bills had been presented to the U.S. Congress by James Wickersham in 1916 and by territorial senator Anthony J. Dimond in 1943. Fifty-eight percent of Alaskans voted for statehood in a 1946 referendum, and President Harry S. Truman gave his support in his State of the Union address that year and in a long message to Congress two years later. Nevertheless, a 1950 bill died, after passing in the House and being revised in the Senate.

The statehood movement faced powerful opponents: the Seattle-based fish-canning industry, which was making millions out of Alaska; southern politicians, who feared that an Alaska delegation to Congress would vote for civil-rights legislation; and President Dwight D. Eisenhower, who thought Alaskans would elect Democrats and wanted to protect the small Republican majority in the House. In 1954, a fourteen-member delegation from "Operation Statehood" chartered a plane and flew to Washington where they met with the president and convinced him of their determination.

To further show their readiness to govern themselves, Alaskans chose delegates for a convention, which in seventy-five days in 1955 and 1956 drew up a state constitution. The convention also followed the example of Tennessee in choosing an unofficial congressional delegation—which for the next two years effectively lobbied in Washington. Finally, with Eisenhower's request that Congress admit both Hawaii and Alaska, a bill passed the House in May 1958 and the Senate in June. Alaska formally entered the Union on January 3, 1959.

Oil and Troubled Waters

Two cataclysmic events marked the new state's first decade. On Good Friday, March 27, 1964, the largest earthquake ever recorded in North America hit Southcentral Alaska. Although even the federal government's official figures vary, an estimated nine Alaskans were killed directly by the quake and another 106 by the resulting tidal waves, or tsunamis, which then killed at least another twelve much farther south on the West Coast. The quake devastated Anchorage, Whittier, Valdez, Cordova, Seward, and Kodiak and caused at minimum $311 billion in property damage. (*See* The Bad Friday Quake, *page 201.*)

The second cataclysm was of an entirely different and longer-lasting nature: the discovery of a vast oil deposit at Prudhoe Bay on the Arctic coast by Atlantic Richfield in 1968. The following year, in one dramatic day, the state auctioned leases on 450,000 acres on the North Slope. Suddenly, Alaska had $900 million in the bank and could anticipate annual royalties on an estimated 9.6 billion barrels of oil at Prudhoe Bay. But it soon became apparent that the oil would remain in the north until an economical way could be found to transport it south. Three oil companies formed the Trans-Alaska Pipeline System (TAPS) and began the long process of overcoming objections and obstacles to a pipeline transecting the state. Chief among these obstacles were Native land claims.

Land disputes had been virtually guaranteed by the statehood act, which had given Alaska the right to select 103.3 million acres from vacant, unreserved, and unappropriated lands. At the same time, the act protected the rights or title to lands held by Eskimos, Indians, or Aleuts. As the state Department of Natural Resources made its land choices, the Natives, perceiving the threat to their way of life, protested the selections and filed their own claims. In 1966, the indigenous peoples founded the Alaska Federation of Natives to pursue their collective interests. In 1969, Secretary of the Interior Stewart Udall pressured the federal government to be fair to Natives in addressing their land claims. As Donald Craig Mitchell, the federation's former vice-president and general counsel, writes in *Sold American: The Story of Alaska Natives and their Land*, Udall signed an order that "withdrew 262 million acres of 'unreserved public lands in Alaska' from selection by the state of Alaska, as well as 'all forms of appropriation and disposition under the public land laws' so that the lands would be available 'for the determination and protection of the rights of the native Aleuts, Eskimos, and Indians of Alaska.'"

Realizing that Native claims would block their project, various oil companies lobbied for the Alaska Native Claims Settlement Act (ANCSA), which was passed in 1971. The federation saw the act as a solution as well: it settled Native land issues that had been recognized, yet remained unresolved, in various previous acts. By 1973, the year of the Arab oil embargo, Alyeska Pipeline Service Company (which had originated as TAPS) received permission to build an 800-mile-long pipeline from Prudhoe Bay to Valdez. Opened in 1977, the line zigzags south over three mountain ranges and under hundreds of rivers and streams. Oil first flowed into the line on June 20, 1977, and took thirty-eight days to reach its seaport destination. (*See* Prudhoe Bay, *page 234*.)

While the ANCSA abolished aboriginal rights, it compensated Alaska Natives with $962.5 million and title to one-ninth of the state—44 million acres of land, where they are free to hunt, fish, and trap. Natives living in Alaska were enrolled as stockholders in one of twelve regional corporations and, if they were villagers, in one of 200 village corporations. A thirteenth regional corporation was created for Alaska Natives living outside the state. The corporations received a share of the compensation payment to capitalize business ventures.

The act was an attempt to give Alaska Natives the means and the expertise to survive in the modern world, and to an extent it has done that. Some regional corporations have been successful in market terms; some have chosen to earn less money in order to employ a higher percentage of their shareholders. As they went into the new century, the twelve regional corporations and three of the

Helping celebrate 50 years of the Alaska Highway in 1992: Fred and Sandra Tremblay's 1915 Cadillac.

largest village corporations had assets of $2.8 billion, not including the value of the millions of acres of land they own. (*See* The Native Way, *page 119.*)

The ANCSA contained the source of another battle over land use. The d-2 controversy, as it is known, arose from a paragraph in the act that allowed the Secretary of the Interior to hold up to 80 million acres of federal lands as possible wilderness. Alaskans were infuriated by Washington's interference, but they were also divided among themselves about land use, with environmentalists pitted against developers. The issue was complicated by the ambitions of four federal agencies: the National Park Service, the Fish and Wildlife Service, the Forest Service, and the Bureau of Land Management. The upshot was the Alaska National Interest Lands Conservation Act of 1980, which has been called "the conservation vote of the [20th] century." It increased the national conservation areas by 106 million acres and struck a balance between natural and human use of the land, assuring the preservation of wildlife and wildlands while protecting traditional uses such as subsistence hunting. Today 75 percent of the state's land area of 365 million acres is in 235 federal or state conservation units, which include forests, parks, monuments, preserves, wildlife refuges, and wilderness areas.

In the early years of the new millennium, the wilderness/development debate flared anew as President George W. Bush pushed an energy plan that would open a slice of Alaska's Arctic National Wildlife Refuge to oil and gas exploration. Targeted are 2,000 of the 19 million acres in the refuge that lies between the Yukon border and the Beaufort Sea. At a time when the nation wanted to lessen its dependence on the Middle East—especially given the terrorist attacks on New York and Washington, D.C., of September 11, 2001—the refuge was looking mighty attractive, possibly holding the biggest supply of crude found anywhere in the past three decades. Pitted against the administration were environmentalists who saw possible drilling as the thin edge of a development wedge that would despoil the refuge, home to the 120,000 Porcupine caribou that swarm in from Canada as well as polar and grizzly bears, musk oxen, and millions of migratory birds. The fate

The Alcan—Or the Canal?—Highway

When Fred and Sandra Tremblay of Vancouver, British Columbia, drove the Alaska Highway in 1992, they had a rougher ride than most people do these days. The highway's 50th anniversary was celebrated that year with more than 200 events, including the car rally in which the Tremblays participated. They found the road to be surprisingly smooth, now asphalt-surfaced from Mile 0 in British Columbia through Mile 1,520 at Fairbanks. Their problem was that shock absorbers were not standard equipment on 1915 Cadillacs. By far the oldest entrant in the rally, the sturdy Caddy made the one-way trip in a week at a dignified, if bone-shaking, pace of 45 miles an hour.

The $150-million Alaska-Canada Military Highway has been called the major engineering feat of the twentieth century. In eight months and a dozen days, 11,000 U.S. soldiers and 16,000 U.S. and Canadian civilians punched a 1,422-mile road from Dawson Creek in B.C. to Delta Junction, the official terminus. There the road joined the Richardson Highway for a final 100-mile run to Fairbanks.

President Franklin D. Roosevelt approved construction on February 11, 1942, and Canada acquiesced two days later. Working from the Alaska and Canadian ends, army engineers sought the easiest path through unbroken wilderness and five mountain ranges and over more than a hundred streams. Wherever possible, they detoured around the dreaded muskeg (which accounts for the still meandering route). This boggy material insulates permanently frozen subsoil. To get to a firmer footing, the roadbuilders tried scraping the muskeg off or covering it with gravel. Either way, the permafrost melted, and the roadway became a truck-swallowing canal. The solution was to place logs on the muskeg and build a gravel roadbed over this corduroy surface.

On September 24, the north-going crew met the south-going crew at a place now known as Contact Creek. The road was officially opened on November 20, but needed another 11 months of work to make it passable and to repair the 150 bridges washed out the first spring. In 1947, the road opened to unrestricted travel.

of the refuge promises to be a polarizing issue throughout the first decade of this century.

Whether or not extensive drilling ever happens there, the fortunes of the state's residents will continue to depend primarily upon oil. If the world price drops, so do state revenues, 85 percent of which come from royalties and taxes on North Slope crude. When prices were high, legislators abolished personal income tax. Seeing the state strapped for cash in 1993, a former governor commented, "Eliminating the income tax entirely was probably the dumbest thing we ever did."

Alaskans have attempted to preserve their oil income by establishing a trust fund. The Alaska Permanent Fund, built up from mineral-lease rentals and royalties, had assets of nearly $26 billion in 2001, making it the largest pool of money in the nation. Residents receive an annual remittance from the fund.

Boom or bust has been the story of Alaska's economy ever since the days of the Russian fur hunters. But like them, Alaskans have always believed that the prize was worth the pain, the pay dirt repaid the drudgery. The reality of the 49th state has more than matched its promise.

THE LURE AND LORE
OF THE INSIDE PASSAGE

It is the longest sheltered inland waterway in the world, a thousand miles of protected Pacific Ocean from Puget Sound in Washington state to Skagway in southeastern Alaska. The longest, and one of the most seductive such channels in the magnitude and magnificence of its land- and waterscapes, its 50,000 square miles of mountain, sea, and ice. Carved by glaciers between the Coast Range peaks of mainland British Columbia and the umpteen offshore islands to the west, the Inside Passage is so extraordinary that the usual superlatives sputter out. Even someone as eloquent as the pioneering American naturalist John Muir seemed at a loss for words reporting his trip through the Passage in 1879: "Day after day, we seemed to float in a true fairyland, each succeeding view seeming more and more beautiful…. Never before this had I been embosomed in scenery so hopelessly beyond description."

In the day and a half it takes most large cruise ships to ply this passage serenely northward, through straits and narrows to Ketchikan, you will have been gradually introduced to the grandeur of the Pacific Northwest coast, which reaches its crescendo in Alaska—the inconstant sea in all her humors, the endless armada of uninhabited islets, the rain-forested flanks of sky-poking mountains, the slow-moving fields of ice, and the fretwork of steep-sided fjords indenting the coast (which, if straightened, would stretch about 17,000 miles). You will soon begin to pick out wildlife from this distracting backdrop: posses of sunbathing sea lions; pods of whales, humpbacks breaching and killer whales hunting; and loons and herons and a lone bald eagle circling the salmon'd sea. Beyond Vancouver, the signs of human life will be scant: in only a few spots along the Passage do roads link with the rest of civilization. You'll spot some fishing and logging towns, a few isolated Native hamlets and abandoned fish camps, unmanned lighthouses, and the broken bones of long-ago boats.

There will be the occasional lonely vessels threading through what is really not one marine highway but an unknowable labyrinth of large and small channels. Most frequently you'll see fish boats seeking crab, herring, halibut, cod, sole, red snapper, and five species of salmon. Crab boats of about 120 feet set their traps for Dungeness and Alaska kings. Halibut schooners two-thirds that size pay out miles of lines studded with hooks. Forty- and 50-foot seiners spread their saucer-shaped nets to enclose a school of salmon like a massive purse. Smaller trollers long-line like the halibut boats. Other workhorses navigate these waters: tugboats towing rafts of logs or barges topped by loading cranes; local ferries scooting across the channels; large B.C. and Alaska government ferry vessels carrying cars and passengers. And sometimes canoes and kayaks, sailboats, and other pleasure craft brave the Passage, little cousins to the twenty-one or more cruise ships that make at least 330 sailings between Vancouver and Alaska each summer.

Centuries-old History

This sparse if constant stream of human traffic evokes the history of this place. Imagine the dugouts and sailing ships, the steamboats and fishing schooners. For centuries, the Inside Passage was a Native pathway—in particular, the route of the Haida, whose warriors raided and traded its length and who still traverse the worst of its waters from their northerly home in B.C.'s Queen Charlotte Islands. The white man came from opposite directions. First, the Greek explorer whose Spanish name was given to the southern Strait of Juan de Fuca, a century after Columbus arrived in America. Then the Russian fur traders from Siberia who reached the northern end of the Passage in what is now Alaska. Next, Spanish ships sailing north, seeking a way through the continent, though Spain

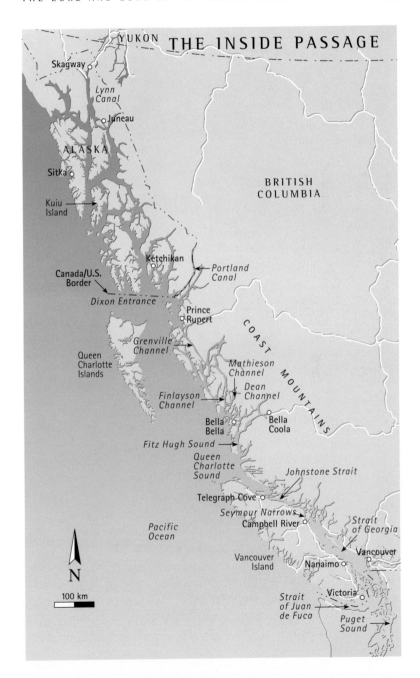

THE INSIDE PASSAGE

YUKON

Skagway

Lynn
Canal

Juneau

ALASKA

Sitka

Kuiu
Island

BRITISH
COLUMBIA

Ketchikan

Portland
Canal

Canada/U.S.
Border

Dixon Entrance

Prince
Rupert

Grenville
Channel

COAST MOUNTAINS

Queen
Charlotte
Islands

Mathieson
Channel

Dean
Channel

Finlayson
Channel

Bella
Bella

Bella
Coola

Fitz Hugh Sound

Queen
Charlotte
Sound

Johnstone Strait

Telegraph Cove

Seymour Narrows

Campbell River

Strait
of Georgia

Pacific
Ocean

Vancouver
Island

Nanaimo

Vancouver

N

100 km

Strait
of Juan
de Fuca

Victoria

Puget
Sound

would cede its claims in 1795 to ever-venturing Britain, personified by Captains Cook and Vancouver. (*See* The Pacific Coast of George Vancouver, *page 51.*)

The first steamship to run the Passage continuously was the S.S. *Beaver*, launched in England by the Hudson's Bay Company in 1835. The elm-keeled paddle wheeler, 101 feet long, had several lives: for twenty-six years, trading for the fur company, with a cannon and large crew to keep the peace; for another eight, surveying the coastline for the Royal Navy; and for her final twenty years in private service, towing lumber and coal ships, supplying lumber camps, and toting passengers. Refitted with fresh boilers at least five times, grounded and holed more than once, the *Beaver* ran aground finally in 1888 at Prospect Point off Vancouver's Stanley Park, where cruise ships now pass as they enter and leave Burrard Inlet.

The Inside Passage had increasing traffic after 1867, as seal hunters and some settlers headed for the new U.S. territory of Alaska. The first cruise ships to carry sight-seeing passengers as well as cargo for the villages and canneries along the waterway were lavishly fitted Pacific Coast Steamship vessels. The *Idaho* took the initial batch of tourists to view Glacier Bay in 1883 (*see* Eliza, Alaska's Intrepid Tourist, *page 15*), and other paddle wheelers like the s.s. *Ancon* followed in her wake; within a year, there were 1,650 people cruising up here. A decade and a half later, the coast was awash in mostly American stampeders lusting after the gold in Canada's Yukon Territory. The Trail of '98 began in the Lower 48, usually in San Francisco or Seattle. By early that year, forty ships were running regularly to Alaska from San Francisco—"greater in point of numbers, efficiency and carrying capacity than any fleet ever collected in any harbor in the world to engage in a specific enterprise," the local *Examiner* said. The enterprise: to carry six million tons of freight and 100,000 gold seekers in a mad rush to the Klondike via Skagway, Alaska, the opportunistic settlement newly born at the end of the Passage.

The gold rush ebbed within a couple of years. And it was well

"A true fairyland": the seductive channel of the Inside Passage

into the twentieth century when entrepreneurs voyaged up the Passage in search of other resources in which it was (and remains) rich: fish and lumber. Some of them stayed on this coast, living isolated lives on the islands, the mainland, or even on the water in floating camps.

You'll catch glimpses of their successors in communities along the way. Cruising north from Vancouver—past the urban oasis of Stanley Park and beneath the graceful span of Lions Gate Bridge, named for the leonine-like peaks behind it—your ship enters the Strait of Georgia. Twenty miles wide, the strait begins in northern Washington and extends 100 miles and more until dissolving into a confusion of channels off the city of Campbell River (population 29,000), halfway up Vancouver Island. Your route is through Discovery Passage, where ships must always be cautious. Here, between the big island and Quadra and Maud Islands, tides of up to 17 miles

For half a century, the S.S. *Beaver* ran the Passage in many guises.

an hour rush through Discovery's skinniest, trickiest stretch: Seymour Narrows. Beset with shifting currents and whirlpools, it's only 800 yards wide and makes a turn of almost 90 degrees.

The Blasting of Ripple Rock

Until the late 1950s, the narrows were perilous because of the submerged mini-mountain at their center. That year, in one of the most extraordinary feats in Canadian engineering history, the largest manufactured, non-atomic explosion of its time blew Ripple Rock apart. Old Rip had two pinnacles—one 160 by 300 feet, the other 150 by 200—lurking at most only 19 feet below the water's surface at low tide. Conflicting records report that at least 114 people had died here when an equal number of vessels, including fourteen large ships, were sunk or damaged. The first known victim was the American gunboat U.S.S. *Saranac*, in 1875. Surprisingly, some people wanted the rock to remain as a natural base for a potential bridge between Vancouver Island and the mainland. Mariners' demands to blast it away proved more persuasive. The idea was to drill a half-mile-long tunnel from Maud Island under the narrows and up into Old Rip, and there plant a special new high explosive so carefully that the resulting shower of shattered rocks would land in deep underwater holes—to avoid later dredging. The $3.1-million project used 1,375 tons of Nitramex 2H, enough to lift the Empire State Building a mile high. On April 5, 1958, as the world watched on television, engineers lit the 5.3 miles of fuse. Within moments, an estimated 350,000 tons of rock shards and 370,000 tons of water erupted a thousand feet into the sky. The explosion sheared at least 40 feet from Ripple Rock's peaks. Seymour Narrows was suddenly much safer.

Eventually every ship and boat voyaging up the Passage has to contend with Johnstone Strait. About 60 miles long, it lies just above Discovery Passage, off Vancouver Island, roughly between the port communities of Rock Bay and Telegraph Cove. It's a wide, windswept, choppy channel in a glorious mountain setting. The

**The 1958 explosion of Ripple Rock to make
passage through Seymour Narrows safer.**

loftiest summit to the northeast, near the head of Knight Inlet,
is Mount Waddington, second-highest peak in British Columbia.
Where Vancouver Island's Tsitika River emerges, a dozen miles
below Telegraph Cove, is the recess of Robson Bight, an ecological
reserve where killer whales gather and rub themselves against the
cliffs—the world's premier place to view orcas. Just north of Telegraph Cove, on Cormorant Island, the Kwakiutl Indian community
of Alert Bay still has some of the world's tallest totem poles.

From here you cruise through Queen Charlotte Strait, passing the town of Port Hardy near the top of Vancouver Island,
and enter the lone unsheltered patch of the Passage, open wide to
the Pacific—Queen Charlotte Sound. The names on the map are
expressive: Storm Islands, Cape Caution, Hope Island. Vessels have

The Pacific Coast of George Vancouver

Capt. George Vancouver found the Pacific Northwest coast a "dreary and uninteresting" place, but he was focused less on scenery than on the intricate task of mapping every foot of its convoluted indentations and naming 400 bodies of water or points of land.

On his first voyage in 1792, after exploring Puget Sound and the site of present-day Seattle, he anchored in Birch Bay just south of the 49th parallel and rowed north into Boundary Bay, 'round Point Roberts and into Burrard Inlet—becoming the first European to see the site of what is now Vancouver. Having charted between Vancouver Island and the mainland, he entered Queen Charlotte Sound, harboring at Calvert Island where he decided to return south for the winter. In the following year, he began where he'd left off. A little north of Bella Bella, Johnstone's crew ate mussels for breakfast in a cove off Mathieson Channel, and immediately became sick. One of them died a few hours later, an unwitting victim of paralytic shellfish poisoning. That summer's work advanced the survey only 300 miles north, ending at Cape Decision on the southern tip of Kuiu Island, one of the islands of the Alaska Panhandle.

In 1794, Vancouver sailed directly to the Gulf of Alaska and proceeded southeast toward the Panhandle. Too sick to do the work himself, he sent out crews under Joseph Whidbey and James Johnstone. The charting of Cook Inlet, which proved it was not the river Cook had assumed, took four weeks in April and May. Here, Vancouver ignored the repeated requests of the Russian-American Company's Aleksandr Baranov for a meeting.

In July, the expedition entered Cross Sound, north of Chicagof Island, and found it filled with huge chunks of ice. Whidbey reported a glacier at the entrance to present-day Glacier Bay. Now close to finishing, Whidbey and Johnstone charted Icy Strait, Lynn Canal (named for Vancouver's birthplace, King's Lynn, Norfolk), Stephens Passage, and Chatham Strait. When the two met in Frederick Sound south of Admiralty Island in August, they realized that the survey was complete and celebrated with a double portion of liquor. Vancouver returned to England and died four years later at the age of forty.

to traverse Queen Charlotte's unruly 40 miles to reach Fitz Hugh Sound and Fisher Channel and dart between Hunter and Denny Islands and up past Bella Bella. This fishing village, on Campbell Island at the mouth of Dean Channel, is named for its local band of 1,200 Natives who belong to the Heiltsuk First Nation. An ingenious people, their ancestors built a boat in the nineteenth century modeled after the S.S. *Beaver*, scooping out a tree trunk 30 feet long and carving and painting it to resemble the Inside Passage steamship. Today their houses, which you can easily see on the port side traveling north, ascend a hillside community that has revitalized itself in recent years, developing businesses that include harvesting herring roe on kelp, a delicacy in Japan.

Big Lynn

You then wind through Seaforth Channel, Milbanke Sound, and the Passage's deepest waters, Finlayson Channel, which descends nearly a half-mile, and then cruise through several reaches and the steep, treed cliffs of Grenville Channel. At the far northern end of the Canadian Passage, the channel is the aerial scene photographers love to capture: 45 miles long, narrowing to less than a quarter-mile, a canyon between cone-shaped peaks heaving straight up from the water, layer after layer of them, edging ever closer as the ship creeps up the channel, fat clouds curling around them. Conservationist and fly-fisherman Roderick Haig-Brown of Campbell River, one of the world's great writers about the outdoors, has written, "The first almighty fact about British Columbia is mountains." If so, the second is the sea. And here, along the archetypal path of the Passage, these two facts of nature meet and meld with grandeur. Later, as you pass through Chatham Sound, you might catch a nighttime glimpse of Prince Rupert, the biggest city on the B.C. mainland coast above Vancouver. Founded by an American, Charles Hayes, this major fishing port of 17,000, only 90 miles south of Ketchikan, is the northern terminus of the B.C. Ferries system.

Soon you're into the broad reaches of Dixon Entrance, passing

Dundas Island and crossing the unmarked Canada-U.S. boundary into Alaska. The next morning, along Tongass Narrows, you'll disembark at your first stop, Ketchikan. From here, cruise ships of various sizes travel individual routes and berth at different ports along the Inside Passage as far north as Skagway. If you reach this terminus of the inland waterway, you'll have gone up the 90-mile straightaway of the Lynn Canal, a wide cleft gouged by glaciers during an early ice age. One of Alaska's most scenic fjords, it's lined with tall mountains streaked with glaciers and waterfalls. In a modern vessel during the cruise season, when the still blue water reflects like a looking glass, you won't taste the canal's reputation for trouble. But give a thought to those who came before you who had to face the Big Lynn's worst conditions in lesser craft.

When Captain Vancouver's expedition sailed by in the late 18th century, present-day Glacier Bay was sealed by ice.

GLACIERS: THE POWER
AND THE GLORY

For more than a century, Hubbard Glacier in southeastern Alaska had been advancing gradually, but relentlessly. Then in 1986, icy tributaries of the longest valley glacier in North America began to accelerate into Disenchantment Bay. As this expansive stream of ice spread forward from its head in the St. Elias Mountains, the glacier blocked off Russell Fjord. The ragged ice dam trapped porpoises, harbor seals, and otters in what became an instant lake, which grew with glacial meltwater and threatened to spill over into a prized salmon river that was the economic lifeline of a remote community. The international scientific excitement about this phenomenon focused less on the imaginative rescue efforts to free the sea life and more on the still-mysterious nature of glaciers themselves, especially on the mechanisms by which they move: advancing and retreating, and often inexplicably surging and galloping.

As wildlife rescuers guided seals across an earth bridge and lowered them on stretchers into salty water, glaciologists were intent on studying the factors that made the 95-mile-long glacier advance. At first they speculated that they were witnessing a true surge, when glaciers can extend themselves at a hundred times the normal pace in a process that is just starting to be understood. Well after the dam broke in an hours-long deluge and the lake became a fjord again, scientists declared that Hubbard's Valerie tributary had truly surged while the main glacier had been perturbed by a flow instability.

**A helicopter ferries cruise-ship passengers
onto Mendenhall Glacier.**

It was another compelling reminder that Alaska's glaciers, like others around the world, are among nature's most destructive forces: flows of living ice that can ruthlessly crush and carve the landscape and alter people's lives. In the words of an admiring nineteenth-century scientist, they are God's Great Plough. Glaciers contain within their frozen clutches 90 percent of the globe's fresh water; if they were to melt, most major ports would disappear, and the whole of Florida, for instance, would survive as only a few small islands. The world's glaciers are like immense icy currents caught in the freeze frame of a camera—and nowhere can they be better captured by eye and lens than in Alaska.

Glacial ice cloaks one-tenth of the earth's surface, but in southeast Alaska geographical and meteorological conditions combine in ideal equilibrium to facilitate the viewing of glaciers. Outside the polar regions, they and their handiwork loom largest here. Glacier Bay, a stop on some cruise voyages, may be the most magnificent example anywhere of a glacially sculpted complex of fjords, and its St. Elias and (misnamed) Fairweather ranges are the most elaborately glaciated mountains. Alaska is one of only a few places in the world where spectacular tidewater glaciers can be conveniently observed and heard, as the sound the native Tlingit called "white thunder" announces a calving—the breaking off of huge chunks crashing dramatically into the sea.

A Century of Visitors

In size, Alaska's estimated 100,000 glaciers range from leftover fragments of less than a square mile to tremendous sheets of ice that spread for hundreds of square miles. In accessibility, they can be as close at hand as the Mendenhall, just outside Juneau, which can easily be reached by land and helicopter. Or they can be as remote as the glaciers in the high peaks of the Brooks Range north of the Arctic Circle. Among the most approachable, in terms of sheer comfort, are the St. Elias's thirteen tidewater glaciers in Glacier Bay National Park and Preserve, which visitors have been viewing from the decks of tour ships for more than a century. On July 7, 1890, the American naturalist John Muir noted with bemusement the arrival of the steamer *Queen* at the base of the glacier named for him: "She arrived about 2:30 P.M. with two hundred and thirty tourists. What a show they made with their ribbons and kodaks!"

John Muir, who had been visiting here since 1879, was the first to write extensively and eloquently about Glacier Bay and its rich lode of glaciers. His passion for them is expressed in this typically poetic passage from *Travels in Alaska*: "The whole front of the glacier is gashed and sculptured into a maze of shallow caves and crevasses, and a bewildering variety of novel architectural forms, clusters of glittering lance-tipped spires, gables, and obelisks, bold outstanding bastions and plain mural cliffs, adorned along the top with fretted cornice and battlement, while every gorge and crevasse, groove and hollow, was filled with light, shimmering and throbbing in pale-blue tones of ineffable tenderness and beauty. The day was warm, and back on the broad melting bosom of the glacier...many streams were rejoicing, gurgling, ringing, singing, in frictionless channels worn down through the white disintegrated ice of the surface into the quick and living blue, in which they flowed with a grace of motion and flashing of light to be found only on the crystal hillocks and ravines of a glacier."

Muir, the Scottish-born conservationist and crusader for national parks, was in Alaska to continue investigating the new theory of glacial erosion. In the continental United States, he had attributed the configuration of Yosemite Valley to such erosion, after painstakingly crawling around on all fours with a magnifying glass to document suggestive scratches in the bedrock. At Glacier Bay, he traveled by steamer, in canoes with Tlingit Indian guides, and on foot with his faithful dog, Stickeen (named for a local Indian tribe). One day, dog and master were alone on a glacier when they encountered a crevasse, which Muir could traverse only by chiseling foot- and finger-holds across a narrow bridge of ice. At one point this sliver of a span was

With the roar of "white thunder," the Columbia Glacier calves into Prince William Sound. ▶

a mere 4 inches wide, and Stickeen howled in panic at the thought of crossing it. Only at the last moment did he chance it—"with a nervous spring he whizzed up and passed me out on to the level ice, and ran and cried and barked and rolled about fairly hysterical in the sudden revulsion from the depth of despair to triumphant joy."

In risking his life, Muir was reaping the joy of chronicling a place that barely existed only a hundred years before, when Captains Cook and Vancouver, on separate voyages, had sailed right by a mammoth glacier then sealing the mouth of the bay. Cook, who had seen glaciers in the Antarctic, didn't even recognize this one. But Vancou-

A Little Glacier Glossary

Ablation: The combined processes—including melting, calving, evaporation, erosion—in which a glacier loses ice and snow. The opposite of accumulation.

Bergy seltzer: Also known as ice sizzle, this is the simultaneous loud popping of the bubbles, under pressures of more than 750 pounds per square inch, that break when glaciers and icebergs melt.

Crevasse: A deep, steep-sloped open fracture in the upper ice, created by the stresses of a flowing glacier. In the illustration, a glacier is passing over a mound of bedrock, and the bending of the ice opens up crevasses in the brittle top layers to a maximum depth of about 100 feet—beyond which the pressure of the glacier keeps the lower ice more pliable.

Drumlin: A low, smooth mound of glacial drift deposited beneath a glacier.

Firn: Transitional ice grains, between snow and glacier ice.

Foliation: Layering within a glacier as its snow is transformed into glacier ice, with irregular bands usually alternating between fine- and coarse-grained ice or bubble-rich and clear ice; can be seen at a glacier's face.

ver, while exploring College Fjord in Prince William Sound in 1794, did record the first account of an Alaska glacier calving. The British explorers were preceded in the area not only by Russians but also by a Frenchman, the Count of La Pérouse, who precisely located five nearby glaciers and whose name now graces a mountain and ice stream on the coastline of Glacier Bay National Park. By 1879, the bay's ice sheet, at points thousands of feet thick, had retreated 48 miles from the mouth—one example of a rate of glacial retreat that remains the fastest in the world. Today, only two of the glaciers are advancing; the rest remain stable or continue to withdraw.

Glacial drift: All rocky debris, from mud to boulders, carried and deposited by a glacier.

Glacial flour: Bedrock ground to powderlike silt by the pressure of flowing ice; suspended in meltwater, it becomes a light-colored glacier milk.

Hanging glacier: Usually a small glacier that clings high on the wall of a U-shaped valley.

Icefall: Area where a glacier plunges over a steep slope, creating a heavily crevassed surface and a flow of ice triple the normal rate; the most hazardous part of a glacier.

Moraine: A ridge or group of ridges and mounds created from an accumulation of glacial drift. An *end* moraine is a ridge or hill that can become several hundred feet high when the end of a glacier melts and its terminus stays in the same place for a long time. (*Terminal* moraine denotes a glacier's farthest advance.) A *lateral* moraine is composed of material eroded from valley walls as the glacier moves. A *medial* moraine, found in the middle of a glacier, originates from a rock outcrop or converging lateral moraines of two or more ice streams.

Till: A stew of unsorted glacial drift deposited directly by a glacier and not reworked by meltwater. Glacial till compressed into rock is *tillite.*

God's Great Plough

At Glacier Bay, Muir was following in the scientific footsteps of French naturalist Louis Agassiz and his predecessors, who had only recently propounded the theory that moving sheets of ice, carrying outsized rocks along with them, had scarred and restructured vast surfaces of land throughout the world. It was Agassiz who described a glacier as God's Great Plough. This was heretical to early nineteenth-century scientists who still attributed the cause of most geological anomalies to the biblical flood. Of course, nobody had yet seen the enormous ice sheets of the Antarctic. Agassiz's theory of an ice age—a "Siberian winter" in which glaciers from the North Pole grew to envelop much of the northern hemisphere—was scoffed at until the 1840s, when his scientific work in the mountains of Switzerland and the highlands of Britain secured his reputation. By mid-century, he was ensconced at Harvard University and would become one of the most popular American scientists of the era.

Louis Agassiz was not entirely correct. There had been not one but as many as twelve periods of major glaciation around the globe over the past million or so years that define the Great Ice Age of the Pleistocene epoch. But eras of glaciation date back as long ago as seven hundred million years and as recently, in geological terms, as 150 years ago, when the Little Ice Age ebbed after five and a half centuries of glacial expansion.

Among the glaciers that had grown during this latest period were Alaska's. Then, when the world's mean temperature began to rise by about one degree Fahrenheit during the nineteenth century, they started to retreat. In the middle of the twentieth century, as the northern hemisphere was recooling, 7 percent of them began to advance again—and today in total this minority holds more ice than all the rest of the state's glaciers.

Such movement is the very definition of a glacier, which is a flowing body of natural, land-borne ice—containing meltwater, algae, pollen, and the debris of rock torn from mountains and valleys, not to mention ice worms and snow fleas. (*See* Ice Worms and Snow Fleas, *page* 65.) Ice itself is a mineral, or monomineralic rock, created from soft snow which builds up in layers. Over the years, its massive weight and extreme pressure compacts snow crystals at a depth of about 200 feet into solid ice crystals, which can form up to a foot in length. Although much glacier ice looks white, some appears blue. The reason: as daylight passes through the dense ice, light waves at the red end of the color spectrum are absorbed, causing the human eye to perceive an enhancement of blue light.

Alaska offers textbook conditions for the growth of what scientists call temperate or warm glaciers (as opposed to the cold ones of Greenland and Antarctica). In the southeastern stretches of the state, the warm Japanese Current flowing through the Gulf of Alaska encourages precipitation, which at the 5,000-foot level becomes snow throughout the year. (The Juneau Icecap has an estimated annual snowfall of 100 feet.) In summer, the temperature of most of these glaciers remains just at freezing, 32 degrees Fahrenheit, which enables meltwater to flow through the ice and form the spectacular ice caves characteristic of warm glaciers. The chilly summers allow snow to survive annual melting and become solid granules, known in their second year as firn.

Alaska's glaciers are born in alpine regions, valleys, and piedmonts—the flatlands at the foot of a mountain where one or more streams of ice spread out. A sheet of glacier ice, usually dome-shaped, with the flow radiating from the center, is called an ice cap. A large area of connecting valley glaciers is an ice field, such as the well-studied Juneau Icefield, where the Mendenhall flows. Islands of bedrock projecting through an ice field are called nunataks.

A Mystery Being Solved

For most of the century and a half that science has been studying glaciers, their movement has been a mystery. Recent research has now identified two basic methods: internal deformation (alteration of form) and basal slip or sliding. Cold glaciers in the polar regions move because their ice acts like minerals and metals under stress, which can deform and actually "flow." Most of the movement of warm glaciers, like Alaska's, depends on a base of meltwater that—although it may be only a mere fraction of an inch thick—acts like a lubricant to reduce friction as gravity and the weight of the ice send a glacier downhill. Crevasses are created when a descending glacier crosses bumps in its bedrock path, causing it to bend and open up long cracks in its upper layers to depths of up to 100 feet.

Along the way, a glacier manhandles everything in its path. It bends around, while roughing up, the largest rock barriers. It freezes onto smaller loose rock, dirt, and other detritus that gathers along its sides, creating black borders called lateral moraines. Sometimes glaciers merge, and the debris of each one produces a black stripe, which identifies the individual glaciers within the collective mass. As the glacier moves, the debris becomes its instrument of destruction and creation. Gravel frozen into the ice wears away the terrain, boulders gash the land and dredge up and drag along more rock.

The ice always moves downward, following the line of least resistance. When glaciologists talk of glaciers retreating, they aren't suggesting that the ice actually backs up a slope. But when the distance between the head of the glacier and its terminus begins to shrink—through melting and calving—it is said to be in retreat. Alaska has seen the world's most rapid retreats. In the eighty-five years between George Vancouver's and John Muir's visits, Glacier Bay ice had retreated 48 miles; by 1916, Grand Pacific Glacier had backed up to 65 miles from the bay's mouth and exposed the face of Johns Hopkins Glacier. Since then, Grand Pacific has been unpredictably to-ing and fro-ing across the adjacent Canadian border.

Advancing glaciers—those that grow longer—most often also move forward only a fraction of a yard a day, the glacial pace that has become a metaphor for slowness. Some, however, surge and gallop. In 1936 the retreating Black Rapids Glacier, amid the high Alaska Range in central Alaska, suddenly, inexplicably, began to surge forward with an ice face more than 330 feet high. Before it stopped—only a mile and a half from a lodge along the Richardson Highway—it had traveled 4 miles in three months. Alaska and neighboring northwest Canada have about 200 of these galloping glaciers between them. In 1982–83, an international scientific team

Ice Worms and Snow Fleas

Wolves and bears, moose and caribou, Arctic fox and wolverines have all braved Alaska's glaciers. So have mice and shrews, and even bumble-bees and hummingbirds. But perhaps the most intriguing creatures on these icy stretches are the minuscule and mysterious ice worms and snow fleas.

Although they were first recorded on a Canadian expedition to Greenland in 1872, and an American one on Muir Glacier five years later, ice worms were long thought to be a practical joke on newcomers to the north. (Alaskan shops sell postcards labeled "ice worms" showing strands of spaghetti curling on the snow.) In fact, they are a relative of the common earthworm, black, and usually no more than an inch long—about the length of a spruce needle and the diameter of a darn-ing needle, says one scientist. They wriggle through crystals in partially thawed ice or through firn—transitional ice grains, between snow and glacier ice—and lay their eggs in water. The colder it gets, the deeper they burrow into the glacier. It's assumed that they dine on pollen or red algae in the snow. And various birds dine on them.

Spotting the worms can be difficult. A member of the U.S. Geologi-cal Survey saw them early one morning in 1891 on Malaspina Glacier off Yakutat Bay: "These creatures were wiggling over the snow in thousands, but as soon as the sun rose and made its warmth felt, they disappeared beneath the surface." A few summers later on the same glacier, another observer watched them start moving sluggishly around 4 P.M. and stay on the surface until dawn.

If ice worms are hard to believe in, consider the snow, or glacier, flea. A member of the order Collembola, it's a blue insect that hops around the surface of melting snow in late winter and early spring and lives on a vegetarian diet of conifer pollen and red algae—and perhaps even dead ice worms.

studying the Variegated Glacier at Yakutat Bay on the southeastern Alaska coast observed an 8,000-foot surge in progress, speeding along at 200 feet a day. They theorized that a buildup of meltwater increased hydraulic pressure, raising the glacier slightly off its bed and escalating the rate of basal sliding. And glaciologists camping atop it spoke of the cracking and thumping of the surge.

Surging or snail-like, a glacier keeps moving, inexorably, until it reaches a point where the ice at its margin either melts or reaches tidewater. At its snout, a tidewater glacier can lie deep underwater where it deposits rock debris to create a protective shoal enabling it to advance in the water. Meanwhile, it will continually calve to form icebergs or ice shelves.

Bergs, composed of fresh water and floating seven-eighths submerged, come in all shapes and sizes. They range from an ugly black or brown from the stony debris called moraine, which the glacier has collected along the way, to the clear white and blue that John Muir described as ineffably beautiful, "in which the purest tones of light pulse and shimmer, lovely and untainted as anything on earth or in the sky." In size, icebergs in Alaska waters can be chunks just large enough to float a few seabirds or huge floating islands.

The immense power of glaciers has carved U-shaped valleys, islands, lakes and rivers, and the fjords of the Inside Passage, Glacier Bay, and Prince William Sound. It has ground granite and limestone into a fertile mix that, borne by meltwater and blown by winds, has created what became the world's richest agricultural lands. And well beyond the ice ages, the influence of glaciers continues. The cold air above the major ice sheets affects global weather patterns. As efficient storehouses of water, glaciers power hydroelectric facilities, especially during the winter, in Scandinavia, Switzerland, and parts of the U.S. And they are effective outdoor laboratories for the arctic sciences as well as glaciology. The Juneau Icefield Research Program, which began in 1948, not only provides training for university and high-school students but also offers professional scientists—among them, climatologists, biologists, botanists, and specialists in polar medicine—field experience and long-term research opportunities.

For the visitors to Alaska who view them from a cruise ship or on-shore tours, glaciers can be appreciated simply as one of the most wondrous manifestations of the natural world.

Where to See Glaciers in Alaska

Juneau Icefield   One of the most intensively studied ice fields in the world—site of the Juneau Icefield Research Program—covers 1,500 square miles of land along the crest of the Coast Mountains, from the Taku River to just east of Skagway, and dips into British Columbia. It comprises many smaller glaciers and at least thirty-eight larger valley glaciers, all of them retreating except for the advancing Taku. Just north of Juneau, the *Mendenhall,* its 1.5-mile-wide terminus rising 100 feet above the surface of deep Mendenhall Lake, is slowly retreating (at a pace of about 70 feet a year) and filling the lake. Scientists have found the 12-mile-long glacier a superior source of big single-crystal ice samples. Visitors who come by vehicle, or land by helicopter a mile or more onto the glacier's face, find it a fascinating way to begin comprehending the size and structure of glaciers.

Glacier Bay National Park and Preserve   Ringed by the superbly glaciated Fairweather Range to the west, the Chilkat Range to the east, and the St. Elias, Alsek, and Takhinsha Mountains to the north, the bay is 62 miles long and 10 miles at its widest. Located about 65 miles northwest of Juneau, it became a national monument in 1925 and a national park and preserve in 1980. Early in the new millennium, a federal court judge in Alaska ordered a reduction in the number of cruise ships allowed into the park and preserve each season, in an effort to minimize the environmental impact on the sensitive bay.

The most dramatic modern event in Glacier Bay's history was the 1899 earthquake that shook the Alaska coast, destroying the front of Muir Glacier and sending others into fast retreat. The Grand Pacific backed off to 65 miles from the mouth of the bay and exposed the face of Johns Hopkins Glacier. All of this activity attracted scientists from around the world, who have since turned the bay and its thirteen tidewater and seven freshwater glaciers into a natural laboratory.

Grand Pacific Glacier, along with neighboring Margerie, plugs the extreme upper end of the bay. During John Muir's time, when he camped on "the crystal bluffs of the vast glacier," the two ice flows were actually fused. Grand Pacific may be advancing now, but during the 1920s it had retreated across the adjacent Canadian border for more than a mile. Three decades later it had moved back again into Alaska, where it remains today—the longest glacier in the park, its face 260 feet tall and 1.5 miles across.

Margerie Glacier, which routinely calves for cruise-ship passengers in Tarr Inlet, is smaller but has the sharp features of a classic glacier. Its active calving and the resulting swells keep small boats and kayaks half a mile away from its mile-long face.

Johns Hopkins Glacier, christened for the university whose glaciologists were pioneer researchers here, began advancing out of the Fairweather Range about 1930. It chokes the inlet of the same name with ice that keeps most vessels four miles away.

Yakutat Bay   Northwest of Glacier Bay, at the top of the Panhandle, lie Yakutat Bay and, at its far end, Disenchantment Bay—into which *Hubbard Glacier* continued a century-long advance until it temporarily dammed Russell Fjord in 1986. (Scientists estimate that it had last advanced into the bay in the twelfth century.) Now, the continent's longest valley glacier is continuing a slow advance, and its calving at mid-tide is a sensational event. Glaciologists predict that in the next few decades the Hubbard will again dam the fjord—and this time, once the dam is in place, it will remain for hundreds if not thousands of years.

Prince William Sound   In the Gulf of Alaska, south of Valdez, Prince William Sound has more than twenty active glaciers amid forty fjords, the most of any one area in Alaska. You can view abundant sea life here, from seals and sea otters to porpoises and whales.

College Fjord's six glaciers were named for eastern colleges by the 1899 Harriman Expedition of geologists affiliated with the institutions: Harvard (the most active) and Yale in two arms at the head of the fjord; Smith, Bryn Mawr, Vassar, and Wellesley on the western side. The inlet, 20 miles long, lies within the Chugach National Forest. Approaching from a wide channel lined with dark-green mountain slopes, you enter the fjord to find peaks white with snow even in summer and a series of glaciers that appear almost side by side. The big one, dead ahead, is Harvard and off to starboard is Yale, rising sharply up the mountain valley. Nearby *Harriman Fjord* has a dozen glaciers, including the advancing Harriman (the longest) and Surprise, so-called because it was the first to be spotted by members of the expedition. The drama here is not only observing mighty Harvard but also seeing so many other glaciers so close together in one place.

Since the mid-1980s, *Columbia Glacier* has retreated 8 miles into its fjord. It remains, however, the largest and most majestic in the Sound, spread across 400 square miles from its head in Mount Einstein (elevation 11,522 feet). Its 3-mile-wide terminus (only half-visible from the middle of the bay) is in the tidewater of Columbia Bay near the port of Valdez, where the Trans-Alaska Pipeline fuels oil tankers. Scientists have been studying the glacier's energetic calving—which can produce flat-topped icebergs 200 feet long—because of the long-shot possibility of a collision between berg and tanker. At some points, Columbia's ice front lies several thousand feet below sea level. As the ice retreats, the bottom of the bay is falling away under the glacier's snout. Although you might think the water could become deep enough to float the glacier, Dennis Trabant of the U.S. Geological Survey says this is unlikely to happen: "The glaciers of Alaska are warm glaciers. Warm glaciers aren't stable when approaching flotation. They calve quickly, eliminating the potentially floating parts."

Harding Icefield   Amid the Kenai Mountains, in the Kenai Fjords National Park southwest of Seward, lies 35-mile-long Harding Icefield. This remnant of the Pleistocene age, about 300 square miles of ice, generates more than forty sizable glaciers, four of them longer than 15 miles. Tours through this magnificent area of thickly treed slopes take in some of the most impressive of the ice field's progeny, including *Exit Glacier*, which is accessible by road along the Seward Highway.

Worthington Glacier   North of the oil port of Valdez, a frequent stop on a cruise voyage, a tour-bus trip can take you into the Chugach, America's second-largest national forest, to view the *Worthington Glacier*. Climbing Thompson Pass, which rises to 2,771 feet, you catch a glimpse of the glacier on the left, a bit of blue ice poking up in the green folded slopes, and eventually a fuller view of the ice flowing out of the mountains. A state recreation site has an information area that points out how the Worthington's northeast exposure protects it from the sun and, if global warming continues, how it could be the last surviving glacier in the area. If you are willing to ignore the "Glaciers can kill you" signs, you can walk right up to its terminus, which rests on black rock. As enormous as it is, this receding glacier has the look of something dying, a deflating monster in a newly vegetated sweep of valley.

Portage Glacier   The most popular attraction in the state lies within driving distance of Anchorage. *Portage Glacier* occupies what was once a low pass across the Kenai Mountains, which Alaska Natives and Russian explorers traversed before Vancouver's time. Even after the glacier filled it, the pass continued to be used as a highway by the U.S. Army at the turn of the century. As you approach the area, the awesome vista of Portage appears suddenly. Boat tours on Portage Lake present a fine close-up view of the glacier's face, and in the visitor center you can wander through a simulated ice cave and even stroke a real iceberg.

And Now, the Weather

There's a strange if extremely rare weather phenomenon in Alaska called the *fata morgana*. Named for the legendary half-sister of King Arthur, who made her submerged crystal castle appear as a mirage above the waves, the Alaskan version can happen during temperature inversions when several layers of warm and cold air project images in the air of objects that may be well below the horizon. The most celebrated mirage, in the late 1800s, was the recurring vision of a populated city of gardens and tall spires that appeared in Glacier Bay.

As a cruise-ship passenger, you're not likely to experience the *fata morgana*, though it might be fun to see the Silent City hovering above Muir Glacier. The truth is, Alaska can be a most pleasant place to visit during the regular tourist season. The state remains green half the year, with virtually no snow in summer except on the hills and mountains; summer days are exceedingly long (on June 20–21, daylight hours in Ketchikan, Juneau, and Anchorage range from 17 1/2 to nearly 19 1/2); and occasionally the usual temperatures in the 50s and 60s leap into the 80s and 90s. Anchorage has a climate similar to the Great Lakes region; Ketchikan, lying at the same latitude as Glasgow, Scotland, has relatively mild weather distinguished mostly by the rain that makes it one of the wettest places on earth (though the rain and sun may alternate throughout the day).

Generally, May and June are the driest months in Alaska. July and August can be shirt-sleeve weather. The leaves of willows and birches begin yellowing in August. Fall may be the best of all, when the days are crisp and cold.

So what should you wear on a cruise to Alaska? Aside from the attire you take for shipboard life (travel agents and cruise brochures will guide you there), plan on casual, comfortable clothing that you can easily shed or layer back on as the weather fluctuates. The basics are good walking shoes (but probably not sandals or other open-toes), sweaters, medium-weight pants, and a lightweight, water-repellent coat. Bring a hat and an umbrella, but skip the mukluks and sealskin parka.

WILD ALASKA

For a lover, or mere admirer, of the wild—of sea life, animals and birds, plants and flowers, the wild land itself—Alaska is America's most rewarding place. At least a half-dozen of its thirty-eight kinds of sea mammals, including the most immense on the planet, are seen in Alaska waters and nowhere else. Here too are some of the world's largest land mammals, in some of the largest groupings. There is one grizzly bear for every eight Alaskans; there are as many caribou as there are people. Golden and bald eagles, trumpeter swans, and red-faced cormorants flourish in this northernmost state among more than four hundred species of birds. Wildflowers grow so prolifically in summer that they can be difficult to sidestep. And the plant life of the tundra is so diverse that one biologist compares it to the lushness of a tropical rain forest a few inches tall. What you will not find here, thankfully, are rattlesnakes and poison ivy.

Life in the Sea

Whales An Alaska without whales would not be Alaska, says Dr. Victor Scheffer, the internationally renowned American zoologist. One of the most exciting events on a summer cruise in the state's southeastern coastal waters is the sighting of these leviathans—often the show-stopping leaps or the high-arched tail flips of that most acrobatic of whales, the HUMPBACK. This migrating species shares one characteristic with many of the cruise ships that enable so many of us to see them: most humpbacks spend their summers in Alaska and winters in Mexico and the Hawaiian Islands. Up to three-fifths of the world's 10,000 humpbacks summer here. Feeding on herring and other fish close to the shore, they can be seen in Glacier Bay, Prince William Sound, and especially around Admiralty Island.

You can distinguish them by the telltale hump of their black-and-white bodies; their oversized flippers, the largest of any whales; and the wartlike bumps on their snouts, each holding a single hair, which scientists believe may be a sensor. Breaching, they fling their 35-ton, 45-foot bulk out of the sea in a series of twists and turns. In their dramatic descents, they flash the white flukes (or lobes) of their winglike tails, which bear markings so distinctive that they are as identifying as fingerprints.

Although humpbacks may be the whales most often spotted by cruise-ship passengers, they are only one of fifteen species that make Alaska the best whale-watching state in the U.S. They are members of the order Cetacea, which also includes dolphins and porpoises, all of them descendants of warm-blooded, lung-equipped land mammals that adapted to the sea as far back as 100 million years ago. (Some researchers see parallels between the mating habits of humpbacks and Rocky Mountain bighorn sheep.) Cetaceans are either toothed (Odontoceti), with conical teeth adapted for seizing fish and other sizable prey, or baleen or moustached (Mysticeti), so called because of the flexible, bristle-fringed plates of their enormous jaws, which filter water as they entrap much smaller sea life. Most baleen whales—the blue, fin, sei, minke, and humpback among them—have pleated throat grooves, which extend as they feed. The humpback has another remarkable feeding technique: after using its blowhole to create a "net" of large bubbles that encircle and baffle its quarry, it plunges through the net—its massive mouth gaping as much as 90 degrees—and gulps up its panicked prey.

The BLUE WHALE—blue-gray in color—is the largest animal on the planet. Larger than even the mightiest dinosaur was, it has been known to grow to 150 tons and 100 feet, though most today are 10 to 30 feet shorter. Its heart alone can weigh in at half a ton (an adult

human could squeeze through its arteries), and its belly can take in two tons of seafood. For all its size, it feeds in shallow waters on an exclusive diet of minuscule shrimplike crustaceans called krill. The blue is seen on occasion in Prince William Sound.

The slightly smaller FIN WHALE—less than 70 feet long—has a sleeker appearance, a more diverse diet, and travels even faster than its cousin. Its back is darkish gray or even black, its undersides white, and two chevrons of white stretch diagonally from behind the blowhole down the sides to its tail. The fin, which has been observed in the Aleutians and Prince William Sound, cruises up to 6 knots, with spurts of more than 20. Its food includes anchovies and squid as well as krill. More sociable than the blue whale, the fin swims in pods of from ten to 100.

Among the more commonly sighted whales, from May through September, are the gray-backed SEI (pronounced *say*, from the Norwegian word for a fish that migrates at the same time in Scandinavia), a bottom-feeder with a pointier snout than the fin whale and a speed fleeter than any of its kind—38 knots or more; the MINKE (pronounced *min*-key), not much bigger than a killer whale, with a gray-black back, sometimes seen romping gregariously around ships and boats; and the equally friendly PACIFIC GRAY, christened for its mottled appearance and known for migrating the longest distance of any mammal. During their 12,000-mile return trips from the lagoons of Mexico to the Bering Sea, increasing numbers of grays can be seen along the shoreline of the Pacific coast. (In 1988, the world watched on TV as the Alaska National Guard, oil industry personnel, and Eskimo hunters carved breathing holes in the ice near Barrow on the Arctic coast to help two of three trapped gray whales reach the open sea.)

Most whales have been hunted commercially, often near the point of extinction, but the BOWHEAD remains an important source of food and oil for Eskimo whale hunters. (Its horny baleen, or whalebone, was once prized for use in corsets). Eskimos fancy a

A killer whale in the Inside Passage performs a sea-going ballet.

delicacy called *muktuk,* made from the whale's outer layers of skin and blubber. The bowhead, growing to 60 feet or longer, has a stocky body and an upwardly bowed mouth in a head that extends one-third its length. It leaps high and lands on its side, and sometimes groups with a dozen others in an efficient V-shaped pod, like geese in flight, to hunt prey. Cruise passengers who take land tours to the Bering, Chukchi, or Beaufort Seas are most likely to sight this endangered species, which by international law can now be hunted only for subsistence by Arctic Eskimos.

KILLER WHALES, or orcas—which are technically members of the dolphin family—until recently have been given a bad rap, one that endowed these highly social creatures with their distasteful name. In fact, there has been no recorded case of these black-and-white "wolves of the sea" ever willfully attacking humans (as any visitor to an oceanarium show would guess). In the wild, however, hunting in packs and wielding their two-dozen conical teeth, they are savage and quick-witted predators of birds, fish, turtles, squid, seals, sea lions, porpoises, and even the big blue and gray whales. And they can turn on their own too: two orca-literate biologists aboard a ferry in British Columbia's Inside Passage once saw a pack of locals brawling with three transients in what they suspected was the first recorded killer-whale "rumble."

Marine experts consider orcas even more intelligent than dolphins, who earned such flattering reviews for *Flipper* and other TV appearances. Zoologists have watched two killer whales tilt an ice floe with their backs and dump a seal into the awaiting mouth of a third orca. Others routinely liberate black cod from fish boats' longline hooks.

Mature males can grow up to 30 feet and 8 tons. The orcas' singular dorsal (back) fin, which may work like a keel, is triangular and can reach 6 feet in height. Orca water ballets have entertained hundreds of thousands at aquarium shows where their streamlined bodies, showing characteristic white bellies and flanks, take to the air and land with a calculated splashing of the audience. But they are never more gymnastic than when the male courts a female, leaping like a Baryshnikov and churning the water to froth. The resulting families bond over long periods of time; orcas have the most stable society of any mammal. A B.C. ferry captain has described how a pair of killer whales kept a bloodied young orca calf afloat after it had been cut by the ship's propeller; fifteen days later, they were still there trying to save the victim.

Dolphins and Porpoises   PACIFIC WHITE-SIDED DOLPHINS are the other stars of the world's oceanariums, vaulting well out of their pools, sometimes turning somersaults, and splashing down on their sides or backs. They perform the same hydrodynamic stunts in the open sea while traveling in herds of up to several thousand, from the Aleutians' Amchitka Island through the Gulf of Alaska and as far south as Baja California. Feeding near the shore on squid, anchovy, hake, and other fish, they can be identified by their tall black-and-white hooked fins. As jet black and snow white as killer whales, but with a pair of gray suspenders along the back, they are about a quarter the size of the orcas—with whom they sometimes hang around in the wild, hitching a ride in the wake of a killer-whale pod.

HARBOR PORPOISES are many times more bashful than their dolphin cousins. Although tending to congregate in the shallow waters of harbors, they are seldom seen for more than a moment in their Alaska hangouts, which range as far north as Point Barrow, around Prince William Sound, but mostly along the coasts of the Gulf of Alaska. The smallest of the cetaceans, half a dozen feet long, these blunt-nosed porpoises with small back fins are also hard to spot because of their prosaic brown-and-gray coloring.

DALL'S PORPOISES (named for American zoologist William Dall) are among the speediest of cetaceans, jetting along in bursts of up to 30 knots. While some are entirely white or black, most of these small-headed animals are black with white flanks. No longer than the Pacific white-sided dolphin, but a lot bulkier in build, they streak through Prince William Sound, the Gulf of Alaska, the Pribilof Islands, and as far north as Bering Strait. Occasionally, like dolphins, they ride the waves at the bow of a ship for several hundred yards.

Seals, Sea Lions, and Walruses These are all members of the fin-footed pinniped family, which share big eyes and snouts, spindle shapes tapering at both ends, and great diving ability. The shy PACIFIC HARBOR SEAL hides out from predators and humans by plunging up to 200 feet for more than twenty minutes at a time. It can slow its heart rate by three-quarters, to fifteen or twenty beats a minute, and constrict its blood vessels to conserve oxygen. Harbor seals' keen vision is better undersea than ours is in the air. Living on land as much as in water, these relatively plentiful seals are common along the Pacific Coast from Baja California to Alaska, especially on the reefs, sandbars, rivers, and estuaries of the Inside Passage. They breed in the water, exuberantly; the female's nips on the male's neck and shoulders appear far more brutal than mere love bites. They give birth in summer on rocks and icebergs, sometimes near tidewater glaciers like those in upper Glacier Bay. About 6 feet long and weighing up to 250 pounds, adults can be colored almost white or black but are usually a bluish gray, spotted with black and erratic white loops and rings. They are now legally protected in both the United States and Canada. But because they go after the same food that fishing boats track—shrimp, squid, herring—they're often considered a nuisance and killed.

The calisthenic STELLER'S SEA LION (named for German naturalist Georg Steller) is as surprisingly mobile on land. Waddling and lurching, it cavorts in rookeries on Benjamin Island in the Lynn Canal near Juneau and Forrester Island at the southwesternmost tip of the Panhandle. There, while the males can be triple the size of females—at 10 feet and more than a ton—the females can be ten times more abundant. Males are tan or the color of cork, darker on the chest (though they look white underwater); females are lighter but darken with age. The pups are silvery black. During the two months or more of summer breeding, the males do not feed, but they may have more than a dozen biting, battering fights with other raging bulls, and mate with a harem of up to thirty females.

A lone harbor seal basks on an iceberg calved from the Columbia Glacier.

In recent years, Steller's sea lions have been declared a threatened species, their numbers having declined from 150,000 in the 1950s to an estimated 25,000, possibly because of a shortage in herring, capelin, and other preferred food.

The PACIFIC WALRUS, which is more plentiful than it was a century ago, inhabits the Bering and Chukchi Seas. Eskimos in Nome and other centers still hunt them for subsistence meat as well as the ivory of their tusks, which they carve. Every summer, as many as 15,000 walrus bulls, up to 2 tons apiece, gather on the Bering's tiny Round Island before going north to meet their mates and calves. There they swarm together like college kids trying to squeeze into a telephone booth.

The walrus's warty hide and impressive tusks (each tusk can weigh as much as 12 pounds) make it unmistakable. After molting, the bumpy, hairless skin looks white in the water but pink in the sun. The walrus's scientific name, *Odobenus rosmarus*, comes from its habit of "tooth-walking": using its tusks to pull itself into position on an ice floe. On the sea bottom, those tusks, more than a yard long on the males, may be used like the runners of a sled as the walrus burrows in the mud to actually suck out from their shells the 150 pounds of mollusks an adult can dine on every day. And the walrus's sensitive whiskers help it find and sort the food. Less evident in looking at a walrus are the twin air sacs in its neck, which add resonance to its mating and communication sounds and also inflate to let the animal sleep with its head above water.

Otters The Russians called them "sea beavers" and referred to their valuable velvety fur as "soft gold." In hunting down SEA OTTERS, the Russian, and later American, traders nearly annihilated them. Once almost as thick in the water as flocks of sea birds, these affable mammals are resurfacing in southeastern Alaska, where ship passengers occasionally spot them. Several hundred were brought there in the late 1960s because of the underground nuclear testing on Amchitka Island in their traditional Aleutian home. These members of the weasel family are the smallest marine mammals: the adult male weighs no more than 100 pounds and measures less

The Rhyme of the Ancient Humpbacks

Dolphins send out sound waves for bouncing off any fish within their range to identify where and how far away and how big it is. Tests show that they can discriminate between objects about the size of BB-gun shot or a corn kernel at fifty paces. Killer whales' screams—called pulsed calls—keep members of a pod in contact with one another at long distances; each pod has its own dialect as well as at least one distinctive scream of its own. But the most fascinating sea-mammal communication may be the songs of humpback whales—which intrigue musicians and mammalogists alike.

The trumpeting, low-frequency pulses of the humpbacks in Alaska differ from those in Hawaii, where as they mate and calve they sing complicated songs that can last half an hour and be repeated for nearly a day. Some researchers believe that the songs are one way a female humpback chooses the right sire; others suggest they're symbolic weapons as males fight one another for the attentions of the females.

We now know that though the songs can differ widely from year to year, each whale always sings all the verses of the same current song. Which leads to the most intriguing hypothesis: humpbacks may actually use a kind of rhyme as a key to remembering the verses. Biologists Linda Guinee of the Long Term Research Institute of Lincoln, Massachusetts, and Katharine Payne of Cornell University's Laboratory of Ornithology captured linear pictures of hundreds of the songs on a spectograph. Sorting them into themes with phrases and sub-phrases, they noticed that a certain sub-phrase would frequently appear in the same place in adjacent themes, just as a rhyming pattern links lines of a poem. And they found these rhymes showing up most often in the more elaborate and harder-to-remember of these ever-changing songs—a discovery that Katharine Payne calls "one of the nicest examples of cultural evolution that has been gathered from any species in the animal kingdom, including man."

than 5 feet long. Its dense dark-brown or black fur may have almost a billion fibers. Feeding on the bottom of shallow waters, the sea otter uses uniquely rounded teeth to crush the clams and snails it carries to the surface in pouches that stretch from its forelegs right across its chest.

Sea otters are sometimes mistaken for their more detectable cousins, RIVER OTTERS, which also frequent salt water. Check the tail to identify which is which: the river otter's has a thick base and is more than half as long as its body: the sea otter's, which is flattened, is only a third of its length.

Stalking the Land

If there's one sight in the Alaska wilderness that embodies all of the state's grandeur, it's the vision of a 7-foot-tall, 1,600-pound giant sauntering down a hillside to draw water from a glacier-fed stream, its 70-pound antlers bobbing as it drinks. Faced with the spectacle of a full-grown Alaska moose, pioneering naturalist Charles Sheldon thought he had caught a glimpse of a dinosaur. Certainly, for him, "the sight of the moose among the spruces evokes a sensation of the creations of the long past." The antediluvian armature of the moose is less a throwback to the Jurassic past and more an emblem of the way the state's mammals have adapted to its multifaceted terrain. When the earth began heating up 14,000 years ago, the mammoths, saber-toothed tigers, and lions inhabiting Alaska disappeared. Moose—with long legs that let them graze above the snow line and impressive antlers to defend themselves—thrived. Meanwhile, in thick interior forests, northern flying squirrels evolved side pouches, stretching from forefoot to hind foot, which allow them to swoop from tree limbs in search of prey. On the northern ice, polar bears set up dens whose inner chambers can be as warm as steam baths. The barren ground caribou survived by developing their endurance and mobility as they roam the northern plains in an incessant search for calving grounds and their lichen of choice, caribou moss.

Moose While other mammals burrow or rely on camouflage as winter approaches, the MOOSE has taken the route of gluttony, giving it the sheer bulk to take on—or at least scare off—the grizzlies that often share its territory (the Kenai Peninsula, the Alaska Range, and Denali National Park and Preserve). Throughout the summer, moose browse on aspen and birch, though they'd walk a mile for a willow, their favorite tree. As the first flakes of snow start to fall on the upper limbs, most moose forgo sleeping and will spend twelve-hour days eating up to 60 pounds of leaves. During the winter, bulls and cows are hard-pressed to find foliage and are often driven to scrape through packed snow for a handful of lowbush cranberries. Their ceaseless browsing draws them toward towns, where the living is sometimes easier, but also across highways, where a frontal collision with a vehicle is often fatal to both man and beast. (An underpass was built beneath a six-lane highway leading to Anchorage to prevent such encounters.)

More than 160,000 moose are scattered throughout the state, showing their donkey ears and dangling noses almost everywhere except the southeastern Panhandle. They are shambling, affable creatures—except when in rut. Then the males, lean after a winter of avoiding the Alaska Railroad's cowcatchers, are ready to joust. Cows mingle nearby like half-amused courtiers, until two bulls square off, lowering the 7-foot spread of their antlers to charge. Antler tines often make their mark, causing serious or fatal gouges. All in all, it's a relatively chivalric affair—a browbeaten loser can step down, though there's no question of taking his pick of the onlookers.

Bears Moose, like most of Alaska's herbivores, are no danger to visitors, whom they take care to avoid—especially when there are calves around. The opposite is true of the largest carnivorous land animals in the world, the bears. They are common sights in Southeast, whether waddling up mountainsides with their cubs, gorging on 10-pound salmon adroitly swiped out of streams, or lacerating tents with a casual brush of a paw. Black bears, which can actually be cinnamon, brown, yellow, or even blue, thrive in the Panhandle, especially around Prince William Sound. Grizzlies roam most of the state, especially their sanctuary, the Kodiak Island Wildlife Refuge. On the northern ice, polar bears prowl in search of seals or the occasional stranded whale.

BLACK BEARS, relatively small roadside clowns in national parks from California's Sequoia to North Virginia's Shenandoah, are the aggressors in hundreds of disquieting—and sometimes fatal—encounters in Alaska. In Juneau and Ketchikan, they have been known to saunter up and down streets, inviting caresses that become deadly embraces (Juneau even has an ad hoc urban bear committee to promote safety in dealing with the interlopers). In the wild, their unpredictable behavior is a given. They may seem oblivious to the existence of passersby, allow them to continue on their way, and then suddenly charge at 35 miles an hour, as fast as a horse, often because hikers have approached a hidden cache of food. A sow with her cubs is the most likely to attack. One 175-pound beast in a maternal rage dragged off a geologist, no doubt planning to bury her catch for later consumption—the ursine method of choice for protecting corpses from marauding birds. The geologist was saved, though badly injured, and the bear was shot by rangers, who spared her yearling cub.

Black bears look like pikers next to the BROWN or GRIZZLY BEARS, which can outweigh them by more than 800 pounds, attaining up to 1,400 pounds. Though Alaskans often call coastal bears "browns" and the bears of the Interior "grizzlies," there's no real biological difference, in spite of the grizzly's distinctive shoulder hump. Browns thrive on the Kodiak Island Wildlife Refuge (set aside by President Franklin D. Roosevelt), where they lash out at the abundant sockeye salmon with a seasoned harpoonist's precision. Even heavier than mainland bears, the 3,000 Kodiaks evoke the Alaska that Charles Sheldon described in 1912: "No sight in the American wilderness is so suggestive of its wild charm as that of the huge bear meandering on the mountain-side, or walking on the river-bank, or threading the deep forest. He who still retains his love of wild nature...feels a lack in the wilderness—perhaps the loss of its very essence—when, tramping about in it, he knows that the bear, that former denizen of the depths, is there no more."

Sheldon's fears that the browns might one day be exterminated are so far unfounded. His biggest problem today would be keeping a safe distance from the 20,000 or so of these giants, which can run at least 50 miles an hour. Confronted with a grizzly on the same trail, experienced guides graciously step off the path. On the tundra, they walk away rather than run: browns consider anything that flees to be game, and to them a human being is as delectable as a caribou.

About 100,000 years ago, a group of grizzlies walked out on the arctic ice north of the Brooks Range and never returned. They became POLAR BEARS, white-coated behemoths, as at home swimming around ice floes as they are stalking seals on glaciers. They rove incessantly in search of fish, birds, walruses, and whales trapped in the ice. The only time they pause is beside the breathing hole of a ringed seal, where they'll wait hours for their favorite prey to surface for a lungful of air—then crush its skull with a single blow and haul it from the water.

Since the beginning of the 1970s, many hundreds of polar bears have been tranquilized and tagged by scientists working with helicopter pilots, often Vietnam vets whose military experience helps them dart away from the lunge of a half-dazed bear. Their study has shown that the bears, tracked by satellite, respect no international boundaries; like the 4,400 other polar bears in Alaska, they'll set up a winter den in Canada or Siberia just as readily as in Prudhoe Bay.

They deserve a winter lodge: polar bears walk more than 1,000 miles a year, and wind-chill factors of 75 degrees below Fahrenheit call for a comfortable den. Sows with cubs rest in chambers of mounded snow for up to six months, from October to March, leaving only on brief forays to teach the infants to fend for themselves, including such tricks as covering their black noses with white paws in order to camouflage themselves from seals basking on the ice. The cubs, duly trained and dispatched at about two years, will become independent adults, some of the few remaining predators truly fearless of human beings—mostly because they almost never encounter them.

Elk   The ROOSEVELT ELK lives in more temperate climes, on the islands off the south coast of Alaska, which also means that it is closer to humans—and prone to overhunting. In fact, the seven separate herds of the deer's dark-throated cousin, with its distinctive yellow rump patch, are the descendents of three young couples shipped from Seattle in 1928. Alaskans wanted to see the elk roam through the state as they did before the last ice age, and now there are about 1,300 on Kodiak, Afognak, and Raspberry Islands. This is not many compared to the herds in the lower western states, but elk in Alaska grow to an impressive size, rivaling moose in weight. Since the end of the 1920s, the herds dropped in number and nearly disappeared before recently resurging—especially on northwestern Afognak Island, where the abundance of spruce and the lack of clear-cuts and logging roads prevent overhunting. So far, transition to the mainland has not taken place.

Deer   Though Alaska has no shortage of SITKA BLACK-TAILED DEER, a colony of this relative of the elk was transported to Afognak Island and now abounds there. But Sitkas are far more common in the rain forests of southeastern Alaska and north coastal British Columbia, where the climate is tempered by the Japanese Current. On mountainsides, their black-tufted tails can be seen darting from sedge to salmonberries in spring, gradually moving up the mountain as melting snow unveils new growth. By July, they're feasting on deer cabbage, a protein-rich plant that sprouts at alpine heights. In winter, they descend with the snow, trying to get by on bunchberry dogwood and skunk cabbage. Often, they'll spend all of their short lives—eight to ten years—around the same mountain.

Caribou   The real nomad of the north, the twentieth-century equivalent of the buffalo that once furrowed western plains, is the BARREN GROUND CARIBOU. A caribou is a readily distinguishable deer: both males and females are horned, and their often-striped flanks and white throat patches bleach silver in the arctic sun. They eat on the fly, entering Denali National Park and Preserve at the beginning

A mother grizzly looms on guard, watchful for her cub.

of spring, heading south toward the Alaska Range. When the mothers have time for their knock-kneed calves—their maternal instinct is so weak that they have been known to let their offspring drown in a torrent without glancing back—they grant them the richest milk (containing 20 percent fat) of any land mammal.

A caribou herd crossing the tundra is like a dam-break suddenly flooding a peaceful valley. The animals flow over plains by the tens of thousands, driving snowy owls and peregrine falcons before them, trailed by wolves looking for laggards. Snipping at lichen and sedge, the bulls grunt and roar, relentlessly urging on the cows and calves as they test the wind for the odor of predators. Part of their agitation is caused by nose botflies, the beelike pests that spend most of their life cycle entrenched in the caribou's backs or nasal passages. A caribou's only respite from the sting of the flies is the cooling flow of water as it fords a river. To make matters worse, the female fly invades the nostrils of a caribou to store its larvae, which move on to overwinter in the animal's throat—waiting until spring to emerge, often forced out by the caribou's frantic snuffling and sneezing.

What makes the caribou migration really urgent is the fact that plant life is so sparsely distributed over the tundra. Lichens may grow only a sixteenth of an inch a year, and a willow branch could take two centuries to become finger-thick. In late spring, when the plants of the northern plains start to flourish, the pressure to feed is lessened, but a new imperative takes its place: the search for calving grounds. The estimated 130,000 animals in the Porcupine herd, the most important of the caribou groupings, make a beeline for the tundra north of the Brooks Range each spring, undeterred by rivers, railroads, or mountains. Congregating in the tens of thousands, the bulls watch over the cows, whose horns drop off at about the time they give birth. The calves are active almost immediately, running rings around their mothers, as though eager to start their lives of perpetual wandering.

Musk Oxen   The caribou calving grounds are shared by the horned MUSK OXEN, one of the most astonishing mammals in Alaska. Biologists say that from a distance they resemble giant caterpillars: their skirt-length coats make it almost impossible to distinguish rumps from heads. For the Eskimos, the musk ox was *oomingmak*, "the bearded one," a shoulder-humped source of fur and meat. Traders killed off the last musk oxen native to Alaska in 1865, but in 1930 the legislature had thirty-four of the hoofed mammals brought from Greenland. Gradually, tame animals were released on the Seward Peninsula and Nunivak and Nelson Islands. Their distinctive tendency to huddle in protective circles, horns outward, helped them thrive in spite of harassment by wolves, and restrictions on hunting prevented a recurrence of their nineteenth-century extermination.

Today, more than 1,000 musk oxen live on the tundra and islands north of the Arctic Circle, grazing on cotton grass, willow, and birch. Since 1986, the splay-footed animals have been raised on a farm in Palmer, north of Anchorage, where they graze as peacefully as cattle on a plain. At April's end, farm managers start combing the 900-pound bulls, a three-hour process that yields up to 7 pounds of *qiviut*, their soft underwool. (A single pound of the wool can be spun into a strand more than 25 miles long.) Eight times warmer than sheep's wool, shrink-proof and nonirritating to sensitive skin, *qiviut* is woven into elaborate garments and sold in boutiques throughout the state.

Dall Sheep The coat of the DALL SHEEP, the only white wild sheep in the world, is equally remarkable. Three inches thick in winter, its hollow hairs channel the warmth of the sunlight toward the sheep's body. Dall sheep can be seen jumping from cliffs to peaks on all the major mountain ranges of Alaska. Constantly on the lookout for wolves, they will graze nervously on low pastures and then make a sudden—and unexpected—dash for the safety of a jumble of craggy rocks. The rams have curling horns up to 50 inches long, which are more useful in establishing dominance during mating periods than in standing off a wolf pack. It's only through constant vigilance, keen eyesight, and a sure-footed grasp on rocks inaccessible to predators that the 3,000 Dall sheep of Denali National Park and Preserve manage to survive.

Mountain Goats   The only animals that can be mistaken for Dall sheep are the MOUNTAIN GOATS of Southeast. The goats' horns are much smaller, however, and black rather than golden brown. They are even more agile than the sheep, with cushioned, skid-proof pads on their black hooves. Hunters and hikers have tried to follow the goats up coastal mountains, only to find themselves trapped on a rocky face, unable to descend or continue upward, while the goats continue to jump from cliff to cliff.

Wolves   Alaska's WOLVES hunt with moderation. Running in packs of thirty, they'll take on Dall sheep, caribou, and even moose, but the sheep can outleap them, the caribou can outrun them, and a bull moose can drive them off with its antlers and sharp front hooves. The approximately 7,000 wolves of Alaska (which weigh up to 75 pounds each) are significantly larger than the endangered gray wolves down south. They can be found throughout the state, in

The northern light illumines the
antlers of a caribou in velvet.

Musk oxen gather in a characteristic
circle of defense.

dense rain forests, on northern tundra, or trotting along high ridges
in Denali National Park and Preserve. They have been a source of
fear and controversy for generations, but scientists are coming to
understand that wolves are hardly indiscriminate or rapacious kill-
ers. In the mid-1990s, Alaskans overwhelmingly voted to ban aerial
hunting of wolves and wolverines (and, surprisingly, the state has
fewer hunters per capita than places like Wyoming, Montana, and
even Georgia).

Wolf packs are highly complex groupings, led by a male and a
female who control the breeding of other couples. If food is scarce,
the dominant male will prevent others from mating, communicat-
ing his authority through growls, bared teeth, or simply a grim-
eyed stare. Wolves rarely fight among themselves, and the whole
pack participates in the feeding and rearing of pups. As the pups are
weaned in summer dens, the pack shows that it really is an extended
family: aunts, uncles, and grandparents all help nourish the young.

A group of wolves bonded together by lines of authority and
family ties defends its territory from other packs, preventing intruders

or lone wolves from crossing strictly marked boundaries. In Denali National Park, the packs control areas of up to 800 square miles, leaving "scent posts" by urinating on rocks or trees to mark the limits of their land. During the hunt, an encounter with another pack might lead to a standoff and an angry dispute; more often than not, the outnumbered pack simply backs off.

Ranging forth from its den, the pack hunts for twelve hours at a stretch, usually encountering several groups of prey: mountain goats, caribou, Dall sheep, moose, deer, and lots of mice. In most cases, the hunted animals outrun or outmaneuver the wolves: a caribou can easily outdistance a wolf, even when it's trotting at 25 miles an hour. Moose stand their ground, and unless the animal is obviously weak, the pack usually withdraws—the kick from the front legs of a bull moose can send a wolf flying 15 feet. Because the animals that wolves succeed in bringing to the ground are usually sick or lame, their hunting only rarely interferes with the healthy population of herds. When wolves do manage to make a kill, they tend to gorge, and each can bolt down as much as 20 pounds of meat at a time.

Returning from a successful hunt, wolves wag their tails, start to whine, and eventually one of the pack raises its muzzle and howls. The others join in gradually, shifting a note or two, creating chords. The mournful chorus is one of the most haunting sounds in the Alaska wilderness. Its echoes delineate the contours of surrounding cliffs, valleys, and mountains, serving as a reminder of the vastness of the surrounding landscape.

Small Mammals   Alaska is host to colonies of smaller mammals, whose range and populations often fluctuate wildly. The periodic peak in the numbers of SNOWSHOE HARES is one of the more spectacular examples. In ten-year cycles, the population grows until thousands can be seen on a single field, gnawing on power poles when they've stripped the bark from all the available trees. The hares that survive the summer competition for birch and willow turn completely white in winter; they wildly search the snow for vegetation as they're pursued by their chief predator, the LYNX. This

3-foot-long feline lies in wait, flat to the ground, as bands of famine-crazed hares pass by, leaping out only at the last minute. The lynx's feast ends the spectacular explosion, and in turn the cats die off as the hare population crashes.

BROWN and COLLARED LEMMINGS—the 5-inch-long rodents that range most of the state with the exception of southeastern Alaska—are even more astounding breeders. If food is abundant, the females can have seven litters of up to eleven kits each time per year. In a boom year, lemmings inevitably strip the surrounding grasses and sedges bare. After the typical four-year population rise and crash, only one lemming per acre may remain for every fifty that crowded underground nests the year before. If vegetation has been completely gnawed away, lemmings often move on in a mass exodus, snapped up by predators or dying of hunger or exhaustion along the way. The Eskimo word for the lemming is *kilangmiutak*, "the one that comes from the sky," a traditional way to account for the torrents of rodents that seem to have fallen from the clouds.

If there's one predator in Alaska willing to kill at the drop of a hat, it's the WEASEL. The agile, 7-ounce bundle of fur will attack hares that outweigh it several times over, gripping their throats until they bleed to death. It will pounce on fish in rivers, leap for birds on the fly, and even threaten humans who come too close. One biologist saw a weasel attack an eagle, relentlessly clinging to the bird's neck as it was borne aloft. The ERMINE, or short-tailed weasel, ranges through most of the state, turning brilliant white in the winter. It often moves into cabins, where it can mop up the entire mouse population in a couple of days.

Masters of the Air

At Bella Bella, as the ship threads through the Inside Passage's narrowest channel, they wheel overhead like traffic helicopters. When the floatplane lands on Rudyerd Bay in the wilderness of Misty Fjords National Monument, at least one of them is waiting, atop the tallest hemlock, its golf ball of a head lazily turning. And high in the woods of the national park in Sitka, looking like figures torn from the totem poles that line the pathways, they are there.

Bald eagles—10,000 to 15,000 of them in Southeast alone, more in this part of Alaska than in all the other states combined. America's national symbol, struggling back from a population of only 3,000 in the Lower 48 two decades ago, seems to be everywhere in Alaska. But while the state's biggest bird may be the most obvious master of the air here, it merely symbolizes one richness in Alaska's bird populations. Among them are such permanent residents as the submersible American dipper; the state's official bird, the willow ptarmigan, which has an enlightened male spouse; and the smallest visitor to summer here, the pugnacious rufous hummingbird, whose female partner can be vicious.

For bird-watchers, Alaska is next to nirvana, as they begin to realize soon after their cruise ships dock in Ketchikan, the traditional first port of call. Here, during migration flights, are sleek green-black cormorants, seabirds with skinny bills and four webbed toes; and long-legged, long-necked sandhill cranes, a wading species, which ranks among the world's tallest birds. Many species are resident in the state (or in Siberia) and few other places, including the whiskered rhinoceros auklet and the red-legged kittiwake gull; and others from Asia make their only North American visits here, such as the eyebrowed thrush and the red knot sandpiper. The summer visitors come in unimaginable waves of waterfowl followed by shorebirds and finally land birds, all intent on mating and nesting in the bittersweet briefness of the season. In his brilliant 1986 book *Arctic Dreams*, Barry Lopez describes astonishing concentrations of bird life in the southwest around the Bering Sea: 24 million migratory waterfowl and shorebirds summer on the delta of the Yukon and Kuskokwim Rivers, including all of the continent's emperor geese and rapidly declining spectacled eider ducks. One day in May 1982, the people of Nome watched whole flocks of sandhill cranes en route to Russia as they flew over the town virtually nonstop for two hours.

"One of the most exciting aspects of watching birds in Alaska," writes Brina Kessel, former curator of the museum at the University of Alaska, in her foreword to Robert Armstrong's *Guide to the Birds of Alaska*, "is that there is so much yet to be learned about them. We are still at the frontier of knowledge about so many aspects of Alaska's bird life that any observant bird watcher has a good chance of contributing new and valuable information about them...."

Because there are at least 443 species in the state, we have confined our descriptions to a sampling of some of the most common and interesting birds likely to be seen by cruise passengers.

Birds of Prey Anywhere else, the display in the Alaska State Museum in Juneau would be impressive: you walk up and around a life-sized eagle's nest, 8 feet wide and 12 feet deep, typical of the sticks-and-moss aerie this bird of prey expands year after year atop old-growth spruce and hemlock. Then you visit the Forest Service building next door to watch a film about a fledgling eagle's first clumsy attempts to fly. Anywhere else, museums and movies as well conceived as these would be satisfying of themselves; in Alaska, they are a mere adjunct to the reality of observing BALD EAGLES in the wild.

Come spring, a visitor to Alaska can see a pair locking talons as they cartwheel in aerial courtship, swooping as low as a couple of feet from the ground. In summer, ship passengers approaching Sitka through the narrows in Neva Strait may count nearly 100 eagles. Later in the year, the world's largest convention of the birds—more than 3,000—gather at the Chilkat Bald Eagle Preserve near Haines, where these noble raptors lose most of their dignity gorging on a late run of spawning chum salmon. Balds bond for keeps, generally occupying a single nest throughout their thirty-eight-year lifetime. Adults, with their white heads and tails and yellow talons and beaks, stand up to 43 inches tall and have wingspans as wide as 8 feet. They can fly 30 miles an hour, plunge at 100, and detect a trout a mile distant. They will eat small mammals and birds and love fish but as lazy scavengers (some Alaskans call them dandified vultures) they'll dine on carrion and even garbage. Their predators are humans—who slaughtered 100,000 of them between 1917 and 1952—which is why the Bald Eagle Protection Act now makes it illegal to kill or possess any part of an eagle or disturb its nesting site.

GOLDEN EAGLES look like immature bald eagles (which also don't have white heads), but these slightly smaller raptors have gold on their crowns and the back of their neck and on the leg feathers that stretch to their feet. Common in central Alaska, they are celebrated in many Native cultures as the Thunderbird or Great Spirit. And, unlike the balds, they generally eat live prey.

NORTHERN HARRIERS, the only hawks to nest on the ground, are sometimes confused with SHORT-EARED OWLS. Both wing their way through the wetlands and salt marshes of Southeast in spring and fall, hunting the ratlike voles by day. Both have similar facial disks and bodies shaped like an ice cream cone. But the gray-and-brown harrier, or marsh hawk, has a long tail, a white patch on its rump, and flies in a series of smaller flaps of its long narrow wings, interspersed with a glide—whereas the smaller buff-to-brown owl makes more exaggerated mothlike flutters.

Seabirds Of all birds, ARCTIC TERNS are *the* long-haul flyers. They are known to make an annual 22,000-mile round trip between the Antarctic coast and the western hemisphere's northernmost reaches. On their layovers in Alaska, they breed anywhere from beaches and tidal flats to rivers and marshes, and even on glacial moraine. They dive below the water to catch small fish with their sharp-pointed beaks. You can glimpse these 15-inch-tall birds—with their characteristic black cap, white body, and red bill and feet—throughout the south of the state anytime but winter. One hangout: Potter Marsh, at the Anchorage Coastal Wildlife Refuge, just south of the city.

Members of the auk family are the North American equivalent of penguins, standing as erect as their Antarctic cousins, but *they* can fly, though awkwardly. Black-and-white, bright-billed PUFFINS, the most prominent of auks, use their meager wings and strong legs, set well back, to swim underwater and catch fish and squid. They come ashore only to breed on cliffsides. Tufted puffins, so-called from the yellow feathers that flourish behind their eyes in nesting season, can sometimes be seen in Glacier Bay (along with the odd horned puffin, its white-bellied brother) and on Saint Lazaria Island near Sitka, one of the region's islands within the National Wildlife Refuge system.

All eight of the North American species of stubby-bodied, short-necked SEA DUCKS spend time in Southeast, the most numerous of the million ducks that winter here. Two of the more eloquently named, which are also on show for the cruise season, are the harlequin, whose blue-and-white body and chestnut flanks are reminscent of the traditional clown's costume; and the very vocal oldsquaw, which has a long, needle-pointed tail.

Shorebirds OYSTERCATCHERS, SANDPIPERS, and PLOVERS are the major families of numerous species of shorebirds visiting and often nesting in Southeast. Many of them migrate here from the southern coast of the U.S. and South and Central America. The vociferous oystercatchers are larger and more colorful than the others; they wield their long, blunt, flat red bills to shuck clams, mussels, and oysters. Sandpipers, snipe, and curlew are wading birds with sewing-needle bills and stovepipe legs on which they walk slowly and relentlessly as they graze the beach. The chubbier, shorter-legged plovers tend to run a lot before stopping to feed with their pigeon-sized bills—and some of them are masters of misdirection, decoying interlopers away from their nests with feigned injuries and pathetic little cries.

Waterfowl The world's largest waterfowl, the legend-inspiring TRUMPETER SWANS, summer in Alaska—12,000 of them, about 80 percent of North America's no-longer-endangered population, flock to the south coast of the state. White as arctic snow, they have sinuous necks and the buglelike cry that christened them. With wingspans the width of eagles', they soar to heights of nearly 2 miles on their migratory flights to the Pacific Northwest. Trumpeters are hard to distinguish from the smaller TUNDRA (formerly WHISTLING SWANS), which usually have a yellow spot on their black bill near the eye. Perhaps ten times as abundant, the tundras frequent Southeast waters.

VANCOUVER CANADA GEESE live and breed throughout the year

A bald eagle delivers a Dolly Varden dinner to its mate and three-week-old offspring. ▶

along the Pacific coast. And all summer long, they abound in the Mendenhall Wetlands; you can see them conveniently in these tidal flats near the Juneau Airport. The monogamous adults leave in April to nest elsewhere, whereas their adolescents remain until late June, when they head to Glacier Bay to molt. By August the whole family is back honking on the tidal flats, a togetherness pattern they'll continue all their lives. The most sizable of Canada geese, they have the typical black head, white cheeks, and long black necks but can weigh 14 pounds. Unlike others of their species, they nest on the ground in thick woods and occasionally even in trees, rather than on water.

The noisiest of all waterfowl, SNOW GEESE—all white as adults except for black wing-tips—are more frequent in south-coastal and central areas during spring and fall. In September they migrate from Siberia to the Seward Peninsula and then the Yukon River delta before heading to California and other southwestern states. (Huge flocks touch down near the international airport in Vancouver.)

Land Birds   The AMERICAN DIPPER's name may be an anomaly under this heading: the lyrical songbird spends a lot of its time underwater, on the bottom of streams where it walks along looking for insects and little fish. The Eskimos call it *anaruk kiviruk*— sunken old woman. And these chunky, short-tailed, gray perching birds are well endowed for their aquatic activities, with glands that create oil to waterproof their feathers, valves in their noses to keep out the water, and ducklike down that insulates them to 40-degree-below-Fahrenheit weather.

STELLER'S JAYS are amusing regulars at bird feeders in Southeast, where they display their street smarts in foraging—often ganging up to bully other species and aping the cries of predators such as eagles to scare away competitors for food. Permanent residents here, they are dark blue with black head and shoulders, and have the high-peaked crest of the common blue jay.

RUFOUS HUMMINGBIRDS, relatively recent arrivals in Southeast Alaska, now journey up from Mexico every mid-April while the snow is still around, then head south by August. They feed first on nectar from blossoming blueberry and salmonberry bushes before the flowering of western columbine and Indian paintbrush, which rely partly on these bird-world midgets for pollination. The rufous, all 3½ inches of them, have needlepoint bills to suck the nectar, and split-end tongues that fold it back into their throats. Male hummingbirds seem all show, with their shimmering burst of orange-red at the throat and their lack of interest in raising their young—a job they leave to the greenish-hued females, who are ferocious in their nestlings' defense against any human or wildlife interloper.

PTARMIGAN, Alaska's most plentiful grouse species, are a close cousin to another famous game bird, Scotland's red grouse. Although rock ptarmigan are more common, local school children cast ballots and made the willow ptarmigan the state bird. Perhaps they were influenced by the fact that the male is a good family man, assailing predators as big as hawks, helping tend the chicks as they hatch by early July, and even assuming the maternal duties if the female should die. Both types—which can be told apart only in summer by the willow's redder hue—were named for the habitat they prefer.

Rain-forest Giants

Alaska has the distinction of possessing the nation's largest and smallest national forest. So small is the latter that its entrance and exit require only one sign: "You are now entering and leaving Adak National Forest." This ambitious cluster of evergreens rises above the flat, windswept land of Adak Island in the Aleutians. Beating the climatic odds against them, thirty Sitka spruce, transplanted from Kodiak Island in 1944, are well formed and healthy, if somewhat shorter than those in Southeast.

Cruise-ship passengers touring outside Juneau, Ketchikan, and Sitka will likely find themselves on some portion of the nation's largest national forest—the 16.8-million-acre Tongass, which encompasses almost three-quarters of the land mass of the Panhandle.

The Rascally, Myth-Making Raven

High atop Mount McKinley, ravens are more than a nuisance. When mountain climbers hide caches of food below the snow, marking them with staked flags to locate them on the descent, they often find the birds have got there first, delving a yard or more to pillage the bags and boxes. On the other hand, the Athabascans in the Brooks Range of northern Alaska claim that ravens will help them find game by uttering a special call—*ggaagga, ggaagga*—and by folding a wing and tumbling in the sky to pinpoint an animal.

Ravens have been bedeviling and bewitching humans throughout history, throughout the world. But it is in the Great Land where the glistening-black, 2-foot-plus raven (*Corvus corax*) still looms even larger in the mind than its presence does in real life. Native peoples here have endowed the raven with mystical powers, symbolized on their totem poles. Elsewhere, it can be an evil presence (as Edgar Allan Poe pointed out), but many Indians of the Pacific Northwest and Alaska long ago considered the raven the creator of the world and—to amuse itself—of people.

With a wingspan 4 feet wide, and a weight about quadruple the American crow's, the imposing raven can also be distinguished from its relative by pointed rather than blunt wings, a long wedge of a tail in place of a square one, and a mostly caw-less vocabulary of calls that may be second only to humans'. They sing musically in choirs and coo to their mates-for-life softly and tenderly.

In scavenging and hunting, they demonstrate their astonishing intelligence. They have been seen working in teams to kill newborn reindeer fawns, with one raven separating mother from infant. And other teams have been observed stalking young seals sunning by their holes in the ice. A raven might fly into such a hole, blocking the escape hatch, while its colleague drives the seal away from the hole and then kills it with a well-directed strike of its powerful bill at the fragile top of the mammal's skull.

Within its boundaries are two national monuments, one national park, and seventeen designated wilderness areas.

Although nearly half of its old-growth stands have been logged, the Tongass remains the least-altered temperate rain forest in the world and the last great expanse of old-growth rain forest in the U.S. Its most common trees are conifers: 70 percent western hemlock, 20 percent Sitka spruce, and the remainder western redcedar, yellow-cedar, mountain hemlock, shore pine, Pacific silver fir, and subalpine fir.

Second in size nationally and the country's most northerly forest, the 5.8-million-acre Chugach National Forest stretches 200 miles from the Kenai Peninsula to the Copper River and sits only 500 miles from the Arctic Circle. And while a third of it is rock and glacier, the portions nearest the shores of Prince William Sound support a fine forest of western hemlock and Sitka spruce. The Kenai Peninsula sustains birch, aspen, white spruce, and black spruce.

The Alaska Division of Forestry manages Haines State Forest (mostly western hemlock, Sitka spruce, black cottonwood, and willow) and Tanana Valley State Forest in east-central Alaska (paper birch, quaking aspen, balsam poplar, black spruce, white spruce, and tamarack), which together cover 20 million acres.

SITKA SPRUCE is Alaska's state tree and was named for Sitka Island (now Baranof Island) where it grew abundantly in the Russian period. Hoping to make the Aleutian Islands more habitable, the Russians created the first commercial forest plantation in North America, introducing Sitka spruce to three small islands in Unalaska Bay beginning in 1805. Unfortunately only a few trees have survived the double hazards of fire and grazing animals.

To find a Sitka spruce in the rain forest, look for a tree trunk with a suggestion of purplish brown in its color. Other clues are bark that seems to have cracked into large loose scales and a trunk splayed at the base. But the surest identifier of Sitka spruce is its inch-long, pointed needles. If you shake hands with a twig, you'll wish you hadn't.

WESTERN HEMLOCK grows well in foggy, rainy conditions and can tolerate the shade that suppresses the growth of other trees. Look for western hemlock seedlings getting started on the trunk of a fallen tree (which Sitka spruce will also do). Nurse logs are good seedbeds, in part because they emerge first from a snowpack and are less encumbered with vegetation than the forest floor. The little trees will wrap their roots around the log as they reach for mineral soil. Western hemlock is characteristically loose in appearance. At a distance, you might spot a leading stem flopping to one side; closer up, notice fanning, downward drooping branches, and short, round-tipped, flat needles, which—possibly because of their different lengths—present a disorderly appearance on the twig.

No tree was more important to the Natives of the north Pacific than WESTERN REDCEDAR, which supplied everything from canoes to diapers. Along the coast, it was known by names such as "Rich-Woman Maker" or "Long-life Maker," names echoed by Europeans who called it the Arbor-Vitae, the tree of life.

The tree permits self-pollination, something that other conifers defend against; it is genetically less varied than other conifers (which are among the most genetically diverse of living things), and its growth is regulated more by temperature than by daylight. Other conifers stop growing as days shorten, but western redcedar will resume growth in a warm November.

Perhaps YELLOW-CEDAR's most interesting characteristic is its seeming reluctance to reproduce sexually. It takes 28 months for its seed cones to release a few seeds, which don't germinate well. Instead, the tree regenerates more efficiently when its drooping branches touch moist soil and put down roots.

Although western redcedar and yellow-cedar look similar because of their flat, braided, scale-like needles, they are quite different trees, belonging to different genera within the cypress family. In Southeast at sea level, you are more likely to see western redcedar. The seed cones of western redcedar are like small rosebuds clustered near the ends of branches. Yellow-cedar cones are nearly round with four or six scales, each with a peculiar triangular spur in the center.

Tundra, Fierce and Fragile

Strolling the summer rain forests of Southeast Alaska, plush with cloud-scraping spruce and hemlock, you may wonder about the barren Alaska of the storybooks. But head just north and west of there, on land excursions that take you to such destinations as Denali National Park and Preserve, Nome, and Prudhoe Bay, and you will begin to appreciate the expanse and allure of the TUNDRA.

This vast, mostly treeless plain (tundra is derived from a Lappish word for "land without trees") stretches across the northern verge of the continent. Swathed for most of the year in hostile snow and ice, each summer it becomes a crazy quilt of hues as vegetation—including more than 600 species of flowering plants—erupts with a sudden glory. The tundra is not homogenous in plant life nor, despite its winter bleakness, monotonal in color. Microclimates and unexpectedly rich soil combine to create startling vegetation vistas, such as the lush meadows of cotton grass that flourish not far from the bare foothills of the Brooks Range.

The transition between the northern forest and the tundra is called the TAIGA. In Russian that means "treeless marsh" and in the Chinook jargon of the Pacific Coast it's "land of little sticks," which nicely describes the pipe-cleaner-thin white and black spruce in Southcentral and the Interior. North of the taiga, the shrubs and stunted trees of the tundra, in tints of flame and gold during autumn, make way for viridescent grassland, which then yields to a polar desert dotted with lichen and moss—and a handful of tenacious perennials with blooms that seem prettier here than the most spectacular displays in the Lower 48.

Among the newest land in the world, tundra emerged when the glaciers retreated as recently as 8,000 years ago. Below most of it lies PERMAFROST, the perennially frozen ground that makes up 82 percent of Alaska. Sometimes only a foot below the soil, it can be 2,000 feet or more thick and often choked with ice. Given this

A splendid view of the tundra against the backdrop of the Alaska Range in Denali. ▶

impermeable base, water has nowhere to drain each spring so it advances across the land while forcing the earth to bubble up in boil-like ruptures. Common to all tundra are PINGOS, ice mounds carpeted in soil and plants, which can rear up like tiny volcanoes to 150 feet and spread thousands of feet in diameter through the expansion of freezing water trapped between permafrost and the surface. Prevalent too are POLYGONS, a series of ice-edged, interlocking landforms shaped like huge honeycombs, created by the endless action of freezing and thawing. Polygons fill with shallow pools of summer meltwater that often swell and spill their banks to become ponds and well-defined, elongated lakes. The land in summer is awash in water despite annual snow- and rainfalls of 20 inches or less.

Trees grow slowly and low to the ground here, to withstand brutal winds; a willow that stands only a foot tall can be 15 feet long and a century old. Arctic plants have developed different techniques to withstand the intensity of their environment. The woolly lousewort uses the insulating hairs on its stems and buds to contain heat. Virtually all of the tundra plants are perennials; they survive the long, bitter winters by reserving their food and energy in bulbs and roots reaching well underground. Primitive lichens combine fungi and algae in a symbiotic bonding: the algae create carbohydrates for the fungi, which then give the algae the necessary minerals and moisture.

Animals too must adapt to the tundra's inflexible conditions. Arctic ground squirrels hibernate for nine months deep in snow burrows that never get colder than 10 degrees Fahrenheit because the squirrels put their doorway below their sleep room, which prevents their body heat from escaping. And the snowy owl is so well adjusted to this land—the hostile yet life-enhancing tundra—that it even lays its eggs in the snow.

A World of Wildflowers

"In whatever direction the eye might look, wildflowers were growing in greatest profusion. Dandelions as big as asters, buttercups twice the usual size, and violets rivaling the products of cultivation were visible around. Berries and berry blossoms grew in a profusion and variety which I have never seen equaled in lower altitudes." That's Frederick Schwatka, a first lieutenant in the U.S. Army and a graduate in law and medicine, rhapsodizing in *Along Alaska's Great River*, his account of an expedition along the Yukon River in 1883. Today you can view about 1,500 species of plants in Alaska, including trees, shrubs, ferns, grasses, and sedges—but of them all, the brief-lived, gloriously painted flowering plants may delight you most.

As in the south, Alaska's wildflowers thrive along lakes and roadsides and across alpine meadows, and you can always find them here in thick throngs on the tundra. The majority are delicate and, like their growing season, short. The official flower, for instance: the fragile-looking forget-me-not (*Myosotis alpestris*) has vivid blue petals around a yellow center; it grows no more than 18 inches while its arctic counterpart never tops 4 inches. But some flowers take terrific advantage of the long days and explode like fireworks. Blooming through the summer, throughout most of the state, are easily identifiable stands of stately, violet-blue lupine, up to 4 feet tall, and magenta fireweed, which can reach 10 feet (and whose shoots helped feed the eighteenth-century Vitus Bering expedition). In meadows near the tides of the southern regions, you can walk through fields of flowers as high as your hips: yellow and red Indian paintbrush, white yarrow, purply blue flag (or wild iris). Along with the blossoms you know from the south—violets and buttercups and wild roses—look for such indigenous delights as the delicate Arctic poppy and the chocolate lily, a purple-brown flower growing 2 feet high in open grasslands, whose nickname Indian rice comes from the edible pellets that coat its bulbs.

The photographs on the following page are a mere sampling of the pleasure that awaits you.

Indian Rice or Chocolate Lily

Arctic Poppy

Fairy Slipper

Western Columbine

Cinquefoil or Tundra Rose

Chiming Bells or Languid Lady

SPORTING ADVENTURES

We were kayaking on Camp Coogan Bay, a fast ten-minute ride in a rigid-hull inflatable across Eastern Channel southeast of Sitka. Our two-person kayaks launched from a floating dock and boathouse into a quiet, mile-long bay with conifers and devil's club growing right down to the water and snow-topped mountains rising in a distant loop around us. Our group of eight followed close to the starboard shore where the guide, Mike, tucked his kayak in under overhanging branches and reached down into the shallow water to pull up a yellow sunflower starfish and an orange leather starfish. Paddling along, we viewed dozens of jellyfish, some as big as bread plates, others reminding us of wontons. Just about then, Mike commented appropriately that we could eat anything we found below the water.

Food was the farthest thing from our minds as we kept looking for a bear on the flat grassy shore at the head of the bay. We had to settle for a belted kingfisher and two blue herons. Then, as we continued our bear watch, the smooth water ahead shivered, punctured by many small triangles—the dorsal fins of salmon. Suddenly we were surrounded by acrobatic fish diving into the air, flashing the pink of their bellies, some moving in straight lines, others in complete circles.

There are various theories about why the fish leap, but Mike told us he likes to think they do it because they're happy to be home in Alaska's waters. For a long time before paddling back to the camp, we floated happily in silence among the joyful fish.

Opportunities like this, combining nature-watching with exercise and sport amid clean air, unpolluted waters, and glorious scenery, find their most dramatic flowering in Alaska. What follow are glimpses of the possibilities that await those wanting to experience the state's sporting adventures.

Sportfishing The fish are big in Alaska—and they can be ferocious too. Consider the experience of Ron Dawson of Juneau, who flies his Piper Cub floatplane to wonderful fly-fishing holes around the Panhandle. One summer he and a buddy settled down on Tracy Arm, a wilderness fjord about 50 miles southeast of Juneau, for a spot of halibut fishing. After hooking a 60-pounder, he had to rev up the engine and take off fast when a strong wind rose on the water—so fast that his friend was still hanging on for dear life to the fish dangling on a line outside the plane. The halibut, which didn't take kindly to this variation on fly-fishing, knocked half a dozen holes in the side of the Piper Cub before the pilot could land the plane—and the fish.

Cruise-ship companies offer their passengers fishing expeditions (as well as packing and shipping services) at several stops along the way in Alaska, especially in Southeast, where the cruise season parallels some of the best runs of sport fish. The whole state is an angler's Shangri-la: five species of salmon remain plentiful, the freshwater trout offer superb eating, the arctic char and grayling are exotic catches, and the halibut are big enough to batter planes.

Normally halibut aren't quite that fearsome, but they—like many other species—can grow enormous. (Ron Dawson had to drag one 258-pounder behind his plane to shore, where he could deal with it.) While an official record is 440 pounds and 97.5 inches, marine biologists speculate that the white-bellied bottom fish could balloon to half a ton here. These flatfish tend to frequent the depths, from which they may demand an hour or occasionally several hours of an angler's time to land. Using octopus and herring as bait—or artificial lures, as we've done—you can find halibut year-round; the waters off Sitka and Skagway are especially good spots.

Salmon offer some of the finest saltwater sportfishing, and you can tackle them by booking trips aboard mini-cruisers in many ports of call, including Ketchikan, Juneau, Sitka, and Skagway. Alaska has the biggest king salmon in the world, nearing 100 pounds—or more, if you believe the word of mouth. You can troll for these giants, known locally as tyee, chinook, and springs, in Southeast saltwalter, where whole or cut herring, spoons, and spinners attract them. More abundant are pinks, the smallest of salmon, averaging little more than 4 pounds. These humpbacks (named for the bump they develop while spawning) like spoons, spinners, herring, and blends of flashers and Hoochies. While sockeye, or reds, can be the tastiest salmon—and sizable, at about 6 to 12 pounds—they're also the trickiest to find and land in salt water, though tiny plastic squid and Hoochies do work. For wet-fly fishing for sockeye on a seven-weight fly rod or medium-weight spinning gear, the Russian River area in the Kenai Peninsula is considered a classic, if crowded, location. Coho, or silver, salmon are swift and smart, average 7 to 10 pounds, and run from midsummer to November. Trolling for them, you might use fresh herring or salmon roe (though the roe is so seductive that some jurisdictions don't allow it). Chum are the least desirable of salmon, despite sizes of up to 20 pounds, because of their reputation as feed for sled dogs—hence their nickname, dog salmon. Roaming as far afield as the high Arctic, they seldom take a lure.

Freshwater fish—which can be caught on independently arranged fishing jaunts as well as some saltwater tours in the south and Southeast—include native rainbow trout, the sea-going rainbows called steelhead, and the cutthroat. Try them on flies, lures, and eggs. All are excellent sport fish and terrific eating. Other angling possibilities include Dolly Varden, a kind of char that react to eggs, spoons, and flies; and the arctic grayling, which go after just about anything, from small spinners to flies to the young salmon called smolt.

River Rafting Running Alaska rivers in inflatable rafts can be sport for everyone, independent of age, size, and even physical condition. Some of the runs offered to cruise-ship passengers are quiet and even soothing; others are breathtaking rides through a rapid's white water. All of them transport you—in more ways than one—through stunning landscapes where your unobtrusive presence might permit close-up views of wildlife and other natural wonders.

Check with your tour organizers for the float trip that meets your needs. Some trips are restricted to those above five years old, others to those above eleven.

Ask whether you should take a camera and what you should wear; warm clothes and thick wool socks (perhaps even an extra dry pair) are usually advised. Experienced rafting companies provide the rest of the gear, including the requisite life jackets and, if necessary, rainwear and rubber boots. The guides are skilled and refuse to take chances with a boatload of passengers, yet manage to create exciting voyages that taste of adventure.

A sampling of some of the float trips offered:

On MENDENHALL LAKE near Juneau, a raft plies the calm iceberg-dotted waters—with a full-frontal view of Mendenhall Glacier—and heads into the glacier-fed Mendenhall River and its brief bouts of gently boiling rapids. Halfway through, there's a stop amid a mountain setting for a snack of such regional food as smoked salmon and reindeer sausage.

The TAIYA RIVER trip, arranged from Skagway, starts with a hike through rain forest and salmon-rich streams along the Chilkoot Trail before you float serenely to a tidal estuary where the walls of the fjord rise to glaciered peaks. A beachside snack is included as you observe seals and eagles looking for lunch.

KEYSTONE CANYON outside Valdez provides a thrilling one-hour, 4½-mile rush through a breach in the Chugach Mountains, past 900-foot Bridal Veil Falls, along the glacially cold Lowe River. It was here in the canyon that guards from the infamous Alaska Syndicate shot five men from the competitive Alaska Home Railroad in the early 1900s.

DENALI NATIONAL PARK offers a choice of runs down the Nenana, one of the preserve's less riotous rivers. A two-hour scenic float for the family down the broad and civilized Nenana lets you watch wildlife while passing through 13 miles of valley, forest, and tundra among the Alaska Range mountains, ending in an explosion

Alaska, an angler's nirvana, offers some of the world's best fishing.

of whitewater. A two-hour, 11-mile rapids run propels you through a straight-sided canyon and a succession of rapids with such suggestive names as Splatter Rock and Royal Flush.

Paddling Expeditions   You don't have to be an expert to float your way along the lakes, rivers, and seas of Alaska. Tour operators use professional guides who offer basic lessons in both mountain canoeing and sea kayaking before setting off with you in safe conditions on manageable waterways.

A typical MOUNTAIN CANOE ADVENTURE begins with a motor-coach trip in Ketchikan to a backwoods lake in the Tongass National Forest. There you're instructed in paddling a twenty-passenger, Native-inspired canoe, which will take you along the rain-forest shore with a stopover for a snack that might include chowder accompanied by sourdough rolls slathered in wild berry jam. Along the way, expect to learn about the Native and natural history of the area in the most pleasurable manner possible. There's also a specially designed teenagers' canoe trip offered in Ketchikan.

SEA KAYAKING is as exciting as it sounds. In Sitka, for example, you can board a Zodiac-style inflatable to reach a floating camp where, after a lesson in paddling techniques, you can spend ninety minutes along the sheltered inlets in reassuringly stable two-person kayaks. The bonus might be sightings of brown bears and black-tailed deer on land, harbor seals and sea otters on the water, and bald eagles and marbled murrelets in the air. Kayaking is also available in the Juneau area to sites such as the Mendenhall Wetlands in the shadow of the imposing glacier of the same name, around the Tatoosh Islands and Whiskey Cove off Ketchikan, and through Duck Flats near Valdez. And teens can take a wilderness kayak jaunt off Sitka.

World Eskimo–Indian Olympics   Many of the twenty events sound like something out of the Marquis de Sade's fevered imagination: the Ear Pull, in which competitors twine dried seal gut around their ears and yank their heads back sharply, occasionally losing these organs in the process; the Ear Weight, which has them walking up to half a mile with a load of lead as heavy as a bowling ball hanging from their ears; and one of the most painful, Drop the Bomb, where an individual is picked up by wrists and ankles and his rigid body toted around until it collapses in agony.

If you happen to be in Fairbanks during the second-last weekend in July, you can witness all this—and lots of other unusual sports that depend more on strength and endurance than a high pain threshold. Since 1961, the World Eskimo-Indian Olympics have attracted thousands of spectators and international media each year to watch hundreds of men and women representing every Native group from across the state, Canada, Greenland, and Siberia.

Sports in this case include cutting up salmon, high-kicking, and walking a greased pole. All of which gives a hint of what inspired these centuries-old athletic contests: crucial life skills and perseverance, a combination that equals survival in the North's ferocious living conditions. Obviously, speed in cleaning fish and mammals was vital in vicious weather. Strolling a bumpy log slick with vegetable oil harks back to the time not long ago when Indians had to negotiate a slippery tree trunk that led to a fish-catching wheel far out in a frigid river. And high-kicking? The astonishing leaps of well over 6 feet to touch a suspended ball with the feet is a sporting version of the jumps Eskimo whalers made to communicate to those on shore that they'd captured a whale.

Those high kicks are ranked the hardest events, despite the challenges of other contests. Such as the Four-Man Carry, in which an individual stumbles along with a quartet of 150-pounders circling his torso, in a feat that sends some competitors to hospital with dislocated backs. Or the Kneel Jump, in which some contestants can leap nearly 4 feet on their knees. Or the White Man Versus Native Woman Tug o' War, where the women are almost always triumphant.

THE NATIVE WAY

Their homes may be in Anchorage where 19,000 live, or far north in the Arctic National Wildlife Refuge, where the isolated village of Kaktovik has a few hundred permanent residents. Alaska's 98,000 Native peoples collectively own one-ninth of the state and are dispersed throughout it, most in rural areas, some in isolated villages with no road connections to the outside. Their lifestyles combine imported southern comfort and traditional northern toil. Satellite telephones link distant health clinics to a modern hospital; high schools have indoor swimming pools; planes fly in with pineapples and Pampers. While some men might earn $60,000 a year on the oil rigs, both high- and low-income families like to supplement their store-bought food by hunting and fishing. Though they travel to the open sea in snowmobiles and put outboard motors on their modern boats, they will work together in the old way to land a whale. Not long ago, 150 Inupiat from Barrow spent five hours hauling a 50-ton bowhead out of the Chukchi Sea and another seven hours carving and sharing its meat and blubber. Alaska's Native Indians, Eskimos, and Aleuts continue to subsist on and care for the land that sustained their ancestors. As the Yup'ik Eskimos say, the sea is their bank, the land is their life.

Alaska's first peoples have long been political activists. To promote their rights, they formed the Alaska Native Brotherhood in 1912 and the Sisterhood in 1915. Also in that year, Athabascan chiefs convinced Alaska's delegate to Congress that the state should not

Eskimos, though no longer dependent on sled dogs, still cherish their hardiness.

have a reservation system. Native peoples elected a representative to the state legislature as early as 1925. A decade later, they sued the federal government over lost timberlands. They stopped the proposed use of a nuclear device to excavate a harbor on the northwest coast. They tied up the entire state in land-claims litigation and formed the Alaska Federation of Natives to push their claims through Congress. Finally, they allied themselves with oil companies to achieve the Alaska Native Claims Settlement Act of 1971.

The act plucked Native peoples from lives of communal subsistence and plunged them into the business world as stockholders in landholding, multimillion-dollar corporations. It may have taught them to function more like white people but it has paradoxically led to a cultural rebirth. Wendell H. Oswalt, a professor emeritus of anthropology at the University of California, points out that ANCSA required Natives to examine their historical, biological, and geographical connections in order to claim the right to be enrolled in a regional and village corporation and to share in the corporations' moneymaking ventures. As a result, he writes, "a personal identity as a Native Alaskan became a favorable status for the first time in this century."

While Native corporations made and lost millions of dollars in the 1970s and 1980s, some members became increasingly nervous about losing their land, which the corporations owned. If individuals sold their stocks, the corporations would be vulnerable to non-Native takeover. A 1987 amendment to ANCSA prevented the sale of stocks unless a corporation voted to lift the ban. As of 1997, no corporation had taken that step. A survey released in 2001 showed that the twelve Alaska-based regional corporations and the three largest village corporations employed 10,000 workers in the state, made charitable contributions of $8.6 million in 1999, and over a period of ten years had paid about $500 million in dividends to shareholders. The Arctic Slope Regional Corporation, with revenues exceeding $850 million a year, made *Forbes*'s 1999 list of the top 500 private U.S. companies.

On the political side, self-government has been a prominent issue. Many villages removed themselves from the state system of municipal government and chose instead a tribal council chartered under the 1936 Indian Reorganization Act. This movement toward sovereignty offers hope for control and revitalization among people who have been particularly afflicted by modern social ills. Life expectancy among Alaska Natives is astonishingly low: a fifty-year-old Eskimo comments with sadness that in the Yukon-Kuskokwim area he is one of the older people. The suicide rate among young Native men is ten times the national average; the occurrence of fetal alcohol syndrome in Native infants is twice the national rate. Murder, rape, arrest, and psychiatric—admission rates for Native Alaskans are all multiples of those for non-Natives.

On the other hand, there are villages that have banned alcohol, high schools that invite elders to teach traditional skills, communities that keep alive ancient ceremonies. In some cases, tribal councils have stimulated an examination of cultural values. Anthropologist Ann Fienup-Riordan studied one example in western Alaska. In the 1990s, Akiachak, a Yukon-Kuskokwim village, dissolved its second-class municipality in favor of a governing tribal council. The village then helped form the Yupiit Nation, a confederation of fourteen tribal governments. Trying to find a culturally appropriate way to govern themselves, its members researched traditional forms of government and resurrected a respect for their ancestors' ways. Participants in meetings use the Yup'ik language; elders are allowed to speak first and are rarely interrupted; everyone who wants to speak is given a chance. The Yupiit Nation has given its members a forum where, in a traditional way, they can discuss issues such as education, control of land and local affairs, economic conditions, and the survival of their language and values.

The Complex Eskimo Culture

The Eskimos we know from movies and schoolbooks lived in igloos, hunted polar bears, ate raw seal meat, and struggled to survive in a punishing environment. This stereotype, which applied to a small percentage of Arctic dwellers, does not fit Alaska Eskimos generally.

The people anthropologists call Eskimo extend from Siberia through Alaska and Canada to Greenland, but Eskimo isn't what they call themselves. Even the widely accepted meaning of the name—from the Algonquian for "eaters of raw flesh"—is being challenged by authorities who say it is the Chipewyan term for "snowshoe-netter." In Canada, Eskimos prefer to be known as Inuit or Inuvialuit; in Alaska, two broad designations are used: Inupiat and Yup'ik. About 13,500 Inupiat live in Alaska, 3,000 of whom speak Inupiaq, which is both the word for the language and for an individual. The Inupiat live in northern Alaska. Central Alaska is home to 21,000 Yup'ik, the largest of the state's Native groups. About 10,000 people speak the language, which is also known as Yup'ik. Inupiaq and Yup'ik are as different as English and French, and it is easier for an Inupiaq speaker to communicate with an Eskimo in Greenland than with a Yup'ik neighbor.

Early anthropologists found a rich complexity and diversity among Alaska Eskimos, so much so that it was impossible to define a single Eskimo culture. Family-based groups lived in a variety of

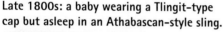

Late 1800s: a baby wearing a Tlingit-type cap but asleep in an Athabascan-style sling.

climates from the relatively warm and abundant islands and shores of the Gulf of Alaska to the frigid desert of the Arctic slopes. Some never saw polar bears. Some hunted great whales, others only caribou. Some scooped salmon out of rivers and were more like their Indian neighbors. For most, their environment, rather than being impoverished, was an ample provider. Even though we picture Eskimos busily gathering enough food to last through a winter, Wendell Oswalt found that many groups had a more relaxed attitude and would let fish go uncaught while they feasted on their dried stores. There was, he says, "no Protestant ethic among Alaskan Eskimos."

If the Inupiat and Yup'ik didn't build igloos, where did they live? Some inland tribes close to the Athabascan Indians fashioned dome-shaped houses with pole frames, but usually Alaska Eskimos established villages of permanent semi-subterranean houses of driftwood, whalebone, and sod, sometimes heated with a fireplace or seal-oil lamp. The inhabitants entered their homes by way of a cold-trapping tunnel, set deeper the farther north they lived. Most houses were equipped with raised sleeping platforms, and some were finished inside with driftwood-plank floors and cupboards. In summer, when families were more mobile, they used portable tepees or campsite shelters.

Yup'ik men and boys older than five occupied a communal residence—a *qasgiq*. Wives brought meals to their husbands in the *qasgiq*, and husbands visited their wives who lived with their young children and other female relatives in a smaller house called an *enet*. Inupiaq settlements had a ceremonial *qargi*, which was a place where men and boys met during the day and families gathered in the evening to socialize.

Both the Yup'ik and Inupiat lived in groups based on blood or marriage kinship. The availability of food affected the size of these family groups. Yup'ik groups were larger, sometimes several hundred people, because food was more abundant below the Arctic Circle. Inupiat groups might grow to fifty family members, with several groups of this size occupying a food-rich territory.

Among the Yup'ik, both parents dropped their own names and were known by the name of their firstborn. Feasts marked a child's achievements: the first time a boy killed anything, even an insect, and the first time a girl picked a berry or provided something the family could eat. Divorce was common. A woman with a lazy husband ended the marriage by refusing to cook for him; a man divorced a wife who hoarded food, perhaps by abandoning her without supplies.

Both the Yup'ik and the Inupiat waged war with neighboring groups. In the far north, the hunting, food-gathering season was an accepted time of truce; fighting would be resumed in the dark days of winter. Long-standing grievances led to surprise attacks in which the goal was to exterminate the enemy, leaving one survivor to tell the unhappy tale. Warriors tattooed their faces and chests to indicate the number of enemies they had killed.

Aleuts: Return from Tragedy

The Aleuts have had a tragic history. In 250 years their numbers have been reduced to one-tenth by contacts with outsiders. When Russian fur traders invaded their windblown homeland between 1750 and 1780, 15,000 to 18,000 Aleuts inhabited the 279 Aleutian Islands. By the end of the eighteenth century, there were perhaps 3,000 left. As American citizens, the Aleuts were unceremoniously herded from their homes in 1942, after the Japanese bombed Dutch Harbor. They were moved to a cannery in Southeast for two miserable years, during which a fifth of them died. In 2001, according to the Alaska Native Language Center, of 2,200 Aleuts on the islands only 300 spoke the Aleut language. Things are looking up, however. Commercial fishing and eco-tourism are rejuvenating the islands of St. Paul and St. George in the Pribilofs, where most of Alaska's Aleuts live. The Aleut Corporation, with more than 3,000 shareholders, owns subsidiary corporations engaged in the development of real estate and natural resources. One subsidiary holds investments in office buildings in Colorado and a hotel in Oregon; another operates a processing plant on Adak Island supplying high-quality seafood to European customers.

In 1805, Russians sketched this sampling of Tlingit
artifacts, including the raven rattle (bottom middle).

Anthropologists believe that at some time after their arrival in North America the Eskimoan people subdivided into Eskimo and Aleut. The Aleuts occupied the 1,200-mile arc of islands—the longest archipelago in the world—that separates the Pacific Ocean and the Bering Sea. In spite of moderate temperatures, the islands are frequently enshrouded in fog or whipped by high-velocity winds known as williwaws. Bushes, grasses, and sedges grow luxuriantly on the almost treeless land. The oldest known settlement in the Aleutians dates back 8,750 years.

The pre-contact Aleuts had a high standard of living. They practiced medicine and surgery. They developed art and music and also mounted elaborate masked ceremonies (the conclusion of which, unfortunately for art history, sometimes meant the destruction of the masks). They lived in semi-subterranean sod houses, which were earthquake-proof and sheltered from the capricious winds. A rich Aleut might have as many as twenty slaves, obtained as prisoners of war. The Aleuts were skilled hunters of sea mammals, and much of their art was created with the hope of ensuring successful hunting.

The Art of Aleuts and Eskimos

Three overlapping motivations categorize Eskimo and Aleut art. In the traditional period before outsiders arrived, spiritual beliefs inspired the crafting of ceremonial and utilitarian objects. Charms carved in the shape of a human face were attached to Aleut hunting weapons to guide them to the animals. Human figures, which seem to be searching the sea for prey, crouched atop Aleut hunters' hats. An Eskimo hunter might make a seal-shaped box to hold his lance points, believing that the tools would become accustomed to being inside a seal.

While this sort of artistic expression continued after contact with Europeans, Eskimos and Aleuts quickly learned to make objects for sale. (When Captain Vancouver visited the Kenai Peninsula in 1794, he was offered model kayaks that had been made as souvenirs.) Throughout the nineteenth century, beautiful objects were produced for personal use and offered for sale. Into the next century, Eskimo and Aleut artists continued to make art for the tourist and gallery markets, emerging from anonymity by signing their work. Only in recent times have they entered a third phase of artistic expression, which steps outside their own culture—making art for art's sake.

Throughout Alaska in traditional times, Eskimos and Aleuts used ivory, stone, wood, bone, grasses, hides, furs, and animal intestines for a dazzling variety of art objects. If you visit one of Alaska's museums, watch for examples of the following items.

Prehistoric stone lamps: Found in archeological sites, especially in the Kodiak Island area, these oval containers were decorated on their outside rims with sculptured animals, whales, or humans.

Carved ivory weapons: The Eskimo believed that an animal should be hunted with beautiful implements because the animal's spirit—its *inua*—would be reborn in another animal and would remember that it had been treated with respect. Their fish spears, toggle-headed harpoons, and harpoon darts, as well as being technically ingenious, were works of art.

The Nunivak tusk: In the 1920s, the Eskimo men on Nunivak Island began carving walrus tusks in a unique way, with animals and birds linked in one long, deeply carved chain.

The Nunivak eye: Many ivory objects are decorated with this dot-within-a-circle motif, which is called "the eye of awareness." It has been explained as a symbol of the ability of a shaman—the spiritual leader who may cure people and tell the future—to journey into another world (through the hole in the circle) or to see into other worlds.

Amulets and charms: Made by both Aleuts and Eskimos, they provided supernatural protection or help. Aleuts most often carved ivory sea otters as charms. An Eskimo might have two dozen amulets, each representing a spiritual helper. Charms were attached to boats or houses.

Ivory drill-bow handles: In the historic period, these drilling devices, which resemble a bow and arrow, were engraved with scenes of Eskimo life, such as ships trading with Bering Sea Eskimos, or important events in the artist's own life.

Engraved ivory cribbage boards: The first boards may have been carved early in this century by Happy Jack, an Eskimo from Little Diomede Island who had lost both feet in a hunting accident. Long, sinuous walrus tusks were used for this popular souvenir.

Ivory, bone, antler, wood, and baleen story knives: A knife was usually carved by a male relative for a young Eskimo girl, who used it to draw on the ground as she told a story, which always began with the sketching of a house floor plan. Girls apparently found it difficult to tell a story unless they were drawing at the same time.

Coiled baskets: Poorly made in the nineteenth century, the grass baskets of Yup'ik women began to improve in the early years of the twentieth century. The technique involves coiling a bundle of compressed rye-grass stems, and stitching together succeeding levels of the coil. Traditional designs were simple geometric patterns.

Wooden masks: Eskimos made a variety of masks representing human faces or half-animal/half-human faces. Worn by dancers in ceremonies rather than in war, masks honored the spirits of animals or birds about to be hunted or evoked angry or dangerous spirits. Some masks covered almost the whole body.

Aleut weaving: Aleut women made exceptionally delicate baskets, mats, boot liners, hats, and mittens using wild rye grass, the blades of which were dried and cured and split with a fingernail. Different weaves developed on Atka and Attu Islands, where the women wove some of the finest baskets in the world. Even exceptionally skilled weavers took fifteen hours to add an inch in height to a 3-inch-diameter basket. Before contact with westerners, baskets were decorated with eagle down, feathers, baleen, and colored grass; afterward, threads of silk and wool were incorporated. To supply the nineteenth-century market, weavers made card cases, covered bottles, and lidded baskets. Production declined in the years after World War I when a number of basketmakers died, but it has since been revived.

Bentwood hats: Made of a single piece of wood, steamed and bent into a triangular shape, these hats were worn by wealthy Aleut leaders. The visorlike front was both blessing and hazard: although it shaded the wearer's eyes when he was hunting at sea, it might have caught a gust of wind and overturned his boat. The hats were painted and decorated with ivory amulets, feathers, beads, or bristles of a sea lion (of which each animal has only four; hats aquiver with bristles indicated the owner's hunting skill).

Gut parkas: Made from sea lion, walrus, bear, and whale intestine carefully seamed in horizontal strips, these Aleut garments were lightweight and completely waterproof. They were called *kamleikas* by the Russians who, impressed by their efficacy, wore them. Some were decorated with strips of sea-lion esophagus and loops or patterns of tufted and embroidered hair.

The Indians of Alaska

Historically, the two groups of Indians in Alaska—the Athabascans of the Interior and the Haida, Tlingit, and Tsimshian of Southeast—were as different as socialists and capitalists.

The Athabascans are thought to have been the first peoples to cross the land bridge to North America and are related to the Navajo and Apache far to the south. In Alaska, they settled along Interior rivers and around Cook Inlet or the Gulf of Alaska. Today, Alaska had almost 6,500 Athabascans, who speak eleven different Athabascan languages.

The seafaring Haida, whose homeland was the Queen Charlottes, settled on Prince of Wales and Dall Islands before contact with Europeans. Their language is a linguistic loner, totally unrelated to any other. The Alaska Native Language Center estimates that fifteen of the 600 Haida in Alaska still speak the language. The largest Haida village in Alaska is Hydaburg, founded in 1911 when four smaller villages consolidated to build a public school. The Hyda Corporation has 700 shareholders.

The Tlingit (*klink*-it), whose language is in the Na-Dene family of Athabascan tongues, occupied the territory from Yakutat Bay to Portland Canal, including portions of Prince of Wales Island that were not controlled by the Haida. Fierce warriors, they fought the Russians and were never defeated. Undaunted by seeing their village at Angoon on Admiralty Island wiped out by the U.S. Navy in 1882, they sent two war canoes to Seattle a few years later to recover a totem pole stolen by a tourist. About 10,000 Tlingit remain in Southeast; another 1,000 live in Anchorage.

The Tsimshian arrived in Alaska in historic times. A group of 823 left Prince Rupert, British Columbia, and followed their leader, Anglican missionary William Duncan, to Annette Island, southwest of present-day Ketchikan. There, in 1887, they founded New Metlakatla, a model community where they operated a sawmill and cannery. Annette Island is the only reservation in Alaska, and its 1,000 Tsimshian were the only Natives who exempted themselves from the Native Claims Settlement Act.

Artists and Acquisitors

Life for the inland Athabascan was hard. Famine was frequent and cannibalism was not unknown. Their territory was the subarctic coniferous forest that the Russians call taiga. They were forced to keep moving to hunt caribou, moose, and rabbit—sources of food that were always on the move. They also caught salmon, using a trap that funneled fish into an enclosure.

Though they created permanent villages, their mobility called for a variety of portable or temporary housing, including ice caves. The Gwich'in-speaking Athabascans, whose territory extended well into the Arctic Circle, built villages of log houses with gable roofs. To live on the land, they carried a *nivaze*—a domed tent of caribou or moose hides over a spruce framework, which two families would use—or a tepee of four poles and a single skin. Because the Athabascans had to survive in freezing temperatures, they wore carefully tailored clothing of caribou and moose hides, which they decorated with beads and quills. Expert in making snowshoes and dogsleds, they were a migrating people who did not accumulate the artifacts they created.

Great artists that they were, the Haida and Tlingit in Alaska were above all else capitalists. Creating, accumulating, and displaying wealth ruled their existence. Living in the naturally abundant Panhandle, they had both the means to get rich and the leisure to make magnificent works of art that declared their wealth. Their societies were hierarchical: things were ranked (interior houseposts were more valuable than exterior ones) and so were people—from the lowest slave to the leader of a house, who constantly strove to maintain his position.

Tlingit and Haida tribes were divided into two groups that anthropologists call moieties. The Tlingit moieties were Raven and Wolf (or Eagle in the north); the Haida divisions were Raven and Eagle. Individuals inherited the moiety of their mother, and had to

Potlatches honoring the dead and elevating the living were fading away by the twentieth century.

marry a member of the opposite—in other words, the father's—lineage. The leadership of a house (which was a grouping of several families living together) passed usually to a maternal nephew.

The moieties were obliged to perform certain tasks for one another. For example, when a man wanted a crest carved, his wife's brother did the work or paid an artist to do it. When a man died, members of his wife's lineage dressed his corpse and cremated it. If he had been an important individual, they would tear his house down and build a new one for his family. Obligations, once met, had to be reciprocated. Funerary services, for instance, were repaid with a potlatch.

Christian missionaries saw in the potlatch an excess of feasting and wasteful gift-giving. They did not understand its complex roles. Among the Tlingit, the ceremony maintained social order and defined the relationships among people. One impetus was to honor a dead relative and to pay the debts incurred by his funeral. At the same time, the right of the host to succeed the deceased was declared and witnessed by the guests.

Among the Haida, the ceremony fulfilled the role of our credit unions and life insurance policies. By potlatching them, a Haida repaid members of his own moiety who had helped him in some way. Giving his wealth away was an investment because in a few years, the guests would repay him with interest. If he died, they would care for his orphaned children. The totem pole raised at a Haida potlatch validated what had taken place.

Outlawed in Canada between 1884 and 1951, the ceremony simply faded away in Alaska by the turn of the century, only to resurface later. One great potlatch was a cross-racial revival held in Wrangell in 1940 to commemorate the restoration of Chief Shakes Tribal House on Shakes Island in the inner harbor. To pay for the event, at which he was named the seventh Chief Shakes, Tlingit Charlie Jones adopted the Wrangell Chamber of Commerce into his tribe and accepted its financial contribution.

Like their neighbors to the south, the Athabascan tribes developed decorative art to a high level. They excelled in beadwork and tailoring and made containers of birchbark and woven baskets. The Haida, Tlingit, and Tsimshian surrounded themselves with art, their best-known works being monumental wood carvings. Most visitors to Alaska will encounter at least one totem pole, if not one park where groups of poles are dramatically displayed. (*See* How to Read a Totem Pole, *page 136–37.*) Native Indian artifacts of note in museums include the following:

Chilkat blankets: The Chilkat, a northern Tlingit group, were masters of weaving these blankets from the wool of mountain goats. It took the wool from three goats to make one blanket. They twisted bark of yellow-cedar trees with strands of spun wool to form the warp threads. The geometric totemic designs were woven by women following pattern boards painted by men. Materials such as hemlock bark, iron, wolf moss, woolen trade cloth, and urine produced the yellow, black, and blue dyes. Chilkat blankets had a higher status than button blankets.

Coppers or tinnehs: These 2- to 3-foot-long plaques of beaten copper covered with black paint or graphite, with engraved or carved crests, were always made in the same shieldlike shape. They can be recognized by ridges that form a T. Among the southeastern Indians and particularly among the Tlingit, they seem to have been used like money, their value increasing as they were traded or sold. Their symbolic value was also powerful; individual coppers had sentimental names, and their histories were remembered. At feasts, as a demonstration of his wealth, a chief might break off pieces, which themselves became valuable and might be bought by a rival who would attempt to accumulate the whole copper. Sometimes, insults were avenged by giving a piece of a copper to the offender. Coppers are sometimes incorporated into a totem pole carving.

Labrets: Women of high rank inserted these oval wood or stone ornaments into a slit in their lower lips. They can be seen on several totem poles in Alaska.

Ceremonial spoons: Families treasured these carved and decorated wood or horn implements, which were used to ladle food at feasts and ceremonies.

Masks: Southeast Indians always carved masks to be worn in ceremonies. Their masks are less complicated than those of the south coast; there are fewer mechanical masks but more minimally painted portraits. Tlingit shamans were buried with their religious paraphernalia, which included masks they had worn while practicing their healing and ceremonial arts.

Bentwood boxes: Made of a single plank, kerfed at the corners, and steamed and bent into shape, these boxes were watertight and could be used to store liquids or to cook foods (by heating liquid inside the box with hot stones). They were elaborately painted with family crests.

Beadwork: Athabascan women were expert at decorating skin clothing and footwear using porcupine quills (which they flattened with their teeth) and carved wood beads or seeds. Later, they incorporated shells and glass beads in trading with Southeast Indians and westerners.

Baskets: Athabascans cooked food or carried water in birch-bark containers. They also made coiled and geometrically decorated baskets of willow roots, carefully dug and split. Tlingit spruce-root baskets, in twined weaving, were decorated with colored patterns. Some baskets had lids that rattled because loose stones had been hidden in the weaving.

A watchman figure tops this pole in Sitka National Historical Park.

How to Read a Totem Pole

The totem pole was the perfect expression of lofty status among the hierarchical Indian societies on the northwest coast. Standing tall in front of a house, a pole made a public declaration of ancestry, affiliations, and real or imagined events that had shaped a family's history.

The Tlingit, Haida, and Tsimshian raised several types of poles. An early form was inside their longhouses, where as many as four poles supported the roof. Outside, a frontal pole framed the doorway or sat to one side of it, flush against the house. Memorial poles, with one figure at the top, or with top and bottom figures, were erected to commemorate a person or an event. Mortuary poles had the same function, but also contained a box or niche for the body or the ashes of the deceased.

The totem pole reached a peak of artistic expression in the mid-nineteenth century. Carved of cedar by a commissioned artist, totem poles were raised by wealthy leaders and stood in front of, but not right up against, their houses. At a feast or potlatch after the raising of a pole, the owner would explain the significance of the figures.

Begin examining a pole at the top where you'll likely see the crest figure of the owner, the common ones being Raven, Eagle, or Thunderbird. The legend of Raven and how he gave the world light by stealing the sun from a stingy chief is depicted on several Alaska poles. Raven sits on the box in which the chief kept the Sun. Another figure you'll easily recognize at the top is the Watchman. In the body of the pole, look for the figures described below.

Raven: The large and straight beak is the key. The figure is usually upright, with wings close to its sides.

Eagle: Again, look to the beak. Eagle's is shorter than Raven's, curved, and comes to a downturning point.

Thunderbird: Though the beak resembles Eagle's, curved horns on top of the head are unique to Thunderbird. The wings may be outspread. Kolus, Thunderbird's younger brother, has straight, horizontal tufts.

Watchmen: These crouching human figures sit atop Haida (and sometimes Tlingit and Tsimshian) poles surveying sea or land to warn of approaching danger. They wear high hats that look like segmented stove pipes. The segments, called skils, might indicate the number of feasts or potlatches given by the chief for whom the pole was carved. Skils sometimes appear as part of the body of the pole.

Bear: Flared nostrils or a short snout, a full set of squared-off teeth (and perhaps some sharp incisors), and a protruding tongue are the tip-offs. Bear's ears are small.

Wolf: Wolf can be distinguished from Bear by its longer, slender snout and ears, and its many large teeth.

Beaver: With its two big incisors, a stick between its paws, and a crosshatched tail, Beaver is easy to identify.

Frog: Crouched in sideview or diving, Frog shows a toothless mouth, a goofy grin, and big round eyes.

Whale: Look for blowholes carved as human faces. The gray whale has a short fin on its back and long side fins. A long back fin, short pectoral fins, and fiercer expression indicate a killer whale.

Mosquito: A long, downturning proboscis is the obvious clue.

Human beings: People usually don't wear clothes, though a chief may sport a hat with a number of skils. Europeans are dressed and may have heavy, wavy beards. Uncle Sam is readily identifiable atop the Centennial Hall pole in Juneau; Abraham Lincoln is the top figure on a Saxman Village pole.

Transformations: Check out a creature's limbs; they may be clearly human. You may be seeing an animal with human characteristics or a human with animal characteristics—and getting a glimpse into the spiritual world of Southeast Indians where magical transformations took place, and animals became human by shedding their skins.

BRINGING ALASKA HOME

For more than a century, visitors have been coming to Alaska as tourists, and residents have willingly been offering them keepsakes to take back home. In the nineteenth century, visiting naturalist John Muir complained about the steamer passengers who arrived at the glacier named for him in Glacier Bay and "turned from the great thundering crystal world of ice to look curiously at the Indians that came alongside to sell trinkets." But most Alaskans were grateful for the opportunities that tourism provided a boom-and-bust economy, and Native people in particular sold everything from reindeer moccasins to the elaborate baskets that became a North American fad in the first decade of the twentieth century.

Today there are many ways of keeping Alaska alive in your memory, from buying meaningful souvenirs to taking still photographs or making videotapes, from keeping a cruise diary to reading about the state before, after, and during your voyage there.

Souvenirs

Perhaps the most meaningful Alaska memorabilia you can bring back home are authentic traditional and contemporary Native art and crafts. The aboriginal peoples have been creating souvenirs—such as model kayaks—almost since the first European set foot on this land. You can be assured that the works are genuine if they bear an emblem of a silver hand and the words "Authentic Native Hand-craft from Alaska."

As detailed in "The Native Way" *(pages 119–37)*, Alaska Natives have long been creating practical tools and works of art from wood, grasses, and seeds; the skins, quills, and intestines of animals; and bone, ivory, and even fossils. Only they can legally possess raw ivory from the walruses they hunt or fossilized ivory from the tusks of walruses, mammoths, and mastodons, but they are allowed to sell only ivory that has been handcrafted.

What are Native artists and craftspeople creating today? Well, don't overlook the exciting work many are doing in the modern idiom, transcending their heritage and stretching old styles to create contemporary—often multimedia—sculpture, paintings, prints, and jewelry. Others continue in the traditional modes, using traditional materials, such as the popular etched ivory called scrimshaw.

The Inupiat Eskimos of the Bering Sea and Arctic Ocean sculpt walrus ivory and baleen (whalebone); create masks of hide and baleen, and baskets of birch bark and baleen; fashion garments of local furs; and continue a craft that's at least 2,000 years old: the

A beautifully crafted miniature Eskimo whale hunter.

making of dolls for little girls. Some dolls of museum quality may take months to make, with faces and hands carved of wood, eyes of ivory and baleen, and hand-sewn parkas of fur.

The southwestern Yup'ik Eskimos craft dolls too (their history recounts taboos limiting the occasions girls could play with them), along with miniature dog sleds and kayaks of local materials. They also carve walrus-ivory sculptures and spirit masks, as well as weaving fine baskets of beach grasses and using age-old patterns to hand-knit scarves, sweaters, and other garments with *qiviut*, the warm, shrinkproof, and rare musk-oxen underwool.

The Aleuts of the Aleutians and the Pribilofs use strong, sinewy rye grass to weave their superb small baskets and bigger, more practical ones. They also use feathers to make their famous birdskin parkas, and wood for their highly decorated visor hats. Athabascan Indians in the Interior specialize in working with beads of seeds, shells, quills, and wood to adorn moccasins, mittens, jewelry, and garments made from furs and hides. Their other creations include dolls, baskets of willow root and birch bark, and carvings of wood and soapstone.

Southeast's Haida, Tlingit, and Tsimshian peoples are acclaimed for their totem poles and other wood carvings such as ceremonial masks; their silver jewelry, beadwork, and art prints; and their red-and-black felt blankets, decorated with buttons and beads and sometimes woven of mountain-goat wool and cedar bark.

Non-Native Souvenirs

Meanwhile, authentic local souvenirs created by non-Native artists and craftspeople can be identified by the symbol of the circular figure of a bear and the words "Made in Alaska." Among the most popular items are gold-nugget jewelry and carved local jade, which comes in a variety of colors from the expected green to red, yellow, brown, and even black and white. The inspiring landscape can spur Alaska artists to impressive heights in creating eminently collectable works in oil and watercolor or limited-edition prints.

Non-Native arts and crafts: Prints and original paintings, along with
the art of resident photographers, weavers, and potters working
in local clay. Gold nuggets fashioned into pendants, rings, and
earrings; and jewelry of blue topaz, hematite, and a trademarked
stone called Arctic Opal. Art works of porcelain, lead crystal,
Alaska coral, and stained glass. Carvings in ivory, jade, wood,
and soapstone, as well as miniature totem poles and birch bowls.
And a variety of souvenirs with Alaska motifs, such as Christmas
ornaments, belt buckles, collectors' pins, pewter figures on fool's
gold, and painted gold pans.

Tools and other practical items: The semi-circular *ulu* (oo-loo), a skin-
ning and filleting knife, now made with a stainless-steel blade and
handles of ivory, jade, and walnut; wallets and purses of fish-skin
leather; and folding and rigid kayaks, in finished or kit form,
which can be shipped home.

Clothing: T-shirts featuring such local events as the Iditarod sled-
dog race; sheepskin slippers, mittens, and earmuffs trimmed
with farm-fox fur; slippers of beaver and seal, and seal and lamb;
Eskimo-style summer and winter parkas; fur-trimmed and wool
vests; and other garments of fur and leather.

Food: Caribou and reindeer sausage; jams, jellies, sauces, and even
candies made from local wild berries; smoked salmon and halibut,
king crab and scallops—all of which can usually be packed and
shipped to your home address anywhere in the world.

Printed materials: Old local maps and nautical charts.

Russian souvenirs: Nesting dolls, hand-painted icons dating back to
the seventeenth century, lacquered boxes, Ural stone carvings,
Ukrainian Easter eggs, and porcelain figurines.

Buyer Beware

The caveat for shoppers in Alaska is that not everything you buy will necessarily get to sit on your mantelpiece. Art or craft objects made from the body parts of wild animals are subject to international regulations regarding trade in regulated species, about which shopkeepers may not always be forthcoming.

Because these regulations govern goods crossing an international border, American citizens traveling directly from Alaska to the Lower 48 can acquire most souvenirs or art objects made from animal parts. However, problems arise for Americans if they attempt to carry their purchases through Canada, because the regulations established under the Convention on International Trade in Endangered Species (CITES) will apply. The situation for Americans is further complicated by U.S. legislation regarding marine mammals and endangered species. Under these laws, certain goods that might be brought into Canada will not be allowed to re-enter the U.S. *The advice for American travelers who will be entering Canada is simple: send souvenirs made of wildlife parts or products home by mail from Alaska.*

Although whale parts *are* restricted under CITES, Americans may purchase non-edible by-products of Alaska whales taken for subsistence by Natives and handcrafted. Walrus ivory or parts may be sold in interstate commerce only if they are part of an authentic Native handicraft; polishing the ivory or carving a signature on it does not qualify. Under U.S. law, it is a felony to sell parts—such as feathers—of migratory birds. All wild birds, except ptarmigan and grouse, are protected.

Anyone—American, Canadian, or another national—arriving from Alaska in a Canadian port with souvenirs made of whalebone, whale teeth, baleen, or fossilized whale will have the souvenirs confiscated and will be subject to prosecution.

Canadians returning to Canada from Alaska and other nationals who must cross an international border need to be more concerned about CITES regulations. They may not transport products made from animals on the most-endangered species list (CITES Appendix I) unless they have both import and export permits. Import permits, which must be obtained before travelers leave their own country, are given only if the item is to be used for educational purposes or for scientific research, or if it has been inherited and can be proven to be a family heirloom. In other words, an import permit for an Appendix I animal is almost impossible to obtain.

In effect, that means Canadians and other nationals returning from Alaska must forgo souvenirs such as carved whale teeth or carved baleen and that old whalebone found lying on a beach (fossilized whale and walrus are subject to CITES permits). Mastodon or mammoth ivory can be imported, but since sometimes only an expert can distinguish mastodon ivory from elephant ivory (which is a no-no), be very sure about what you are buying.

The regulations are less strict for Appendix II and Appendix III animals, which include walrus, bear, wolf, otter, eagle, owl, hawk, bobcat, lynx, and cougar. If you are shipping Appendix II and Appendix III animal-product souvenirs to Canada, you will need a CITES export permit from the United States Fish and Wildlife Service or the State of Alaska Fish and Wildlife Branch. However, you can carry these souvenirs into Canada in your accompanying luggage under a personal exemption as a tourist souvenir; a CITES export permit is not necessary.

Travelers entering British Columbia should be aware that the province prohibits traffic in bear gallbladders and paws.

Canada Customs has the power to seize any item for which proper permits are not available—and it does so, frequently. The Canadian Wildlife Service will not issue after-the-fact permits for Appendix I items. If the seized items are noteworthy, they will be given to a museum or school. Otherwise, they will be destroyed, which would make them a sad souvenir indeed.

(Canadians may apply for import permits to the Canadian Wildlife Service branch in their province or to the Administrator, CITES, Environment Canada, Ottawa K1A 0H3. For more information, check Environment Canada's website at http://www.ec.gc.ca/cites/html/eng/sct4/sct4_1_e.htm. Travelers from other countries should check their countries' regulations before leaving home.)

Photography

When Danny Lehman photographed Denali National Park and Preserve for a *National Geographic* feature back in 1992, he spent four months off and on in one of the world's grandest wildernesses and came back with 600 rolls of film to create a stunning portrait of the park. But he believes that cruise passengers need only do some thoughtful planning, expend a little time, and shoot intelligently—not extravagantly—to record images that will remain memorable.

Lehman, who has since been visiting Alaska regularly to photograph for the major cruise lines, has known both ships and the state since the start of his commercial and documentary career. He grew up in New Mexico, where he still lives, and earned a degree in business administration and then another in photography from the esteemed Brooks Institute. As a student he worked on a tramp freighter off Africa for twenty-five cents an hour and as a young professional in 1975 took his first pictures of Alaska for what was then the Orient Overseas Line's *Universe*. On that initial assignment, he chronicled the wonders of Glacier Bay and began to learn some of the secrets of photographing the state, such as timing his shots to capture the singular light of this land.

When we talked, he had just returned from a two-week Alaska photo expedition. "I was up at two-thirty in the morning to catch the ship at sunrise in the Lynn Canal," he says. "Cruise passengers may miss the best scenery because they don't get up early enough or stay up late enough to shoot the magic of the sun glowing red on the mountain peaks. People should try to have a catnap and then take pictures—or simply see—the landscape at these special times, when the raking light of a sunrise or the alpenglow of sunset can be much more interesting than the blasting sunlight of midday." He frequently uses a polarizing filter when shooting water or glaciers or working in bright light. At other times, especially an hour after sunrise or an hour before sunset, he uses a warming filter to heat up the color and amplify the wakening or waning rays.

Danny Lehman advises checking your ship's itinerary to determine exactly when it will be at various key locations—on the first evening out from Vancouver, for instance, the Inside Passage offers some of the most spectacular scenery of the trip. You've already broken your routine to take this voyage, so bend it a bit more to be out on deck when others may be inside, "when it's just you and the scenery." Photographing from aboard ship should pose no particular problems because most of the scenery is distant and cruise vessels travel smoothly enough to accommodate shooting at such slow shutter speeds as 1/30th of a second.

Where the problems arise is in establishing context for a photo, such as showing how big a glacier really is. "If there's a kayak or another ship or even a loon in the water, you can include it in the photo to establish size. Glaciers can dwarf some of the hugest cruise ships on earth." Frame the picture so that the strong lines of the shore or a mountain range don't split the image into too-neat halves. "You can put more water at the bottom or more mountain at the top. And use an iceberg or the wake of a boat to create texture—or reflections in the water to create interest—in what might otherwise be the blank blue of the sea."

Photographing from a plane or helicopter presents its own challenges: "Don't brace yourself on the frame of the aircraft because you'll pick up vibrations; keep the camera cushioned in your arms. And you can ask the pilot if the windows lift up or slide back so you don't have to shoot through glass." If traveling on a tour bus that stops for a wildlife photo opportunity where you have to stay inside, have a rolled-up towel or piece of foam to cradle your camera while you use the frame of the bus as a steadying support.

Other tips? Filming a glacier, you don't need the sun directly behind your back because other light creates interesting cross-light or texture. To film wildlife, recall his rule about being on the scene at odd times: most animals show themselves in early morning or late afternoon when the crowds have gone. Shooting close-ups doesn't mean lugging an enormous telephoto lens around; an astonishing tableau of a moose in a mountain setting for his Denali feature in *National Geographic* was taken with an 85-millimeter lens. And an expensive digital camera isn't necessary. As a tourist with his wife, Laurie, and their children, he has taken along a simple Instamatic.

Before you leave on a cruise, he suggests, check the camera and the film you intend to use by shooting in a variety of situations and then have the images processed to make sure everything's working. (If you suspect your batteries might run out, bring spares.) During the trip, decide why you're taking pictures: "Ninety-five percent of the time you want photos that bring back special memories, like a friend dancing with his wife on the stern deck at sunset. You can buy slides of beautiful scenics along the way, so include someone special in your landscape—a mountain isn't going to change much in 10,000 years, but your traveling companions will, and you'll have an enchanting record of them in Alaska." Including several different elements in a picture enhances interest: for instance, a sled-dog musher with a husky in front of a log cabin.

Back home again, realize that you can often take your negative film into customizing photo shops to have special photos specially handled rather than machine-printed. And when you decide to show your family and friends the fruits of your trip, remember that less is better. Although Danny Lehman returned from Denali with 600 rolls of film, the final screening at *National Geographic* was a mere eighty images.

And For the Video Photographer...

Panasonic has a few sensible hints for cruise passengers using video cameras:

Drain and recharge the camcorder's battery before leaving on your trip; take along spare batteries and several blank tapes in case the shops along the way are closed. And bring a carrying case to protect the camera and hold supplies, lights, and other accessories.

Tape an establishing, wide-angle shot of a new setting—perhaps of an interesting sign in context—before going for close-ups. Then pan slowly and smoothly rather than taking the usual two-second bursts that most people shoot in fresh situations. If the camcorder comes with an image-steadying device, don't forget to use it.

Minimize your narration; identify what you're shooting but don't describe it in dull detail. Let the subjects of your video talk for themselves. And if you do decide to add narration afterward, you might consider scripting it.

Give a friend or fellow passenger a quick lesson in operating the camera so that you can take home a record of you in the setting—too many people forget to include themselves in their vacation videotapes.

Most of all, don't glue your eye to the viewfinder. Tape the highlights of your trip, not every waking moment, so that you don't miss the actual experience of being in Alaska.

PORTS OF CALL

*Southeast Alaska... is not so much a collection of
separate places as an intricate web of life bound together by
weather and the movement of tides. An eagle
rises with a fish clutched in its talons. Sitka black-tailed
deer move silent as shadows through the lush
undergrowth of the forest. A grizzly prowls a stream bank,
looking for salmon. A pod of orcas, or killer whales,
surfaces and moves in search of seals. This is a corner of
the earth not yet overwhelmed by people.*

ART DAVIDSON, *ALAKSHAK: THE GREAT COUNTRY*

The majority of cruise passengers explore Southeast Alaska, the
Panhandle that forms 10 percent of the state. This strip of land
paralleling the northwestern coast of mainland British Columbia
embraces a thousand islands scattered off the thickly treed shoreline.
It is separated from the Alaska Frying Pan by a mammoth ice field;
by the St. Elias Mountains, among the world's loftiest coastal ranges;
and by the seasonal rain that keeps Southeast fresh and evergreen.

Despite the lushness, this is as real an Alaska as the barren
tundra up north. The belligerent, snow-drenched winter weather,
enveloping wilderness, and capricious seas combine to make life
here raw, unpredictable, on the edge. True, there are 70,000 South-
easterners—including Tlingit, Tsimshian, and Haida Indians, but
no Eskimos—which makes it sound more populated than seekers
of the wild may wish. But to put that in context: the 17-million-
acre Tongass National Forest, America's largest, with its black-tailed
deer, brown bear, and bald eagles, encompasses about three-quarters
of the region. It is literally Southeast's backyard. And there are only

about 50 miles of all-weather roads in the entire region. Even if you travel nowhere else but the Panhandle, you have encountered a true Alaska, unlike anything in the Lower 48.

What follows are mini-portraits of the ports (including Washington's Seattle and British Columbia's Vancouver and Victoria) you can experience by ship or on-shore excursions. Features of special interest to cruise-ship passengers—such as tours and visitor attractions—and specific places they're most likely to visit are indicated by SMALL CAPITAL LETTERS. Although you can fly to Anchorage and cruise southward, we've arranged the ports in the order passengers encounter them on a voyage heading north to Alaska.

Seattle: Livable, Lovable

Think of Seattle, Washington, and the images you conjure up might well be of Bill Gates, Boeing, and Starbucks. Oh, and perhaps Frasier, the hapless fictional radio therapist in the long-running TV series set in this Pacific Northwest seaport. Well, early in this new century the Microsoft empire that Gates created was reeling from anti-trust suits and the meltdown of the dot-com industry while Boeing, the beleaguered aircraft manufacturing giant, moved its headquarters from here to Chicago. Of the trio of Seattle icons, only the coffee colossus of Starbucks (under a corporate name borrowed from a java-loving character in *Moby Dick*) was thriving in town and increasingly around the world. As for *Frasier*, the comedy series might occasionally feature local landmarks such as the Space Needle but in truth it had always been filmed in Los Angeles.

So after the economic downturn, exactly what, besides the ubiquitous Starbucks cafés, was left of the Seattle that the media had labelled variously as Silicon Forest, the Jet City, and the City of Buzz (referring to its residents' caffeine-induced highs)? A whole lot, as it happens. Since 1989—when *Money* named it the nation's Most Livable City and less than a decade later dubbed it the Best Place to Live in America—Seattle has consistently garnered honors from national magazines. *Parade* called it the second Safest City, *American*

Health for Women the #1 City for Women, and *Fortune* the Best City for Work and Family.

Wonderfully livable for its 540,000 residents—among the three million or more in the Greater Seattle/Tacoma area—it's easily lovable for visitors. The city takes culture of all kinds seriously. Fine bookshops (including expansive Elliott Bay Book Company, with its regular book signings, and eccentric Shorey's Bookstore, which has been selling antiquarian books for more than a century). The innovative Seattle Repertory Theatre, and Seattle Opera, world-renowned for its productions of Wagner's Ring cycle. And raunchy local rock groups such as Pearl Jam and Nirvana. Per capita, Seattleites read more books than anywhere else in the U.S., and their city has more arts organizations than any other American center of its size. Among its cornucopia of 2,000-plus restaurants are numerous gems specializing in seafood and Pacific Northwest cuisine lubricated with surprisingly good regional wines. Despite a distressing freeway system that cuts through its heart, the city has an interesting downtown with a stew of historic, human-scale buildings and undistinguished skyscrapers leavened by an abundance of intriguing public art (a civic ordinance of 1973 dictated that a healthy 1 percent of specific capital-improvement funds must be dedicated to such amenities).

But most of all, Seattle and its environs are defined by the splendor of their natural surroundings and the moderate coastal climate—with temperatures averaging between 70 and 75 degrees Fahrenheit in the summer months, when the omnipresent rain is at its lowest ebb. The city, built on seven major hills, lies on a slim green isthmus between Elliott Bay on Puget Sound and Lake Washington, rimmed by the distant Cascade mountain range visible in the east and the Olympic peaks in the west. Amid the Cascades are two dormant volcanoes, the 14,410-foot MOUNT RAINIER, snow-crested and glacier-hung, and 8,363-foot MOUNT ST. HELENS, which lost 1,314 feet of height when it erupted in 1980; both are destinations for pre- and

A reflected field of cotton grass—one of Alaska's extraordinary landscapes.

post-cruise tours. Among other popular out-of-town excursions are the OLYMPIC PENINSULA, featuring the Hoh Rain Forest and Hurricane Ridge; the CASCADE LOOP to the Bavarian-like village of Leavenworth and frontier-style Winthrop; and PORTLAND AND THE COLUMBIA GORGE, which includes a tour of Oregon's largest city, a paddlewheel trip along the Columbia River, and visits to some of Washington state's fine wineries.

If you depart from or dock in Seattle aboard one of the relatively few cruise ships that make this their home port, you'll understand why the history of the lushly green Emerald City has been determined by its water-girt situation. (Narrated HARBOR CRUISES show off the marine highway of Elliott Bay and the Hiram M. Chittenden Locks, which link the sea with the freshwater Union and Washington Lakes.) Boats for work and pleasure abound in the downtown harbor, as they have for more than a century and a half since the area was settled by white pioneers.

Of course, Natives were here first, harvesting their food from the sea, and the city is believed to be named for Chief Sealth, an arbiter between his people and the European interlopers. Bearing the blood of both dominant local tribes, the Suquamish and the Duwamish, he witnessed the arrival of Britain's Captain George Vancouver on this coast in 1792. For all his diplomacy and conversion to Anglicanism, the chief was later tried in a kangaroo court and lynched. Today, a brief sea voyage through Puget Sound to lovely Blake Island brings you to a reminder of that era of local history: TILLICUM VILLAGE, with its Native cedar longhouse, costumed dancers, and salmon bake.

Seattle's easy water access and tall timber attracted early entrepreneurs who would send logs on wooden skids down to the water in the town's seedy center, which prompted the nickname "Skid Road" for all such urban slums. The port boomed as a supply base for the Klondike gold rush of 1897, garnering a reputation that still exists as the Gateway to Alaska (today, the city is home to Alaska Airlines). Stagnating for much of the first half of the twentieth century, the economy lifted off after World War II with Boeing's commercial aircraft manufacturing as well as shipbuilding. Seattle's

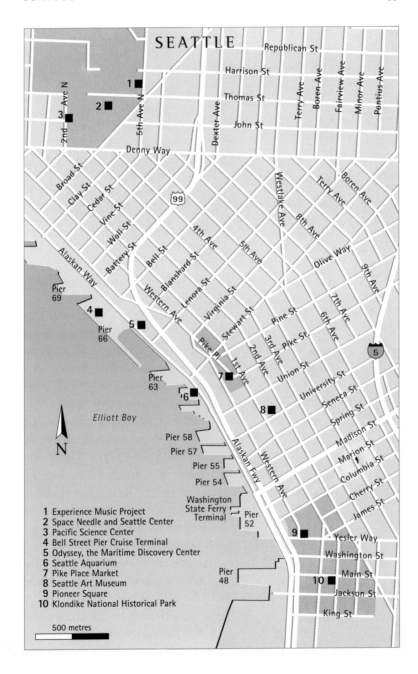

SEATTLE

Republican St
Harrison St
Thomas St
John St
Denny Way
Republican St

2nd Ave N
5th Ave N
Dexter Ave
Terry Ave
Boren Ave
Fairview Ave
Minor Ave
Pontius Ave

Broad St
Clay St
Cedar St
Vine St
Wall St
Battery St
Bell St
Blanchard St
Lenora St
Virginia St
Stewart St
Pike Pl
1st Ave
2nd Ave
3rd Ave
4th Ave
5th Ave
Westlake Ave
8th Ave
Boren Ave
Terry Ave
Olive Way
9th Ave
7th Ave
6th Ave
Pine St
Pike St
Union St
University St
Seneca St
Spring St
Madison St
Marion St
Columbia St
Cherry St
James St
Yesler Way
Washington St
Main St
Jackson St
King St

Alaskan Way
Western Ave
Alaskan Fwy

Pier 69
Pier 66
Pier 63
Pier 58
Pier 57
Pier 55
Pier 54
Pier 52
Pier 48

Washington State Ferry Terminal

Elliott Bay

N

99
5

1 Experience Music Project
2 Space Needle and Seattle Center
3 Pacific Science Center
4 Bell Street Pier Cruise Terminal
5 Odyssey, the Maritime Discovery Center
6 Seattle Aquarium
7 Pike Place Market
8 Seattle Art Museum
9 Pioneer Square
10 Klondike National Historical Park

500 metres

place on the west coast has positioned it well for marine traffic from Asia. More recently, thousands of techies have been lured to town by local boy Bill Gates, who decided to stay at home when he and Paul Allen launched Microsoft in 1975 (with a thousand or more of their employees becoming dot-com millionaires).

You can't tour the sprawling Microsoft complex in nearby Redmond, but before or after an Alaska cruise you can conveniently sample Seattle's downtown delights. The big ships dock at Pier 66, the Bell Street Pier Cruise Terminal, which puts you amid some of the most obvious attractions near the waterfront.

Start with the old-fashioned, well-preserved PIKE PLACE MARKET (Pike Street to Virginia Street on Pike Place). This bizarre bazaar, established in 1907, could easily distract you for a full day, beginning in early morning as more than 500 farmers, specialty-food suppliers, fish vendors, restaurateurs, and booksellers, artists and artisans set up their stalls. You'll find little that's mass-produced, except for coffee from Starbucks, which opened its first shop here in 1971. The fishmongers are particularly appealing as they fling salmon around while chatting you up. Describing all the market's wonders is beyond this book, so go to the official entrance at First Avenue and Pike Street to pick up a self-guided tour map of this two-block-long emporium built mostly on stilts on a bluff above Elliott Bay.

City tours offered by cruise lines will inevitably take you to nearby attractions. Among them is PIONEER SQUARE, along 1st Avenue between Jackson and Columbia Streets. This Native village cum pioneer townsite, destroyed in Seattle's Great Fire of 1889, was nicely rebuilt but languished for the next seven decades until preservationists successfully fought to make it the city's first Historic District. There's an Underground Tour that leads you through the original streets that lie beneath the square's 90 acres, but you'll want to spend more of your time above grade sampling this gracious Old Town of restaurants, galleries, gift and antique shops, entertainment spots, and the unavoidable bookstores. A touch of the far north surfaces here with the KLONDIKE GOLD RUSH NATIONAL HISTORICAL PARK (117 South Main Street), which is really a museum with films, entertaining displays, and informative park rangers to chronicle the city's role in the late-nineteenth-century mania for nuggets.

For an eagle's-eye, rather than a subterranean, view of the town, visit the SPACE NEEDLE and SEATTLE CENTER (between 1st and 5th Avenues North and Denny Way and Mercer Street). They're accessible from downtown on a 90-second ride on the Monorail. A remnant of the profitable 1962 World Fair, this 605-foot tower and entertainment hub ranks among the, um, very top of must-see sights. The Needle, built by private enterprise in just eight months for only $4.5 million, offers a 43-second elevator trip to a restaurant and a big-picture look-out from the saucerlike dome perched on concrete pillars (rest assured, they've handled at least one large earthquake, three years after the tower went up). The center is truly that, a gathering place for the city's plentiful festivals, such as the summer's Bite of Seattle food show, the Bumbershoot celebration of the arts, and the Memorial Day Northwest Folk Festival, biggest of its kind in the U.S. Other attractions here include the PACIFIC SCIENCE CENTER (200 2nd Avenue North), a happy hands-on complex featuring robotic dinosaurs, for the big kid in all of us, and the EXPERIENCE MUSIC PROJECT (325 5th Avenue North), Microsoft co-founder Paul Allen's $240-million homage to rock 'n' roll and one of its knights errant, guitarist Jimi Hendrix.

The Project's outer shell, designed by controversial Canadian architect Frank Gehry, has been called everything from "the wreck of the Partridge Family bus" to "Technicolor mushrooms on a soggy lawn." Inspired by a trash pile from an electric-guitar shop, it bends and undulates in ultra-modernist abandon, painted in wild auto-body hues that range from pastel blues to vibrating reds. The excitement is underlined by having the Monorail line, another world's fair symbol, pass through the structure. Inside, it's indeed an experience: you can watch a film about James Brown while seated on an ever-moving platform, view poignant artifacts from the brief life of the legendary Hendrix, and can even play at being a rock musician on a stage or in a studio.

Another brash building is American architect Robert Venturi's SEATTLE ART MUSEUM, a postmodern work of granite, marble, and clay just a few blocks southeast of Pier 66 at 100 University Street.

Look for the equally bold motorized sculpture called *Hammering Man* at the entrance and the diversely designed galleries focusing on African, Asian, and Northwest Native art. The museum often gets the best of the major shows touring North America.

Less dramatic architecturally, the SEATTLE AQUARIUM, at Pier 59 (1483 Alaskan Way) between the art museum and the cruise terminal, nevertheless exposes you to an enthralling Pacific seascape in a 400,000-gallon Underwater Dome where scuba divers feed reef sharks and other denizens of Puget Sound. Among the aquarium's hundreds of species of fish, marine mammals, plants, and birds are the first octopus born in captivity, 60,000 salmon whose life cycle is informatively exhibited, and a trio of frolicking river otters. Another marine attraction is right at Pier 66, handy for cruise passengers: ODYSSEY, the MARITIME DISCOVER CENTER (2205 Alaskan Way). This interactive waterfront museum is a kids' delight, which their folks will enjoy too as they pretend to fish, kayak, or even take the helm of a container ship. An underlying environmental message warns of the perils of overfishing and pollution in the Sound.

Even first-time visitors know something of Seattle through its professional sports teams: football's Seahawks, basketball's Super-Sonics, and baseball's Mariners. A SAFECO FIELD TOUR provides a behind-the-dugout look at normally off-limits spots such as the press box and luxury suites in the sleek new home of the Mariners, a nearly 20-acre outdoor ballpark with real grass and a retractable roof.

Aircraft buffs will have to wander farther afield to take a 75-minute BOEING PLANT TOUR on Highway 256 in neighboring Everett to see commercial jets under construction in a hangar reputed to have the largest cubic capacity of any building in the world (advance tickets are available at 1-800-464-1476). Or to *oooh* at the superb collection of airplanes and spacecraft hanging from the ceiling of the MUSEUM OF FLIGHT on the old Boeing base south of Seattle (9404 East Marginal Way South). Among the artifacts: replicas of the Wright brothers' first glider and the original Boeing product, the B&W floatplane, as well as the real Apollo and Mercury space capsules.

By now you might concede that Seattle, the birthplace of Boeing, Microsoft, and Starbucks, does offer visitors a smorgasbord of sophisticated urban experiences. But in between all your sightseeing and museum-going, keep taking a good look around you at the city's splendid setting. As Knute Berger, the former editor of the admirable *Seattle Weekly*, has written, "The Microsofts, microbrews, and triple-grande Frappucinos may come and go. Let them. They're not us, despite what the media say.... Look at the Olympic Mountains and take a deep breath."

Vancouver: Sybarite City

Douglas Coupland, the author of *Generation X*, still lives in his Canadian hometown, in the genteel WASPish community of West Vancouver whose inhabitants have one of the highest average incomes in Canada. From his privileged vantage point, the sardonic commentator on the post–baby boomer generation of North Americans looks across the graceful Lions Gate Bridge to the parent city of Vancouver and sees "Everycity...a functioning model of how American cities and neighborhoods were supposed to have functioned in 1961. This is, of course, part of the reason why TV and movie filming here is so popular and easy to do. Many of the factors that stripped the innocence away from other cities never occurred here: freeways were never built and a soul-free edge city never arose because Vancouver has no edge."

Vancouver is the jumping-off point for almost all northbound cruise ships, yet only a relative handful of the 600,000-plus passengers who stream through the city each season take the time to sample its charms. Of any major center in Canada, this is the one most devoted to the pleasures of all the senses, so easily gratified in the region's temperate, virtually snow-free climate. Weather experts consider it the best in the country for sheer human comfort and well-being. Over the last couple of decades, the west-coast port with

Vancouver's downtown Canada Place complex is the major terminal for Alaska-bound cruise ships. ▸

a regional population of two million has matured into a cosmopolitan, soulful—and, yes, sybaritic—city.

Like the ancient Greek inhabitants of Sybaris, Vancouverites are known for their voluptuous living in luxuriant surroundings. Eight decades ago, a prominent visitor said he'd found no other word for the city than "lovely." Sir Arthur Conan Doyle, taking time out from his tales of Sherlock Holmes, wrote of Vancouver: "High, snow-capped mountains dominate the town, and the green-shored bay with its pellucid water makes a wonderful setting...sooner or later Vancouver will certainly be another San Francisco."

In fact, Vancouver has never depended on such comparisons. Few residents ever manage the mythic local experience of skiing on the North Shore mountains in the morning and sailing on the bay beside the city in the afternoon. But it's quite possible—as is hang-gliding the same day from the closest of these summits, Grouse Mountain, or hiking straight up that 4,006-foot peak on the gruelling two-mile Grouse Grind, avoiding the occasional bear and cougar. And then descending to loll against a log on one of the innumerable sand beaches in the urban core; to golf year-round (if often under umbrellas) on seventy regional courses; or to chill a bottle of champagne in the sea on a rope while picnicking beneath lofty virgin evergreens in West Vancouver's Lighthouse Park.

Not long ago the British human-resources consulting firm William H. Mercer tied Vancouver with Zurich as the world's most livable city, based on thirty-nine criteria from entertainment to environment. And over the last few years the local media gleefully reported the results of *Travel & Leisure* readers' polls naming Vancouver the third-best city in North America and the eighth-best destination in the world.

Vancouver's delights are many, only beginning with one of the world's grandest urban situations, rivaling Rio's and Sydney's, sitting as it does so close to the Pacific Ocean that fuels its port economy and backing on to wilderness that's only a brief walk away. This is Canada's largest seaport, where every year ships from around the world load tens of millions of tons of bulk cargo: grain and forest products, petroleum and minerals, coal and chemicals.

VANCOUVER
1 Canada Place
2 Gastown
3 Chinatown
4 Dr. Sun Yat-Sen Classical Chinese Garden
5 Granville Island Market
6 Queen Elizabeth Park
7 VanDusen Botanical Garden

(That yellow "mountain" you can see on the north shore of Burrard Inlet is sulfur.) Some of those vessels, of course, are the world's most magnificent cruise ships, which make this their summer home port for the voyage up the Inside Passage to Alaska. In fact, the major cruise terminal is part of the CANADA PLACE complex in the inner harbor, smack in the middle of downtown. It also houses a hotel, office tower, the immense screen of an IMAX theater, and the Vancouver Trade and Convention Centre.

Because of its pivotal location, Vancouver has become a hub of international trade and investment, with Japan second only to the United States as a trading partner. High-tech manufacturing may soon rival the traditional forestry and mining industries as the city's economic propellant. Tourism already does. And the temperate weather, the surrounding natural splendors, and experienced local movie crews help Vancouver vie regularly with Toronto as the continent's third-busiest film capital after Los Angeles and New York.

Few other cities in North America combine its range of restaurants with the quality of cuisine and the reasonableness of price, accentuated by the low value of the Canadian dollar. The multicultural cast of the city—nearly half its school pupils speak English as a second language—has endowed Vancouver with an *ahhh*-inspiring spread of dining choices. Steven A. Shaw, the opinionated New York food writer who calls himself "The Fat-Guy," claims Vancouver is one of the world's best places to eat fish. "It is also one of the best places to eat just about anything else nature has produced, for the bounty of British Columbia is remarkable."

Cruise-ship passengers often don't get any farther from the Canada Place terminal than GASTOWN, the city's historic original site. In the early 1860s, a sea captain started a sawmill here amid the forests along Burrard Inlet. Logging camps drew Gassy Jack Deighton—christened for his loquaciousness—to set up a saloon on the new townsite of Granville (now the name of the city's main north-south street). In 1886, when the settlement became the western terminus of the nation-spanning Canadian Pacific Railway, it was reborn as Vancouver, after the British naval captain who first saw it in 1792. Two months after incorporation, the 1,000 residents watched it burn down; by year's end, as the railway and the port jump-started the economy, it was rebuilt into a home for 8,000. Vancouver truly began to boom in 1898 when Americans used the city as a way station on the long trail to the Klondike gold rush.

Today, Gastown's old Romanesque and Italianate warehouses and low-rise office buildings are becoming inner-city condos for professionals and artists. But the area remains a visitors' mecca of inviting restaurants and curio shops along cobblestone streets—and it's hard to miss the antique-looking clock at Water and Cambie Streets that blows off steam every 15 minutes and, at the other end of Water, the statue of Gassy Jack in Gastown's first civic center, Maple Tree Square.

Perhaps the most serene of all Vancouver's urban sanctuaries is the DR. SUN YAT-SEN CLASSICAL CHINESE GARDEN (578 Carrall Street), the first authentic Ming Dynasty garden outside China. This is a place of gnarled trees and seasonal flowers, of pavilions and ponds of koi fish, of bridges and sculpted rock, built by fifty-two Chinese artisans from such traditional materials as limestone rocks and colored river pebbles. It's now an integral part of historic CHINATOWN (centered on Pender and Keefer Streets, between Main and Gore), North America's second-largest after San Francisco's. Observers say Greater Vancouver is well on its way to becoming the continent's first Asian city. Already a third of the population in suburban Richmond, home to the Vancouver International Airport, is Chinese in origin, and about 70 percent of all land in Richmond's downtown core is Asian-owned. Meanwhile, the traditional China-town quarter in central Vancouver teems with turn-of-the-century Chinese architecture, restaurants reflecting all the regions of China, and shops selling porcelain and silk, exotic teas and life-enhancing herbs, and glistening barbecued ducks.

Another focus of exciting street life is GRANVILLE ISLAND MAR-KET. This former industrial peninsula (on downtown False Creek below the Granville Street Bridge) has been transformed into a village with its own hotel, community center, art school, brewery, floating-home village, and information office. All that, and art galleries and crafts studios, restaurants and theaters, playgrounds and children's shops—and one of the grandest public markets in North America. The indoor market is a good place to pick up a snack or picnic lunch (the seafood is superb), watch the buskers, or buy handmade gifts and west-coast food and wine specialties.

When Vancouver became a city in 1886, its first resolution was to petition the Canadian government to acquire 1,000 acres of a mili-tary reserve on a forested peninsula along Burrard Inlet. The land became STANLEY PARK, one of the greatest urban oases on the con-tinent and the single must-see tourist attraction in Vancouver. With thick forests of spruce and hemlock, western redcedar and massive Douglas-fir, riotous rose gardens, and 200 species of rhododen-dron, it's at once an unspoiled and yet carefully cultivated natural park. And it sprawls on the fringe of downtown, a few minutes' drive from Canada Place. Here, locals play cricket, soccer, and rugby on grassy fields, swim and fish off its beaches, golf and play tennis, feed the resident Canada geese, and in the odd cold winters skate on frozen Lost Lagoon (named in a poem by Pauline Johnson, the daughter of a Mohawk chief, because the water once disappeared during low tide). The park has restaurants, totem poles, the superb VANCOUVER AQUARIUM and, best of all, a 5½-mile paved path along the seawall. You can walk or cycle in sight of a bevy of the world's ships offshore, awaiting berths, entertained by an abundance of migrant waterfowl and occasional sightings of such marine life as seals and killer whales.

There's a lushness about this rain-forest land (which receives less summer rainfall than any other major Canadian city except Victoria). QUEEN ELIZABETH PARK on Little Mountain (33rd Avenue and Cambie) has waterfalls in sunken quarry gardens, a Henry Moore sculpture, a wide-screen vista of city and mountains, and the BLOEDEL CONSERVATORY under a geodesic dome, with free-flying tropical birds and exotic plants, including an exceptional array of Japanese bonsai. VANDUSEN BOTANICAL GARDEN (37th Avenue and Oak Street) provides 55 eminently walkable acres of lawns, ponds, sculpture, children's garden, plant maze, gift shop, and restaurant, and Canada's biggest collections of rhododendrons and hardy ornamental plants. THE UNIVERSITY OF BRITISH COLUMBIA BOTANICAL GARDEN (6804 S.W. Marine Drive) features alpine, native, food, and Asian plantings as well as the medicinal plants of the sixteenth-century-style Physick Garden. The seaside setting of the major provincial university makes for the most glorious campus in the nation. The monumental MUSEUM OF ANTHROPOLOGY stands here (6393 N.W. Marine Drive), inspired by the cedar houses of northwest coast Natives and showcasing one of the world's most extensive displays of their sophisticated traditional and contemporary art. It's all imaginatively arranged inside the award-winning building and on the totem-strewn grounds, which are planted with grasses and other vegetation the First Peoples once used.

To top off a Vancouver visit, there's nothing more elevating than a skytram trip up GROUSE MOUNTAIN, the 4,006-foot peak in North Vancouver across the elegant Lions Gate Bridge. Along the way, your tour may stop in at the SALMON HATCHERY amid the forests of Capilano River Regional Park, where displays describe how two million salmon eggs are hatched here each year. Another nearby attraction is the CAPILANO SUSPENSION BRIDGE, a 450-foot length of scary-looking wood and cable—the world's longest suspended footbridge—that sways 230 feet above the tumultuous waters of the Capilano River Canyon. The ride in enclosed trams up Grouse Mountain may be even more dizzying, but once at the summit you can hike alpine meadows, which double as winter ski trails; catch a multimedia show and a loggers' demonstration; watch or try out tandem paragliding; snack, dine, or shop for souvenirs—and soak up the unforgettable view of Vancouver the beautiful.

Victoria: Eden on the Pacific

"The place itself appears a perfect 'Eden', in the midst of the dreary wilderness of the Northwest coast, and so different is its general aspect, from the wooded, rugged regions around, that one may be pardoned for supposing it had dropped from the clouds into its present position." In 1842 that was the considered opinion of James Douglas, chief factor of the fur-trading Hudson's Bay Company, after surveying the site for what would become Victoria. That attitude among newcomers toward the British Columbia capital seems as strong today as it was more than a century and a half ago. Readers of Condé Nast Traveler ("Truth in Travel") have actually declared the city's environment the most pleasant of any in the world—and the magazine has ranked Greater Victoria, a region of 380,000 people, fifth-best city overall.

This Pacific port on a peninsula at the southern end of Vancouver Island (the largest island off the west coast of North America) is Canada's westernmost city. It lies 62 miles south of Vancouver across the Strait of Georgia—closer to the United States than it is to

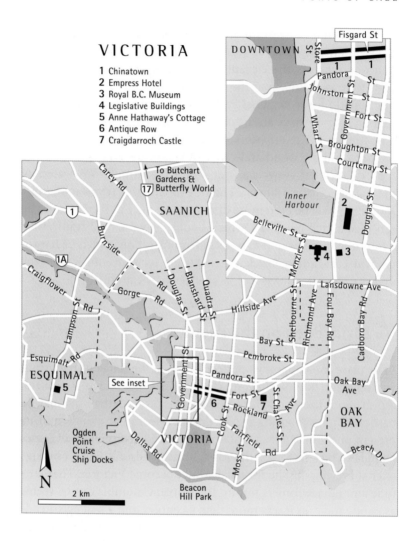

VICTORIA

1 Chinatown
2 Empress Hotel
3 Royal B.C. Museum
4 Legislative Buildings
5 Anne Hathaway's Cottage
6 Antique Row
7 Craigdarroch Castle

the mainland. And in its sheer gentility, Victoria appears as if it had dropped from a kinder, gentler time.

Its low-rise downtown along the humming INNER HARBOUR has a human scale, heritage buildings abound, and its impossibly clean streets brim with hanging baskets of flowers. You can escape the town center in a mere five minutes to be amid lakes and cricket fields, in the company of peacocks and royal swans, and the chickens and lambs of a children's petting farm, at BEACON HILL PARK (between Douglas and Cook Streets along Marine Drive). Such gracious residential areas as OAK BAY and ROCKLAND look like Hollywood's image of middle-class neighborhoods in the 1950s.

Then there's the weather. Victoria enjoys some of the warmest winter weather in Canada, with daffodils trumpeting in late winter among anywhere from one to four billion other blooms recorded in the annual February flower count. And summers here see less rain than any other sizable Canadian city. (James Douglas's assistant complained, mildly: "The climate is perhaps too fine…from June to Novr. we had scarcely anything else, than bright sunny days! Yet we were by no means oppressed by the heat, for the close vicinity of the sea & the cooling breezes blowing thence, made it very bearable.")

This is first and forever a government town, but its other preoccupation is tourism. Victoria has long ridden on its supposed resemblance to Olde England and a reputation as the nation's retirement capital—its refinement and good weather convincing visitors to return to live here. It's true that the inner city ringing the harbor area is overripe with British references. Bruce Hutchison, a distinguished man of Canadian letters, once said his hometown had made the 20 acres of the downtown an altar of the Victorian spirit.

The tourist shops along GOVERNMENT STREET, the main drag, do feature Doulton china and Waterford crystal, Scottish woolens, and English made-to-measure tweed suits. The ferries and floatplanes that land in the harbor (cruise ships and other large ocean vessels berth around the corner at Ogden Point) do have an inescapable view of the city's two turn-of-the-century stone monuments: the LEGISLATIVE BUILDINGS, seat of the provincial government, and the impressively restored EMPRESS HOTEL, still serving daily high tea. Both were designed by an English architect in grand British Empire style (though the lights that outline the exterior of the legislature, strung for the Duke of Connaught's visit in 1910, give it a Disneyland touch).

Look beyond the city's façade, however, and you'll find a multicultural mélange typical of other Canadian centers, which surfaces in ethnic restaurants and the many nations reflected in residents' faces. If the city still lures warmth-starved Prairie farmers to retire here, its population has grown increasingly younger, attracted by high-tech and other progressive industries. In fact, Halifax on Canada's east coast has supplanted it, in percentage terms, as a haven for retirees. Victoria also lures more than four million visitors a year from around the world, most of them American; its inhabitants can see the Olympic Mountains of Washington state, a quick ferry trip south across the Strait of Juan de Fuca.

It was Americans whom James Douglas was retreating from in 1842 when he arrived at the southern verge of Vancouver Island to seek a new site for a fort. The U.S. and Britain had agreed in 1818 to open up the region between California and Alaska to trading by people of both nations. Now American settlers and their political backers were calling for annexation of the Pacific Coast as far north as the Alaska boundary. Douglas of the Hudson's Bay Company—deciding to relocate Fort Vancouver from the mouth of the Columbia River in what is now Washington—found the idyllic site he called Fort Victoria in honor of the contemporary Queen. Three years later, he moved the trading company's Pacific headquarters there and became governor of Britain's new Crown colony on Vancouver Island.

In 1858, discovery of gold on the Fraser River on the British Columbia mainland brought 20,000 hopefuls, mostly veterans of the California gold rush, who stopped in Victoria before crossing the Strait of Georgia to the Canadian Eldorado. Victoria, soon a busy port handling the island's lumber and mineral riches, became a city in 1862; within three years, the muscle-flexing British opened a naval base here (now Canadian Forces Base Esquimalt). After 1886 when the transcontinental railroad made Vancouver boom, Victoria no longer dominated the colony, though it remained the capital when British Columbia became a province five years later.

Thousands of the gold seekers and railroad builders were Chinese from the U.S. and China. By 1884 they numbered nearly 17,000, half of Victoria's population, most of them indentured laborers living in CHINATOWN. The first such Chinese community in Canada, it inspired legends about opium dens, secret tunnels, and what is still the continent's narrowest street, Fan Tan Alley. Over the decades, the flourishing district around downtown Fisgard Street ebbed in vitality; fewer than 100 Chinese remained there by the late 1970s, when young artists were moving in while the city and the Chinese community began to revive the historic quarter. Heralding this renewed Chinatown of shops and restaurants is the Gate of Harmonious Interest, an archway of decorative Taiwanese tiles that spans Fisgard at Government Street.

The place to experience the history and environment of Victoria and the province is the ROYAL BRITISH COLUMBIA MUSEUM (675 Belleville Street near the Legislative Buildings), considered one of the seven best museums in North America. The First Peoples displays are particularly poignant as you hear their celebratory potlatch songs, see flickering old movies of Natives in war canoes, and visit a Kwakiutl longhouse. There are stunningly lifelike dioramas of animal habitats, a simulated submarine tour of the ocean depths, and walk-through re-creations of Captain Cook's shipboard cabin, as well as an Old Town so realistic you might have slipped through a crack in time.

For more peeks into the local past, stroll through the city center, past the heritage brick buildings of the outdoor OLD TOWN along Johnston Street, stopping at the award-winning Market Square complex of shops and restaurants. Or visit ANTIQUE ROW along Fort Street (from Douglas to Vancouver Streets and beyond), where collectibles and old treasures compete with Canadian handicrafts, china, and crystal. In the Rockland area, you can tour CRAIGDARROCH CASTLE (1050 Joan Crescent), the multi-turreted mansion built of local sandstone for Robert Dunsmuir, British Columbia's coal king, and his Scottish wife. He died before the 20,000-square-foot mini-palace was finished in 1889, and in fact, work is still being done to restore its stained-glass windows and inlaid floors to their original beauty.

A lot less local, but still inviting, are thatch-roofed ANNE HATHAWAY'S COTTAGE (429 Lampson Street in Esquimalt), a surprisingly authentic replica of the sixteenth-century home of Shakespeare's wife; and BUTTERFLY WORLD (1461 Benvenuto Avenue in Brentwood

Bay), where some of the world's most exotic live butterflies court, lay eggs, and flutter by to be photographed in tropical settings.

It's just a couple of minutes' flight from the butterflies to what might well be the most astonishing private botanical showcase on the continent: BUTCHART GARDENS. The story goes that flower-crazy Jenny Butchart couldn't tell one bloom from another in 1904 when she and scads of Chinese workers began turning her husband's ugly limestone quarry into a formal, 50-acre garden. To transform it, she even rappelled down rock walls in a swinging ship's chair to plant ivy. Fountains and waterfalls, shrubs and evergreens accent the Japanese, Italian, English rose, and sunken gardens. Spring's daffodils, dogwood, and tulips yield to the roses, fuchsias, and begonias of summer, while dahlias, zinnias, and chrysanthemums flourish in fall. Take tea in the Butchart home, browse the garden shop—and pleasure in a microcosm of the Eden that Victoria still is.

Ketchikan: Salmon, Rain, and Sin

Arriving in Ketchikan—Alaska's southernmost major port and the traditional first stop for cruise ships—you might spot pink salmon literally leaping out of the water around you, in arcs of abandon, perhaps seeking their morning snacks. A good omen, you'll think, if you signed on for a fishing excursion.

This is a town where, they used to say, fishermen as well as salmon came to spawn. Back in the teens of the twentieth century, Ketchikan was called "Uncle Sam's wickedest city." Some of that soiled reputation was due to the presence of Dolly Arthur, its most famous madam, a feisty Idaho waitress who came to Alaska in 1914 and for half a century operated a house of ill repute. "I realized I could make a lot more money from the attentions of men than I could waiting tables," she once recalled.

Today, Alaska's First City is a tamer place, notable for salmon and

Creek Street boardwalk, once the
domain of Ketchikan's famous madams.

halibut fishing, the state's largest collection of totem poles, and its handiness to the feral majesty of Misty Fjords National Monument. But to relive the essence of old Ketchikan, you have only to stroll the boardwalk of south-side CREEK STREET. The Creek still had a score of brothels when local authorities shut them down in 1954. Dolly's House, No. 24, is now a privately run folk museum teeming with her memorabilia, including secret panels to hide money and Prohibition liquor, a discreet nude photograph of the solidly built proprietor, and her equally overupholstered, fringe-and-satin bedroom.

The plank boardwalk of craft and souvenir shops, below Boston Smith Hill, stands on pilings high above the creek that may have given Ketchikan its name. It *may* have come from a Tlingit phrase for "salmon creek that runs through town"; or perhaps "spread wings of a prostrate eagle" for the shape of a sandspit at the creek mouth; or (if you prefer) for the nineteenth-century Tlingit named Kitschk, who had a summer fishing camp here that came to be known as Kitschk-hin-Kitschk's stream. And there are at least three other tales of origin. For certain, it was born as a white settlement in 1887 with the opening of a salmon cannery, the first of thirteen canneries and cold-storage facilities that helped make Ketchikan the self-proclaimed Salmon Capital of the World, the center of a fishing industry propelling the Southeast economy until the mid-1950s. And this is also an Alaska Rain Capital, with more than 13 feet of rain a year, though May through August are the least-wet months, ideal for NATURE HIKES, MOUNTAIN BIKE TOURS, and even BACKCOUNTRY JEEP SAFARIS.

Ketchikan spreads for several miles along the the southwestern verge of Revillagigedo Island (which Captain Vancouver christened for a Mexican viceroy and which locals abbreviate to Ruh-*vil*-la). Revilla, bigger than Rhode Island, is ringed by the 150-mile Behm Canal, one of the most picturesque and fish-rich waterways in the Panhandle. The borough of 14,300 people borders 50-mile-long Tongass Narrows, where cruise ships pull up to docks that rise and fall with the 20-foot tides. (Downtown basements often fall victim to these tides.) Never more than ten blocks wide as it backs up against 3,000-foot Deer Mountain, it's a city of wooden staircases ascending rocky hillsides to ragged rows of houses on stilts, with

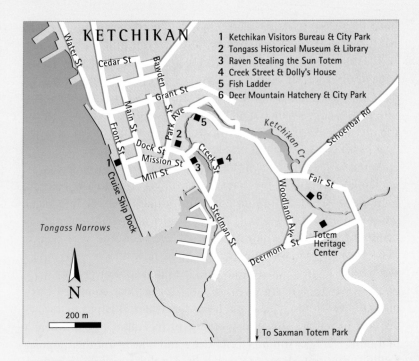

KETCHIKAN

1 Ketchikan Visitors Bureau & City Park
2 Tongass Historical Museum & Library
3 Raven Stealing the Sun Totem
4 Creek Street & Dolly's House
5 Fish Ladder
6 Deer Mountain Hatchery & City Park

Tongass Narrows

N

200 m

To Saxman Totem Park

Walkabout

Totem Heritage Center, a quarter-mile up Deermont Street, houses an intriguing collection of house posts from old Native villages and 33 original totem poles from the nineteenth century.

Deer Mountain Hatchery on Ketchikan Creek, across the footbridge from the Totem Heritage Center, welcomes visitors with a description of the breeding and raising of coho and king salmon. The kings and pinks spawn in the creek in late summer, using the fish ladder to surmount the falls. **The Eagle Center**, offering a chance to see eagles up close, is next to the hatchery.

Tongass Historical Museum, in the library complex at 629 Dock Street, focuses on Native art and craft and the fishing industry, as well as local history; generally open during cruise visits.

A **Tramway** rises up the cliff from Creek Street to a Tlingit-styled hotel, built by the Cape Fox Indian Corporation, which offers commanding views over Tongass Narrows and the city.

steep, dormered roofs and shake-and-clapboard sheathing. The harbor below swarms with floatplanes and pleasure and fish boats.

Ketchikan was once the hub of the north Pacific halibut fleet. Today's commercial fishery focuses on salmon. Although pinks are more abundant, kings and cohos are the prizes here in SPORTFISHING EXPEDITIONS, which might involve fly-casting on a river, or on streams and lakes you reach by floatplane, or on up-to-date charter boats with enclosed cabins and knowledgeable skippers.

You can take other WATERBORNE EXCURSIONS: in jet boats, in sea kayaks around the port and across the narrows to a rain-forest island, in massive canoes on a quiet mountain lake, or in a yacht that motors alongside the city's most historical sites and introduces you to the local fishing industry. You can even do some SNORKELING in a warm wet suit with a guide who will show off the underwater wonders of salmon, sea urchins, and the giant sunflower starfish.

BEAR ADVENTURES start with a trip on a float-equipped bush plane to the salmon hatchery at Neets Bay where you hike to a viewing area to watch black bears gorging, or to Traitor's Cove where a naturalist will take you on a brief drive and hike to another popular feeding ground at Margaret Creek Falls. Another possibility is mountain-goat spotting on HELICOPTER WILDERNESS FLIGHTS to remote areas where the chopper lands on either a mountaintop or an island.

This is an ideal setting in which to absorb Native culture. Either of two land cruises just outside town will bring you face to face with the vivid story-telling medium of totem poles, among 113 in the Ketchikan area. Century-old Tlingit and Haida Indian poles, authentically recreated replicas, and a representative clan house line the shore at the TOTEM BIGHT STATE HISTORICAL PARK, the site of a traditional Tlingit summer camp on Tongass Narrows. The communal house has carved corner posts, an impressively painted façade, and a cedar entrance pole recounting tales of Raven creating daylight in the dark world. On the quiet beach walk beside the poles, there's a chance of spotting seals and other sea mammals, bald eagles, and of course, ravens.

SAXMAN TOTEM PARK, just south of Ketchikan, has more standing totem poles than any other place—over two dozen—and even more in the way of entertainment. Originally the Tlingit village of Fort Tongass, it was renamed for a Presbyterian minister who taught there late last century and drowned while seeking a new site for the community. In the lean late 1930s, the Civilian Conservation Corps brought poles from old villages to Saxman and restored them. The collection has such curiosities as President Lincoln, in a stovepipe hat, as a symbol of the first white man seen by the clan, and U.S. Secretary of State William Seward, wearing a potlatch hat, on a pole that was meant to shame him because he didn't exchange gifts during his local visit in 1869. There's a carving shed where masters of the art create new 40-foot works; a Beaver tribal house, the first clan house to rise in half a century; a handicraft store and interpretative center; and culturally faithful performances by the Cape Fox Dancers.

A flight-seeing tour is a fine way to comprehend the 2.2 million acres of MISTY FJORDS NATIONAL MONUMENT, which even some jaded Alaskans insist is one of the more spectacular sights on earth. There are no roads in; planes and boats are the only options to view

By the 1930s, about 1,200 fish boats fed Ketchikan's canneries and cold storage.

the sheer mountains quilted with snow, hanging valleys, white sand beaches, three major rivers, and countless streams that are among the state's best for rearing fish. The park embraces eastern Revilla-gigedo Island and some of the mainland between the fjords of the Portland and Behm Canals. Protected from logging, its forests are western hemlock, yellow and redcedar, Sitka spruce, a bit of silver fir, and even the northernmost stands of Pacific yew, prized for its use in cancer treatment.

From a floatplane, you can watch twin waterfalls tumble from the bowl of Big Goat Lake, where mountain goats and brown bears ramble. You might fly close to the fortresslike granite flanks of a valley carved by a glacier and land at the head of long fjords to sit silently on the black salt water of Rudyerd Bay. At its entrance, on the Behm Canal, a volcanic plug twenty stories tall vaults from the water, a basking spot for seals. The ubiquitous Captain Vancouver named it New Eddystone Rock for a similar formation on a light-house rock off Cornwall, England. Depending on the excursion you choose, the seaplane might land at a float here and transfer you to a small cruise vessel that will take you up close to eagles and seals.

It's all part of the wonder of a national monument which, given its mist-shrouded enchantment, might just as well have been called *Mystery* Fjords.

Juneau: A Capital City

Every once in a while, the folks up in Anchorage start pushing for an initiative to move the capital of the state from Juneau to a spot more convenient for most Alaskans. To somewhere near Anchor-age, say, where people are supposedly more progressive. As one Juneau resident wrote not long ago, "Media in Anchorage con-stantly bashes us as anti-development, anti-road, anti-capitalist, and anti-Alaskan."

Well, there may be a glimmer of truth to all the charges except the last one about patriotism. Bridget A. Smith, a lecturer in psy-chology on the local campus of the University of Alaska, wrote

1 Glacier Gardens Rainforest Adventure
2 Federal Building & Main Post Office
3 Alaska State Museum
4 Governor's Mansion
5 Juneau-Douglas City Museum
6 Alaska State Capitol
7 The *Windfall Fisherman*
8 Juneau Visitor Information Center
9 St. Nicholas Orthodox Church
10 Marine Park
11 Red Dog Saloon
12 Cruise Ship Terminal

4 km

Walkabout

Juneau Visitor Information Center, 134 3rd Street, a log cabin modeled on the city's first church, has a Walking Tour guide that features historic Juneau.

Public Art: A sampling of many possibilities includes *Harnessing of the Atom Totem Pole* (Calhoun & Main) symbolizing the U.S., Russia, the harnessing of energy, and the Raven Creator; *Windfall Fisherman* (outside Courthouse, Main Street), a full-sized bronze of an Alaska Brown Bear; *Raven Discovering Mankind in a Clam Shell* (City Municipal Building, Marine Way), a wall mural depicting the Tlingit legend.

Juneau–Douglas City Museum, Veterans Memorial Building, 4th & Main: A motherlode of gold-mining lore, hands-on exhibits, and video shows.

St. Nicholas Orthodox Church, 326 5th Street,: Although there were no Russians in Juneau, local Tlingit chiefs asked the Eastern Orthodox bishop in Sitka to baptize them, and this octagonal church was built with Russian funds in 1894. Tlingit families have been worshiping here continuously since.

an entertaining mystery novel called *Death of an Alaskan Princess*, which offers an insider's perceptions about modern-day Juneau and its past. Among them: "...the history of the town can be discerned by the careful observer—narrow streets intended for horses, the absence of right angles as the town grew organically up and around the mountains, the predominance of wood as a construction material giving way to a few buildings built in the thirties of stone when it looked as if it would be a permanent community." Now all this, she writes, is "piously preserved."

Delivering floatplane passengers to the People's Wharf, the chatty woman driving the tour bus comments on the two almighty facts about Juneau—its status as the state capital and its relative isolation as a seaport with no road links to the rest of Alaska: "One out of every two folks in the workforce is employed by the government. We have 31,000 people and about 25,000 cars—going nowhere."

In fact, these complementary insights combine to present what to outsiders seems an attractive portrait of Alaska's third-largest

The New England colonial-style Governor's mansion in Juneau.

city (after Anchorage and Fairbanks). Yes, Juneau may appear a little devout in paying attention to its past, but a lot of its history is still firsthand—with many original buildings standing downtown, recorded in the National Register of Historic Places. Yes, this is a relentlessly government town and it *is* cut off by land, but the security of regular paychecks combined with the sense of separation may explain why there are so many vehicles for only 190 miles of local roads (and why there are 3,000 or so recreational boats). And the comparative wealth and relatively high educational levels of those in government service have obviously given them the discretionary income and the appreciation for things cultural, including an extravagant amount of art on public display in the streets.

Greater Juneau stretches along a skinny bench of land that extends to the Mendenhall Valley, the suburb 10 miles northwest where much of the population lives. At 3,255 square miles, it's the largest U.S. city in area. Of that total, however, 928 square miles are ice cap and 538 are water. The city and borough are squeezed between the Gastineau Channel of the Inside Passage and the 3,500-foot peaks of Mount Juneau and Mount Roberts, which from time to time release avalanches on the community. The Coast Mountains rise to the north and east, the Chilkat Range to the northwest, and the summits of Admiralty Island to the south. Behind the city stretches the 1,500-square-mile JUNEAU ICEFIELD, which feeds thirty-eight glaciers, among them the mighty—and mighty accessible—MENDENHALL. You can visit the ice cap and glacier by bus, plane, jet-turbine helicopter, and high-speed catamaran, and even view it RIVER RAFTING or SEA KAYAKING.

Other outdoor excursions include NATURE WALKS through the Douglas Island and Tongass rain forests and through glacial valleys with tumbling waterfalls; FLOATPLANE FLIGHTS to the historic log-built Taku Glacier Lodge, where you might spot the resident bear, Scarface; NATURE CRUISES to the Taku Glacier and Auke Bay (some by jet boat); and WILDLIFE QUESTS to view humpback and killer whales, among other sea life. For a different spin, there's a three-hour GLACIER HELICOPTER FLIGHT AND DOG-SLED RIDE at a camp on the Norris Glacier.

It was gold that brought a couple of bad ol' boys to Alaska from the mines of the Pacific Northwest in 1879. Richard Harris had been described as "an inveterate drunkard" by one boss, and the word on Joseph Juneau, in those politically incorrect times, was that "between hooch and squaws he never had a cent to get away on." Both in their forties, they landed in Sitka and went to work prospecting for a German mining engineer. After spending all their grubstake and losing their boat, they convinced a Tlingit man to take them back to Sitka. Kowee, related to the local Auk tribe, took them first to a small stream he knew off the Gastineau Channel, where he led them to a vein of quartz bursting with gold. On their second trip there in 1880—the engineer had no one else to send but the hopeless pair—they made Alaska's first major gold strike, which Harris later described: "We knew it was gold, but so much and not in particles, streaks running through the rock and little lumps as large as peas or beans." They staked their claim and a townsite of 160 acres. This was the first Alaska town to be founded after the U.S. bought the territory from Russia. Originally the mining camp was called Harrisburg, but when a horde of competing prospectors soured on its namesake for making multiple claims, they rechristened it Juneau. Dick Harris died broke in an Oregon sanitorium, and Joe Juneau splurged his $18,000 gold earnings within two years.

Hard-rock mining and milling companies superseded the placer miners. Of those working claims on Douglas Island, just across the channel from Juneau, the Treadwell Mine was most successful. For thirty-five years, miners dug out its glory hole—a huge open pit 450 feet deep that led to tunnels half a mile down—until, in 1917, the ground caved in below the flourishing company town of Treadwell, and three million tons of sea swallowed up the mine. In little more than six decades, three local mines produced $158 million worth of low-quality gold using high-tech methods. The last one to close, based on the original Harris-Juneau claims, was the Alaska-Juneau. The A-J's 100-plus miles of tunnels yielded about $4 million worth of gold a year for a decade until a wartime labor shortage shuttered it in 1944. The rusting hulk of its crushing and recovery mill can still be seen on the slope of Mount

Roberts above the site of the GOLD CREEK SALMON BAKE. (You can enjoy another salmon bake at a mountain lodge in the shadow of a glacier.) While ample gold supplies remain in the area—GOLD PANNING is a common visitors' pastime—and there are ongoing plans to revive the mines, the mineral hasn't figured prominently in Juneau's economy since.

Fishing has, however—commercial halibut and salmon fishing is resurging as stocks recover from a decline in the 1980s. A familiar tour destination is the $7-million GASTINEAU SALMON HATCHERY, three miles north of town, where you can watch through underwater windows as pinks and chum fight their way up the largest fish ladder in the state and are checked for maturity. Ripe females are dispatched and relieved of their eggs, which are fertilized with milt squeezed from the males' bellies. Juneau's SALTWATER SPORTFISH-ING is the most popular in Alaska, offering a quarter of all the sport king salmon taken in the sea and the saltchuck. The kings range local waters throughout the summer, with the largest—18 to 50 pounds—peaking in late April through June. Some companies offer another adventure on the water: a LYNN CANAL CRUISE/FLY TOUR to Skagway by sightseeing boat and back by plane. The glacier-dug channel, broad and deep, is 67 miles of Native and gold-rush history; seals, sea lions, humpback and killer whales; and valley and hanging glaciers amid the snow-streaked mountains.

Since 1912, Juneau has been the official capital and, with statehood in 1959, government emerged as the biggest local business. But for more than two decades, the locals had to live with threats to move the capital to somewhere more central—the most active suggestion being the somnolent south-central community of Willow (population 200). The move would have shrunk Juneau's population by two-thirds and shut nearly half its businesses. In 1982, state voters finally decided not to spend $2.8 billion to relocate the capital, and Juneau bloomed anew. By summer, when the cruise ships arrive, the state legislature has finished its session, but you can visit the old marble-columned STATE CAPITOL (4th Street) and admire the white, New England colonial GOVERNOR'S MANSION (atop the Calhoun Avenue hill), which has housed Alaska's governors and their families since 1912. Out front, a totem pole tells the Tlingit legend of the creation of the ubiquitous mosquito.

One of two newer in-town tours is the MOUNT ROBERTS TRAM-WAY, created by an urban Native corporation, which takes you on a six-minute ride 1,800 feet up to the forested peak and a nature center, bar and grill, gift shops, and a theater showing a film on Tlingit culture. (You can walk up or down and take the tram one-way, too.) The other tour is the GLACIER GARDENS RAINFOREST ADVEN-TURE in a 46-acre botanical oasis that is the realization of a dream by a local couple to present an accessible look at both cultivated gardens and natural rain forest. Motorized carts are available to navigate the couple of miles of wide paths that rise 580 feet to gasp-producing overlooks from Thunder Mountain and then loop back down past ponds, waterfalls, and astonishing upside-down trees growing flowers in their exposed root systems. Some tours of the garden end with a tour of the ALASKAN BREWING COMPANY and a sample of a beer first brewed in the late 1800s.

If you have time, one way of savoring the history of Juneau—and the rest of the state—is a visit to the ALASKA STATE MUSEUM (395 Whitter Street). Among its treasures: original sketches from the Cook and Bering voyages, a Tlingit clan house and a 40-foot Eskimo whale-hunting boat, and the engrossing eagle-nesting tree.

And for something slightly less cultural, stop in at the RED DOG SALOON (Marine Way and South Franklin Street), a gold-rush replica with swinging doors, sawdust on the wood floor, and a polished bar with brass beer spigots. It's abrim with wilderness trophy heads, antique guns, nineteenth-century lifebuoys, flags from foreign vessels, and thousands of personal calling cards, some a century old. Joe Juneau's isn't among them.

Skagway: The Lost Frontier

It was Alaska's first-ever city, back in 1900, but that was only because it managed to file incorporation papers just one day before Juneau did. Skagway officials are still gloating: at a ceremony a century later,

1 National Historic Park
  Visitors Center
2 Jeff Smith's Parlor
3 Red Onion Saloon
4 Golden North Hotel
5 Mascot Saloon Museum
6 Moe's Frontier Bar
7 Moore's Cabin
8 Days of '98 Theater
9 Corrington Museum
10 City Museum

Walkabout

The National Historic Park Visitors Center is at 2nd and Broadway. **Skagway Convention And Visitors Bureau** is at 240 Broadway, between #3 and #4 on the map. Both centers have hiking-trail maps and ambitious walking tour maps of downtown.

Strolling Broadway, look for the three-story, yellow onion-domed **Golden North Hotel**, which with an 1898 birthdate might well be Alaska's oldest. It's fitted out with gold-rush furnishings and, yes, there's the fabled ghost of Mary, a gold miner's fiancée, on the premises. The **Days Of '98 Theater**, Broadway and 6th, has the longest-running entertainment in the state: the melodrama featuring Soapy Smith has been involving audiences for eight decades. **Moe's Frontier Bar**, on Broadway between 4th and 5th, is where the locals go to down a few, or more.

local tourism director Buckwheat Donahue remarked, "A hundred years ago, Juneau was upset that we beat them to the punch by being the first incorporated city in Alaska. And nothing's changed. We're still beating them to the punch. Let's party."

Noting the dancehall girls on hand for the centenary, *The Skagway News* noted, "Nothing ever takes place in this historic Klondike Gold Rush town without a floozy or two." Or a cast of authentic Alaska characters who people this town that looks as if it were lifted from a tale by Robert Service.

There's the ivory trader who advertises himself as *Corrington— The Legend—The Man.* The woman who came to visit and wound up buying the Red Onion Saloon, a pint-sized donkey, and a pot-bellied pig. The barmiest of the 850 permanent residents who hired a couple of planes to fly in Big Macs from Juneau's first McDonald's, and others who successfully wielded a petition and a phony newspaper front page imploring Alaska's rural TV network to bring back the eccentric series *The Simpsons*—their soulmates, obviously. And not to forget the kazoo-crazy, award-winning Big Hammer Marching Band, which disrupts every Fourth of July celebration, sending people scurrying from the smoke of their mock nuclear meltdown or neglecting to let the police know about a make-believe bank holdup erupting in simulated gunshots and dynamite blasts.

All of which is one reason why Skagway—at the northern end of the Inside Passage—ranks among Southeast's most popular cruise ports. Amid the imposing St. Elias Mountains, it sits at the head of Taiya Inlet on the 75-mile Lynn Canal from Juneau. Aside from an average annual rainfall of a mere 29 inches (one-sixth of Ketchikan's), the town's most obvious lure is its gold-rush past. During the late 1890s, it was the staging area for the Klondike Stampeders who tried to surmount the wicked White Pass Trail to the Yukon, one of the two Trails of '98 across the Coast Range. As the century turned, Skagway became the starting point of the narrow-gauge WHITE PASS & YUKON ROUTE to Whitehorse—which after several years' interruption in the 1980s resumed its enthralling run over the picturesque pass as a tourist attraction between here and Fraser, British Columbia. (*See* Alaska's Lively Railroads, *page 33.*) Cruise-ship passengers can take a briefer trip behind old No. 73, a steam engine, which eventually gives way to diesels powerful enough to climb to the summit, at the international border with Canada, and wend back down the mountain.

Now, as part of the widely scattered Klondike Gold Rush National Historical Park (with branches in Seattle and Canada's Dawson City), Skagway has enshrined its history. The park service has spent millions on restoration. Although much of the town may be a tarted-up replica of the real thing, every building along two blocks of the main street was put up between 1897 and 1900. The RED LIGHT DISTRICT TOUR will bring you to the Red Onion, which opened in 1898 as a saloon and bordello; now it's a watering hole that often hosts cruise-ship musicians playing jazz on a busman's holiday. Climb the stairs today and you'll be in the period bedrooms of the Brothel Museum. THE MASCOT SALOON MUSEUM (Broadway and 3rd) will tell you almost as much as you wanted to know about gold-rush bars. One of them, at 2nd, JEFF SMITH'S PARLOR, belonged to the town's legendary bad man, Jefferson Randall (Soapy) Smith.

If Skagway has characters today, they descend in spirit from the bearded, beak-nosed Soapy, a con man from the U.S. South. He picked up the moniker in the Lower 48 from his penny-ante racket of selling soap to suckers who hoped to win the $20 and $50 bills supposedly wrapped inside the bars. In 1897, Smith came to a site that had been settled a decade earlier by William (Capt. Billy) Moore, a shrewd riverboat skipper and prospector who had claimed 160 waterfront acres and built a wharf. (MOORE'S CABIN, the oldest local building, is still on 5th Street east of Broadway). With the Klondike gold strike, about 100 stampeders led by surveyor Frank Reid decided to commandeer Moore's land—although he did sell the wharf for $175,000—and lay out a town. It came to be known as Skagway, a Tlingit name variously believed to mean, among other things, "home of the north wind" and "the end of salt water." The day after Smith arrived in the windy,

The White Pass & Yukon Route twists through terrain that's "too steep for a billy goat." ▸

tidewater settlement, he and five fellow crooks rescued a bartender from hanging—Soapy announced there'd be no lynch mobs in *his* Skagway. This pretense at principles made him popular enough that he soon ran the lawless town, operating a crooked gambling parlor and overseeing a string of strongarm men, pickpockets, and rip-off artists. Soapy himself was not above a good swindle, such as collecting $35,000 in contributions for a new preacher in town and then having him robbed overnight.

Meanwhile, Canada's North West Mounted Police were running the Yukon (*see page 254*), and when Supt. Sam Steele visited Skagway in 1898 he was appalled at the difference. The town of 15,000, he said, was "little better than a hell on earth": "At night, the crash of bands, shouts of 'Murder!,' cries for help mingled with the cracked voices of singers in the variety halls...." It wasn't until July 8, 1898, when a new arrival who had been robbed of his gold dust protested loudly, that Soapy's reign ended. At an evening meeting called by more honest citizens to discuss the victim's complaint, a drunken Smith arrived to harangue them—only to be met by Frank Reid, who had helped relieve Capt. Billy Moore of his land. After a shootout, Smith was dead and Reid lay dying.

Skagway incorporated in 1900 and, with Soapy and most of the stampeders gone, it settled down to the business of being a reputable port and a railroad town. For the next eight decades, the White Pass & Yukon carried the natural resources from Canada's North to the coast. But when the Yukon's lead and zinc mines closed in 1982, the railway went down with them. By then the National Park Service had begun restoring the town's boardwalks and false-front buildings. Summer tourist traffic quickly became the major industry. Cruise-ship companies now offer a cornucopia of excursions here. Among them:

A HISTORICAL TOWN TOUR by trolley or 1920s-style sightseeing bus will take you through the compact core (watch for 1st and State, where Smith and Reid killed one another), and perhaps stop at the newish CITY MUSEUM (7th and Spring) which chronicles the town's golden days, including the story of Soapy and his nemesis—who lie buried in the GOLD RUSH CEMETERY just outside town, not far from pretty Reid Falls. Many tours provide an opportunity for photographs at the SKAGWAY OVERLOOK, just on the edge of town, with its inspiring view of the community, the valley, and the Lynn Canal.

THE WHITE PASS TOUR by motorcoach leads to the 3,292-foot summit through the well-named Tormented Valley, a route that runs near the White Pass & Yukon rail line, past glaciers, and on to the U.S.-Canada border. This tour can include a visit to the LIARS-VILLE TRAIL CAMP, a replica of a turn-of-the-century tent town including sled-dog demonstrations, campfire tales, salmon bake, and a chance to pan for gold.

A GLACIER POINT WILDERNESS SAFARI combines a catamaran cruise through the state's deepest fjord with a drive, a walk, and a canoe trip to Davidson Glacier. If you prefer to look down on glaciers, a HELICOPTER EXCURSION offers an exciting view of the alternative Chilkoot Trail to the gold fields, where you may spot contemporary climbers, and lands you on a glacier. Various FLIGHT-SEEING TRIPS, ideal for photographers, explore surrounding glaciers—at nearby Glacier Bay and the Chilkat Glacier system—before touching down a couple of times to marvel at their surface, often while you're enjoying a treat of champagne and Alaska fudge. A DOG-SLEDDING AND GLACIER HELICOPTER FLIGHT transports you to a glacier above the city where you can be a musher or passenger as huskies haul you across the ice.

As in most Southeast ports, SPORTFISHING for salmon and halibut in Skagway is fine, especially from the deck of a roomy cruiser. Some cruise lines offer SEA KAYAKING in the inlets and bays outside Skagway and a CHILKOOT TRAIL HIKE AND FLOAT TOUR, which blends a rain-forest walk with a float trip down a gentle stretch of the Taiya River. The WHITE PASS RAIL AND BIKE COMBINATION is a land-bound package that follows up the train trip to the Klondike summit with a downhill cycle. Four-legged transport is available too, on a YUKON HORSEBACK RIDING ADVENTURE through forests and past a trapper's hut in Canada.

Haines, Where Eagles Soar

The people of Haines are button-popping proud of their eagles and don't cotton to foreigners trying to steal their claim of being the continent's capital of the American bald eagle. The Canadians in Brackendale, British Columbia, just north of Vancouver, have been arguing that they count more of America's symbolic bird every year than the inhabitants of Haines do. Pshaw, says the local chamber of commerce: Brackendale's all-time high in a single day, in 1994, was 3,766 to Haines's record 3,988 in 1984.

There's more to historic little Haines (population 2,400) than eagles, of course. The town perches on the northern verge of the Lynn Canal, like Skagway, yet the two communities don't have all that much in common. Haines is also a port, and although it's not a regular stop on the cruise-ship route, many passengers choose to enjoy a half-hour motor-vessel voyage to the town to take advantage of several intriguing tours.

Haines's first white settler was S. Hall Young, a Presbyterian minister who canoed here in 1879 with his fellow American friend, the great naturalist John Muir, and established a mission that was named for a Mrs. Haines, a secretary to the home mission board. He was ministering to the dominant Chilkat Tlingit.

Historical City Tours, in sightseeing buses and beautifully kept vintage cars, include the American Bald Eagle Interpretive Center, totem poles and Native clan houses, and Fort William H. Seward, the state's first permanent military base. They end with a salmon dinner before you board a motor vessel for the wildlife-spotting trip back to Skagway.

Haines's biggest attraction is the **Chilkat Bald Eagle Preserve** outside the town—where a bus takes you along the coast on an eagle-watching expedition, and large rafts cruise gently down the Chilkat River through the 48,000 acres dedicated to the magnificent birds (see Wild Alaska, page 95). Although the largest concentration of the birds happens between early October and January, more than 200 nest here through the summer, hatching their young between May and July. The best viewing spot is along the flats of the Chilkat River along the Haines Highway—four miles called the Council Grounds, where the eagles fly in for a feast of spawning salmon.

Sitka: Beauty and Culture

The police blotter prepared by the Sitka constabulary is usually indicative of the measured pace of this Southeastern community of 8,600. One typical day's crime: "Police were unable to locate the injured animal reported on Verstovia Street.... Police were unable to locate the dog running at large in the 1400 block of HPR....A driver who pulled in front of a man on a sidewalk was gone from the area when police went to check."

Sitka, which has no roads to the Outside, is more than just a placid, pretty place. As stunningly situated as it is—facing the open Pacific, set amid snow-crested mountains and endless fjords—Sitka has also been a cultural center for centuries. The numerous Tlingit who lived here had developed the most sophisticated civilization of any Natives in the Great Land. Their well-constructed houses, gift-giving potlatches, and elaborate dances performed before long voyages demonstrated the richness of their world. The local tribe lived in the village they called Shee Atika—"people on the outside of Shee," which is the island now known as Baranof, the present site of Sitka. Here, in 1799, Aleksandr Baranov of the Russian-American Company established Mikhailovsk, Fort St. Michael (named for the Archangel Michael). In 1802, the Tlingit slaughtered most of the men and enslaved the women in this fortress colony of Russian fur traders. Two years later, Baranov forced the Tlingit to flee—in their history, only because they misinterpreted the Russians' white flag of surrender for a sign that they'd be erased as clean as snow. A mile west of the old fort, Baranov created New Archangel—more commonly called Sitka, a contraction of the Tlingit name. A hyperbolic writer of the era dubbed it "the Paris of the Pacific," replete as it was with fine art and Flemish linen, good wines and Virginia tobacco, a theater and a multilingual lending library. One Yankee trader described its aristocratic administrators as "highly educated, refined in manners, intelligent, and courteous. Most of the gentlemen spoke French and English in addition to their own language."

Contemporary Sitka has maintained the cultural tradition. Not only has it freeze-framed the past in such artistic ventures as the

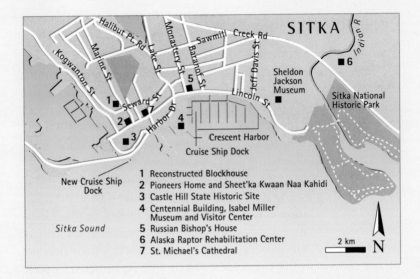

Walkabout

The **Sitka Visitor Bureau**, in the Harrigan Centennial Hall off Harbor Drive, beside Crescent Boat Harbor, has a city map with highlights to see; in the same building, the Isabel Miller Museum shows a detailed model of Sitka in 1867 as well as such historical items as logging and mining equipment and a whalebone chair.

The wooden **Blockhouse**, on a downtown hill at Kogwanton and Marine, is a replica of the original stockade that once separated Natives from the European community. Next to it is the **Russian Orthodox Cemetery** with 400 graves, a century and a half old, among them that of Princess Maria Maksutova, the effervescent wife of Alaska's final Russian governor (who fainted when the Stars and Stripes replaced the Russian double-eagle flag).

The state's first retirement home, **Sitka Pioneers Home**, on Lincoln Street next to City Hall, welcomes visitors who want to chat with aging sourdoughs and buy their handicrafts in a gift shop.

Sheet'ka Kwaan Naa Kahidi, at 200 Katlian Street next to the **Pioneers Home**, is a longhouse where Tlingit dance performances are held throughout the summer and Native artisans are often on site demonstrating their work.

Russian-style New Archangel Dancers and the Tlingit Naa Kahidi Dancers but since 1972 it has also staged a summer classical music festival that attracts superb musicians from around the world, performing contemporary and old-master works over three weeks in June. At the same time, a fine arts camp has kids from Alaska and the Lower 48 practicing their crafts, and the Island Institute's annual Sitka Symposium brings poets and novelists to discuss a central theme and offer writing critiques.

A HISTORIC SITKA AND NATURE WALK will give you a taste of both sides of the city. Sitka, Russia's capital in the New World, was the Russian-American Company's first permanent settlement. The precedents continued: one governor was the first to export Alaska lake ice, shipped in sawdust, to chill the drinks of Californians; another set up the first wholesale conservation program in North America, restricting the hunting of fur seals and the now-endangered sea otters that had brought the Russians here in the first place. And when Russia sold Alaska to the U.S. in 1867, Sitka became the first capital of the new territory of Alaska. (Juneau assumed the mantle in 1900.)

All this compelling history is heralded throughout modern-day Sitka. SITKA NATIONAL HISTORICAL PARK, at the eastern end of Lincoln Street (named for you-know-who), became the first federally designated park in 1910, marking the Battle of Sitka in which Baranov and his Aleut allies had taken the Tlingit fortress a century before. It's an entrancing place today with Tlingit and Haida totem poles theatrically set amid looming hemlock and Sitka spruce in a mile-long seashore loop—the local Lover's Lane. Other cedar poles, rising up to 80 feet in front of the Southeast Alaska Indian Cultural Center, are replicas of those collected for the 1904 Louisiana Purchase Exposition, one of them incorporating the ominous figure of a white man with a rifle. The center offers demonstrations of silver and beadwork and wood carving, and an illuminating ten-minute show of watercolor slides about local history.

Neighboring the park is the SHELDON JACKSON MUSEUM, on the campus of the private college set up in 1878 to train Alaska's Native peoples. The state's oldest educational institution now grants arts degrees and teaching certificates (James Michener based himself here for three summers while researching his popular documentary novel *Alaska.*). The museum is an octagonal structure, dating back to 1895, the first concrete building in the territory. It is named for Alaska's original General Agent for Education, a Presbyterian missionary who crisscrossed the state in the late nineteenth century performing good works, such as introducing reindeer from Siberia to help hungry Eskimos. Along the way, he collected thousands of Native artifacts, from kayaks and reindeer sleds to masks and bentwood boxes—the finest collection of its kind in Alaska and among the most significant in the world.

Across from the Jackson campus (at 1101 Sawmill Road, north of the Indian River bridge) is a unique treatment facility for birds revered by Native people: the ALASKA RAPTOR REHABILITATION CENTER. Every year, volunteers care for up to a couple of hundred injured eagles, hawks, falcons, and owls, sending the most serious to avian experts in the Lower 48, releasing the rehabilitated to the wild, and using non-releasable raptors for captive breeding programs. The majority of cases are bald eagles, 80 percent of them hurt intentionally or accidentally by humans and by such unnatural objects as fish hooks and power lines. One of them was Buddy, a hatchling raised by humans and later abandoned in a Southeast village in 1988. After the center's staff taught him to fly and fed him on "ratsicles" (frozen rats), he became an educational tool for the center, traveling across the U.S. and even—by state ferry—to the annual gathering of balds at Chilkat River near Haines, Alaska.

The RUSSIAN BISHOP'S HOUSE (on Lincoln across from Crescent Harbor)—the oldest intact building in Alaska—is the only one remaining from the Russian colonial era and one of only four original Russian structures still standing in North America. As a missionary in 1824, Father Ivan Veniaminov began fashioning an alphabet for the Aleuts, taught them brickmaking and other trades, and took far-flung kayak trips for months at a time to convert an estimated 10,000 Natives to his faith. American observers referred to him as Paul Bunyan in a cassock. A decade later, he moved to Sitka, where he eventually became Russian Orthodox Bishop of

Alaska before returning home as all-powerful Metropolitan of Moscow and, after his death, being canonized as St. Innocent. The manse he lived in here has been restored, with the help of archeologists and historians, at a cost of about $5 million. The 1842 structure of squared spruce logs and planks features a first-floor museum of Russian-American artifacts; the second story has been authentically returned to its early grandeur, even to the original gold-embossed, crushed-velvet upholstery.

The most imposing reminder of Russian times is the onion-domed, spruce-and-clapboard ST. MICHAEL'S CATHEDRAL in downtown Sitka. America's first Russian Orthodox cathedral stood for 118 years before a fire destroyed it in 1966—but not before local residents rescued its superb iconography and art, including the *Sitka Madonna*, to which miraculous powers have been attributed, and a couple of important two-century-old oils on canvas covered in impressive silver *rizas*. Fundraising in Alaska and Washington

Sitka perches on the open Pacific, against the backdrop of Fuji-like Mount Edgecumbe.

garnered more than $500,000 to painstakingly rebuild a near-replica of the cathedral—recasting the spire's bronze bells from those melted in the fire—but this time incombustible cinder blocks lie beneath its wooden sheathing. The mother church for the 20,000 Alaskans who still follow the Russian Orthodox faith serves a local congregation of about 300, most descended from Russian-Tlingit ancestors. Tours are self-guided, enhanced by the commentary of the resident black-robed priest.

Many shore excursions include a spirited performance of the NEW ARCHANGEL DANCERS, a highly polished group of local women whose repertoire includes heritage dances of Russia, Ukraine, and Armenia. Taught by professional folk-dance specialists, and costumed in such authentic garb as Georgian gowns and Cossack boots, they even pull off the traditionally masculine stunts of sky-high leaps and knee-popping squats.

The small state park of CASTLE HILL (up the staircase beside the post office on Lincoln) handily sums up the three phases of Sitka history. Kiks.adi Natives had their ancestral home here before the Russians arrived, and Baranov built his castlelike headquarters on the outlook. And it was on this site that Russia formally transferred the territory to the United States, which had paid just under two cents an acre for a land twice as big as Texas.

The hill overlooks the quiet waters of Sitka Sound and Mount Edgecumbe, a dormant volcano whose elegant peak reminds many visitors of Mount Fuji. The mountain ascends on Kruzof Island, one of hundreds of small islands whose human-scale fjords lend such beauty to SIGHTSEEING NATURE CRUISES and MARINE EXPEDITIONS. A typical destination is Silver Bay; the 18-mile voyage—during which you may glimpse Steller's sea lions and humpback whales—passes by the remains of the Liberty Prospect Mine, dating back to Alaska's first gold strike in 1872, and one of two modern pulp mills within the Tongass National Forest, a prime plank in Sitka's economic base. In Bear Cove the Medvejie Hatchery offers a fascinating look at how chum, coho, and chinook salmon are raised to supplement the wild stock.

A SEA OTTER AND WILDLIFE QUEST on a jet boat in Sitka Sound

provides a chance to observe and photograph killer, humpback, and gray whales, harbor seals, and the no-longer-endangered sea otters basking like sirens, as well as such land animals as Sitka black-tailed deer and brown bears. (Half your fee is refunded if you don't see a whale, otter, or bear.) More adventurous explorations can start on a Zodiac-type raft that takes you to a floating base camp for SEA KAYAKING. Anglers with enough time will find that the inlets surrounding Sitka are ideal for SPORTFISHING for halibut—and this is a hot spot for the prized king salmon.

Horsepower or pedal power will also get you out of town. A tour called EXPLORING SITKA BY VAN visits a nature-viewing shelter at the stunning Starrigavan estuary for sightings of wetland birds and plant life as well as a drive through Old Sitka and Castle Hill. A GUIDED BIKE AND HIKE TOUR goes to Starrigavan Meadow and then Mosquito Cove for a tramp through the forest while an ADVANCED MOUNTAIN BIKE TOUR climbs 500 feet up to the deep mountain-ringed waters of Blue Lake—or to the Medvejie Hatchery instead, if there are reports of bad weather or grumpy bears on the ride to the lake.

SOUTHCENTRAL ALASKA

Southeast may be only the start of your Alaska odyssey. Venture farther, by luxury train, motorcoach, or plane, and you'll witness other, equally fascinating treasures of the 49th state. The Southcentral region includes the state's major center, Anchorage, a surprisingly urban city rimmed by the wilds. Anchorage's playground is the Kenai Peninsula, where outdoor adventure is easily accessible, especially at its south end around the port of Seward, which is the closest that cruise ships come to Anchorage. And the thriving seaport of Valdez, the terminus of the Trans-Alaska Pipeline, lies east of Anchorage. All of these are regular destinations on cruises or land excursions.

Anchorage: Alaska All Around

Anchorage is the biggest burg in Alaska—a quarter of a million people live here, four out of every ten Alaskans—and in many ways it's a sophisticated, twenty-first-century city, with smart shops and highbrow culture and a cosmopolitan population. If only the bears knew that. Like the chocolate-brown, three-year-old, quarter-ton bear that once made its way through the throngs on the streets of downtown Anchorage and had to be killed. Fortunately, most of the nearly 300 brown and black bears that hang around town roam the leafy suburbs. During one recent summer, the *Anchorage Daily*

The Trans-Alaska Pipeline, here elevated, wends its way from Prudhoe Bay to Valdez.

News reported that they'd "raided bird feeders, ripped into garbage, attacked chickens, chased sheep, killed goats, busted through cabin doors, and chewed up the upholstery of parked cars."

It's just another reminder that Anchorage is still a mere step away from the Southcentral wilderness. There's a standing joke that the city is only half an hour from Alaska. Ringed on three sides by the Alaska and Aleutian Ranges and the Talkeetna Mountains, it juts into the twin arms of Cook Inlet, all of which moderate the snowfall and temperatures. Sealed away perhaps, but more than 240 flights of 20 or so airlines—anchored by Alaska Airlines but including Chinese, Japanese, and Korean carriers—arrive each day at Ted Stevens International Airport. (It's named for the the state's senior U.S. senator, who survived an Alaska plane crash in 1978 that killed his wife.) Recently enlarged to make room for more interstate

Main Street, Anchorage, 1964:
A major earthquake rearranges the city.

The Bad Friday Quake

It was the real thing: the most powerful earthquake ever to be recorded in North America in the twentieth century. At 5:36 P.M. local time on March 27, 1964—Good Friday—the planet's crust burst a seam 500 miles long and 150 broad along the Aleutian Islands and the southern Alaska mainland. The shock waves jarred the earth over half a million miles. A series of tidal waves surged down the west coast. In all, the quake and resulting tsunamis killed an estimated 115 people in Alaska (90 percent of them by the tsunamis) and the huge waves also swept at least a dozen people to their deaths in the Lower 48. About 4,500 Alaskans were left homeless and the damage from the disaster totalled anywhere from $311 million to as much as $500 million (depending on which of the conflicting government figures you believe).

In the Pacific Ocean around Alaska, the plates forming the upper crust of the earth thrust downward at an angle beneath the edges of the plates in the lower crust. When these plates shift suddenly, the seismic energy creates the tremors the state is famous for and, infrequently, a quake. In 1964, the sea bottom here shot up 30 to 50 feet, the largest such vertical lift ever measured. The force of the quake moved local mountains by as much as 50 feet and elevated 50-mile-long Montague Island by at least 30 feet. The shock registered the equivalent of 9.2 on the recently revised Richter scale (eighty times the energy of the San Francisco cataclysm of 1906).

The epicenter was 1,200 feet below Prince William Sound, about 80 miles east of Anchorage, a city with footings of unstable clay. Within five minutes, thirty downtown blocks and a posh new suburb of Alaska's largest and swiftest-growing urban area lay in shambles. On the north side of 4th Avenue—the main street—an entire block of shops dropped 20 feet into a fissure; those on the south side survived. Nearby, an unoccupied six-story apartment crumbled, and the new five-story J.C. Penney store rocked back and forth before its front collapsed, killing two people. At least seventy-five homes in Turnagain-on-the-Sea tumbled down cliffs above Cook Inlet. Because school was out and most stores were closed, and possibly because the city sits 100 feet above sea level, only nine people died directly from the quake.

airlines, the airport is the springboard for cruise passengers heading to Fairbanks, Prudhoe Bay, Nome, Kotzebue, and Seattle.

Relatively youthful, slightly more than eight decades old, Anchorage acts like the older brother of Alaska communities. The only big city in the state seems reliable and a little driven. Born of conventional commerce, a railroad town, it has a much less checkered past than its siblings. Anchorage maintains a cast of respectability despite a few undesirable districts. In cultural terms, this is a highly livable community with many musical groups, among them a symphony orchestra and ballet and opera companies; the highly regarded Alaska Repertory Theater; a museum of history and art; and the creative activities generated by the campuses of the University of Alaska and Alaska Pacific University. The $70-million Alaska Center for the Performing Arts opened in 1988 to a first season featuring Rudolf Nureyev, Itzhak Perlman, and Leontyne Price. In fact, Anchorage has been declared second only to Honolulu in the *Livable Cities Almanac.* The author based much of his ratings on life expectancy, which in Anchorage's case he attributes to a diet high in fish.

Fishing, of course, is what locals and visitors do a lot of here, recreationally, along with the more focused food fishing of Native peoples, who make up 5 percent of the urban population. Anchoragites also rock climb and kayak, ski, and snowshoe. Every second home seems to have a boat or floatplane, a camper or snowmobile, to escape the city's 1,700 square miles for the wilderness on their doorstep. An extensive network of bicycle paths threads through the city, and the TONY KNOWLES COASTAL TRAIL (which the National Park Service designated as a National Recreation Trail) wends 11 miles along the downtown coastline past a lagoon to scenic, wooded Kincaid Park, with its own 30-mile network of paths.

A dozen miles south of the urban core on the Seward Highway, more than 130 species of waterfowl, from arctic terns to sandhill cranes, can be viewed from a boardwalk along Potter Marsh, the ANCHORAGE COASTAL WILDLIFE REFUGE. And the lakes around Ted Stevens International Airport support high flyers of another kind: nesting Canada geese, ducks, and terns. For a safe, close-up look at native animals, including musk oxen, moose, and four kinds of bear, visit the ALASKA ZOO (4731 O'Malley Road, about 8 miles south of downtown).

Before white settlers surfaced here, the peninsula between the Turnagain and Knik Arms of Cook Inlet had been a sometime home to Eskimos, who were displaced by the Tanainas, an Athabascan tribe. You can experience their culture at the absorbing ALASKA NATIVE HERITAGE CENTER (8800 Heritage Center Drive, 10 minutes from downtown by trolley). It opened in 1999 on a 26-acre campus with a quintet of traditional village settings around a two-acre lake and a Welcome House where Native dancers perform historic and contemporary works and elders recount legends and stories about the five branches of Alaska's First Peoples.

The city of Anchorage, the state's transportation hub, started life as a tent town hewn out of the wild to serve the crews building the Alaska Railroad from Seward to Fairbanks in 1915. Much earlier, the Native nomads were on hand to trade sea-otter furs with Capt. James Cook in 1778. Because the British explorer could find no passage out of the inlet's arm, it came to be known as Turnagain. The other arm, Knik (pronounced Kuh-nik), is called by an Eskimo word for fire. Gold brought more white men here, but it wasn't until the railroad came through that anyone bothered to stay. As many as 7,000 laborers and entrepreneurs lived under canvas and later in log cabins before the settlement was officially incorporated in 1920. Although the area had been known as Ship Creek and Knik Anchorage, the settlers wanted to name the port Alaska City—but the U.S. Postal Service settled on Anchorage. Even then, observers were noting that it didn't resemble any typical Alaska town.

A local newspaper publisher once remarked that Hitler, Tojo, Stalin, Mao Tse-tung, and Ho Chi Minh had been the greatest developers of Anchorage. And it's true that the strategically sited town profited from the building of army and air force bases during World War II and further military expenditures in the decades since. In 1957, when oil was found on the Kenai Peninsula south of Anchorage, and later at Prudhoe Bay, there were other booms as petroleum companies moved in and built the office towers that dominate the cityscape. Seven years later, the city—along with many other communities in a 500-mile

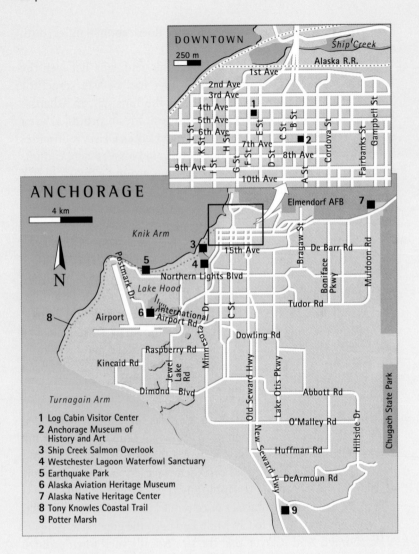

DOWNTOWN

250 m

Ship Creek
Alaska R.R.
1st Ave
2nd Ave
3rd Ave
4th Ave
5th Ave
6th Ave
7th Ave
8th Ave
9th Ave
10th Ave

L St
K St
J St
I St
H St
G St
F St
E St
D St
C St
B St
A St
Cordova St
Fairbanks St
Campbell St

1
2

ANCHORAGE

4 km

N

Knik Arm

Postmark Dr

Elmendorf AFB   **7**

3
15th Ave
Bragaw St
De Barr Rd
Muldoon Rd

5
4
Northern Lights Blvd
Lake Hood
International
Airport Rd
6
Airport
8

Boniface Pkwy

Tudor Rd

Minnesota Dr

C St

Raspberry Rd
Dowling Rd

Kincaid Rd

Jewel Lake Rd

Dimond   Blvd

Old Seward Hwy

Lake Otis Pkwy

Abbott Rd

O'Malley Rd

Hillside Dr

Chugach State Park

New Seward Hwy

Huffman Rd

Turnagain Arm

DeArmoun Rd

9

1 Log Cabin Visitor Center
2 Anchorage Museum of
   History and Art
3 Ship Creek Salmon Overlook
4 Westchester Lagoon Waterfowl Sanctuary
5 Earthquake Park
6 Alaska Aviation Heritage Museum
7 Alaska Native Heritage Center
8 Tony Knowles Coastal Trail
9 Potter Marsh

Walkabout

Log Cabin Visitor Center, 4th Avenue and F Street, is a charmingly rustic trader's dwelling with a green sod roof and, in front, a 5,000-pound boulder of the state's gemstone, jade. Here's where you can find a handy map and other directions for a self-guided downtown walking tour that helps you relive Anchorage's past and directs you to craft shops.

The **Alaska Native Heritage Center**, at Muldoon Road and Glenn Highway, explores the cultures, crafts, and lifestyles of the state's indigenous peoples. A trail from the Welcome House takes you through five village displays around a lake.

The **Tony Knowles Coastal Trail** winds for 11 miles on the city's attractive shoreline along Cook Inlet, between the downtown and Kincaid Park, with views of several other parks, a lagoon, and three mountain ranges.

Anchorage Museum of History And Art, 121 West 7th Avenue, a five-story atrium, with dramatic dioramas of state history, permanent art collections of Native peoples, white exploration, and development of Alaska, and more than thirty new shows every year.

The Heritage Library Museum in the National Bank of Alaska at Northern Lights and C Street, shows Alaska books, artifacts, paintings, and photos.

Ship Creek Salmon Overlook and Waterfowl Nesting Area, off Whitney Road just southwest of downtown, is on the site of the Tanaina Indian fish camps, where spawning salmon head upstream throughout the summer, and geese and ducks hang around all year.

Lake Hood and the neighboring **Lake Spenard**, southwest of downtown, may be too far by foot, but they're a popular tour-bus attraction. The air harbor here is the biggest floatplane base in the world, with 800 or more daily takeoffs and landings in high summer as tourists and locals take sightseeing and fishing flights.

The Alaska Aviation Heritage Museum, 4721 Aircraft Drive, has vintage planes and flight uniforms, historical photos, and half-hour films on pioneer aviation.

swath of southern Alaska—was first shattered by North America's worst earthquake of the century (*see* The Bad Friday Quake, *page 201*) and then revitalized in the aftermath of reconstruction. EARTH-QUAKE PARK (at the far western end of Northern Lights Boulevard), a residential neighborhood flattened in 1964, has an interpretative display of the Big One. In the 1970s, Anchorage became headquarters for many of the large Native regional corporations created under the Alaska Native Claims Settlement Act; one of them, Cook Inlet Region, Inc., constructed a glass-sheathed landmark building.

Today, as oil money ebbs, increasing tourism helps stabilize the city's roller-coaster economy. For example, cruise passengers arriving in Seward and going on to Anchorage can partake of a couple of FLIGHT-SEEING TOURS. One wings over the mountains, glaciers, and lakes in a vintage DC-3 prop plane while big-band music and magazines out of the 1940s complete the time-travel atmosphere. Another trip, in a seaplane, starts from the world's biggest seaplane base, Lake Hood, and flies 70 miles southwest to Redoubt Bay in the Lake Clark National Park and Preserve for a chance to go by foot and boat to watch and photograph brown bears fishing for salmon. The trip ends with dinner at a lakeside lodge.

Many visitors use Anchorage as a base en route to the rest of the state—to the Kenai Peninsula in the south, for instance, or to Denali National Park and Preserve in the Interior. The journey north takes them through Alaska's breadbasket, the MATANUSKA VALLEY, unique in its lush growing conditions. The Mat-Su, as it is nicknamed, was carved during the last ice age, and its fertile soil and long summer days produce Brobdingnagian vegetables—3-pound beets, 10-pound celery, 83-pound cabbages. As the center of the agriculture industry, the valley has experimental farms and, at Palmer (population 3,000), the preserved remnants of the farming colony of transplanted Mid-westerners formed during the Depression.

For others, Anchorage is a way station en route to the rugged east coast or the glacier country to the west. The readily accessible

Anchorage's big-city office towers are humbled by the encircling mountains.

PORTAGE GLACIER, with its all-weather icebergs afloat in Portage Lake, is an hour away; and COLUMBIA GLACIER spreads across 440 square miles in Prince William Sound (*see* Glaciers: The Power and the Glory, *page 56*). Columbia lies off the ice-free port of WHITTIER. This engaging small town of only about 350 people has a rich history: Russian-Native trading, gold mining, and its survival of three tidal waves from the quake that killed an estimated thirteen residents. Perhaps the most interesting piece of its past happened over two years during World War II. Because the saltwater port of Seward was considered too open to Japanese attack, the army secretly dug a total of 3½ miles through the Chugach Mountains to create two tunnels connecting military bases in Anchorage and Fairbanks by a highway to Whittier. (Two crews burrowing from opposite ends met in the middle only six inches off course.) During the Cold War, the armed forces returned, departing finally in 1960. Most of the townspeople now have condos in "the city under one roof," a fourteen-story tower formerly occupied by a thousand servicemen when it was the tallest building in Alaska.

That was then. Now the whole state has grown up, especially its major city. Whittier's high-rise has been supplanted by taller buildings in Anchorage, whose skyline looms like an urban reflection of the mountainscapes surrounding this large but livable city on the very verge of the Alaska wilds.

Seward and the Kenai Peninsula: The Good Land

Mini-Alaska. The whole state on a small scale. Anchorage's Backyard. Alaska's Playground. They've all been used to describe, with only a little hyperbole, the 16,000 square miles of the Kenai Peninsula, a place of mountain peaks and mammoth fields of ice, numberless fjords and fish-choked rivers, a national forest, and state and national parks and wildlife refuges. It begins just south of Anchorage, along the Seward Highway, and residents of the state's largest city often use it as a weekend retreat. Every summer this stampede helps more than double the peninsula's population of 40,000 centered in four main towns. Along with its popularity, there's another reality some visitors might find worrisome upon first hearing. It is in the Kenai that one of the first post-war Alaska oil finds began producing and still plays a prominent economic role. And it was here, along Prince William Sound, that the world's largest oil spill washed up, some of it staining the shores of Kenai Fjords National Park.

Yet the happy truth is that neither oil nor tourism has left much of a mark on the peninsula. You realize, for a start, that this is an area in which Rhode Island, Delaware, and Connecticut could fit quite comfortably. That almost 85 percent of it is under federal protection as the national park, the Chugach National Forest, and the Kenai National Wildlife Refuge. That most of the year-round population is scattered thinly in the towns of Sodoltna, Kenai, Homer, Seldovia, and Seward. That the oil fields are offshore in Cook Inlet, on the far western edge of the Kenai, where cruise passengers on land tours don't usually visit. And that in 1989, winds prevented the spill from the oil tanker *Exxon Valdez* from sullying much of the park's shoreline at the time, so that virtually no visible blemishes are left now. (Nevertheless, the park employees have mounted informative oil-spill displays at their base in Seward.) Given all these factors, the Kenai Peninsula more than deserves its Athabascan name, *Yaghanen,* or the Good Land.

Athabascans and some Eskimos lived here first, and they continue to make up about 10 percent of the population. In 1791, a Russian trading ship following the sea-otter routes reached the mouth of a river the Natives knew as *Kaknu* and the Russians named *Kenay.* There, a village of the Athabascan Dena'ina tribe stood on a cliff above Cook Inlet. Today the town of KENAI is the peninsula's largest (population 6,900), the service base for the inlet's oil fields, and a port for the regional fishing fleet. The Russians, after settling in Kenai, spread across the peninsula, founding Seldovia and then Ninilchik, which became a retirement colony for their hunters who had taken Native wives and refused to return to Mother Russia. The first Americans were pursuing rumors of a richness in coal; the second wave sought gold. Neither promise panned out, although more than 3,000 prospectors flooded into the optimistically named communities of Hope and Sunrise in 1896. You can still pan for gold—mostly for fun—in the Chugach National Forest.

Those who settled here farmed the land, raised foxes for furs, and fished for herring. It wasn't until 1957, when Atlantic Richfield found oil and then gas in Cook Inlet, that the economy heated up. And in 1980, the creation of the Kenai Fjords National Park attracted the attention of visitors from beyond the state, generating the tourist dollars that keep the locals afloat. Tricia Brown, an author and former editor of *Alaska* magazine, lived in Alaska for twenty-one years and always enjoyed her visits to the peninsula. "Soldotna has about 3,700 people, and it's the local sport-fishing capital, where anglers stock up on groceries, buy gear, arrange charters, accommodations, and fly-in-fishing trips," she says. "It has a great visitor center where they've hung the record-breaking king salmon of all time—nearly 100 pounds.

"From here the road splits off to Kenai or continues south to Homer. Homer Spit reaches out 4½ miles into the bay, and all along the single, dead-end road, interesting little shops are perched on pilings. You can buy art, crafts, and fish and chips, watch the action in the commercial boat harbor, arrange a halibut charter, and take a ferry across the water to little Seldovia." One writer who lives in Homer has described his town as "a jumbled-up community of fishermen and computer nerds, hippies and fundamentalists, artists and Cat skinners [bulldozer operators]." This is the town made famous by the author and broadcaster Tom Bodett, whose book and a series on National Public Radio's "All Things Considered" both carried the title *The End of the Road*. Bodett helped launch Jewel in her career as a chart-topping pop singer while she was living on a farm near Homer. Peninsula people generally are an intriguing bunch—among them are a gaggle of libertarians who don't want the government to intrude in their lives and a prospector whose ad in an Anchorage newspaper for a mail-order bride attracted 8,000 replies from around the world.

The *real* wildlife in the Kenai is self-evident once you cross the slender isthmus at Portage and either turn south along the spine of the Kenai Mountains to the national park or continue south and west to Cooper Landing (population 320). Getting to the first of the centers serving the Sterling Highway, only two hours from Anchorage, you pass lookout points for Dall sheep and mountain goats. The Landing, named for a nineteenth-century miner and still rife with log cabins, acts as base camp for half-day RAFTING EXPEDITIONS down the rapids-rich Kenai River. Cruise passengers visiting here also have a choice of HORSEBACK RIDING, FLIGHT-SEEING, HIKING through an alpine backcountry alive with moose, mink, beaver, and bald eagles, or FISHING for red salmon in prime spawning grounds nearby. World-renowned for its runs of king salmon, the river occasionally lures so many anglers that Alaskans refer to the scene as "combat fishing." There's also saltwater fishing for salmon, Dolly Varden, and such bottom fish as halibut from the revitalized deepwater port of SEWARD (year-round population 2,800).

On Good Friday in 1964, it was three strikes—and Seward was all but out. First, the tremors of that terrible earthquake. Then the fires erupting in an oil storage–tank farm near the new port. And finally a series of tidal waves, the second one the worst, roaring up Resurrection Bay: a wall of water 30 feet high, alight with burning oil, surging into town at more than 100 miles an hour, flinging aside boxcars and their engines like so many model trains. Houses lay shattered, cars squashed, boats snapped in two. A 4,500-foot swath of waterfront sank into the bay. No one was killed, but the combination of quake, fire, and tsunami left the port and the rail line—the region's economic underpinnings—in ruins. Ironically, Seward had been slated to receive an official All-America Cities Award for industry and civic improvement the following week. It took the city a couple of decades to recover and rebuild, with a $10-million, supposedly earthquake-proof, dock; and the railroad returned to its pre-quake strength. Today, one of the few reminders of the disaster is the slide show SEWARD IS BURNING, which you can view at the public library (5th Avenue and Adams).

A more ambitious local attraction, symbolic of Seward's progressiveness, is the ALASKA SEALIFE CENTER (301 Railway Avenue).

The first coldwater marine-mammal research center in the western hemisphere, the $56-million facility attracts scientists from around the globe and entertains and informs visitors through thirty-plus species of birds (yellow-tufted puffins, red-legged kittiwakes), mammals (sea lions, sea otters, seals) and other sea life (including an amiable red octopus). A dramatically designed viewing area lets you observe the mammals, most of which were rescued after being injured or falling ill at sea. And kids like the touch tanks where they can caress sea anemones and starfish.

Seward, in the vitality of its renewed economy, could well be at least a contender for an All-America award again. Not that all of it is a model small town, by any means: the low-slung, frontier-style main street may have more drinking establishments per capita than anywhere else in the state. But step outside to absorb the views of the bay in front and Mount Marathon behind and you might agree that the surroundings still earn the encomium of one of its founders, John Ballaine. He recalled "that shining afternoon as we glided easily in those majestic scenes up to the timber-covered site I had chosen for the future terminal city—the future gateway in and out of Alaska's great interior."

It is that: a year-round ice-free harbor for ships to and from Outside; the southern terminus of the Alaska Railroad leading to Fairbanks and beyond, and also the gateway to the increasingly popular Kenai Fjords National Park. In 1903, Ballaine was the first agent of the Alaska Central Railroad, which decided to use Resurrection Bay as the sea terminal. He suggested naming the new townsite for Secretary of State Seward. The rail line made a couple of false starts before evolving into the Alaska Railroad in 1923. Seward was also the original start of the Iditarod Trail to the bountiful gold fields of Nome, a dog-sled course blazed through the land during 1910–11. (In 1916, forty-six dogs pulled a record ton and a half of gold south to the port.) Today, the annual Iditarod Trail Sled Dog Race runs from Anchorage to Nome (*see* Nome—No Place Like It, *page 243*), but you can see Mile 0 of the first trail marked on a plaque at the southeast corner of 4th and Railway.

Three blocks southwest of Mile 0 is the SEWARD RAILROAD CAR

(3rd and Jefferson), the Pullman dining car in which President Warren C. Harding rode to drive the last golden spike of the Alaska Railroad. Now it's the Chamber of Commerce Information Cache, which offers a walking-tour map of such areas as MILLIONAIRES ROW, the half-dozen elegant houses the founders built from materials shipped in from the Lower 48. Mount Marathon rears up 3,022 feet over the city; every July 4 since 1915, suicidal runners have raced up the peak and down, some in less than forty-five minutes.

The restored SMALL BOAT HARBOR, at the north end of 4th Avenue, is action central of Seward's fishing industry, which operates the largest halibut-receiving station on the U.S. west coast. (Fish can grow so big here that they're often shot upon landing to prevent them from damaging the boat.) Throughout the summer, there are derbies for halibut, king salmon, and silver or coho salmon (first prize for the latter is $10,000 and one specially tagged fish can net the angler $100,000), with the entries weighed in at the harbor. And sometimes out on the water, beyond the fish boats and sailing vessels, you might spot sea otters.

Near the Harbormaster is the Kenai Fjords Visitor Center, with its fine displays of the Harding Icefield and the less-visible attractions of nearby KENAI FJORDS NATIONAL PARK. Few federal parks in America seem as protected as Kenai, surrounded as it is by the Caines Head State Recreation Area to the east, Kenai National Wildlife Refuge to the west, Chugach National Forest to the north and east, and Kachemak Bay State Park and State Wilderness to the southwest. Near the park entrance, a typical first stop is EXIT GLACIER. One of eight large glaciers formed in the Harding Icefield, Exit flows into the Resurrection River valley, which reveals all the typical levels of plant life found on glacier-carved land. Beware of ice falling from the face: in 1987 a half-ton chunk killed a California woman who came too near.

While the park itself may be one of the state's smaller ones, its steep-sided fjords and the range of sea and bird life make it one of the most sublime. But because so much of the land is uncongenial for the casual visitor, it's best seen by boat. Your sea voyage girdles Kenai, taking you along Resurrection Bay near the forest shoreline where Aleksandr Baranov, who named the basin, launched Alaska's first shipyard. Here he built small but sturdy boats in the 1790s to compete against the sea-otter hunters of other nations. Guides will likely point out artifacts of the more recent past—concrete bunkers that supported gun emplacements and searchlight stations during World War II. They might even mention that it was here on this bay—and not a fjord near Murmansk, Russia—that Sean Connery's nuclear submarine cruised at the start of *The Hunt for Red October*.

But the man-made pales beside the natural world. This can be one of the finest places in Alaska for viewing marine life. A couple of thousand sea otters cruise the region, and you'll often see some, along with Dall's porpoises, harbor seals, sea lions, orcas, and a variety of whales, including fins, seis, and minkes. And many of the 200,000 or so sea birds that make this their summer home—auklets, tufted and horned puffins, cormorants, and even kittiwakes (with their black wing tips and yellow bills). Black bears and grizzlies prowl the shores and mountain goats pose on the slopes, where waterfalls plummet beautifully into the bay.

A gem of a park. Or in the words of a frequent visitor, a former state fishery biologist, it's nothing less than the crown jewel of the Kenai Peninsula.

Valdez: Little Switzerland

The city you visit now is not the Valdez destroyed in the great earthquake of 1967. Old Valdez lay four miles east, and today there's little there left to see. Gold had launched it in 1897, copper kept it alive for a while, and now another natural resource, oil from Prudhoe Bay, is pumping life through the arteries of the new city that rose to replace the pioneer Southcentral town.

About 120 miles due east of Anchorage, Valdez earns its name of Little Switzerland as one of Alaska's more beautiful urban settings—with a port off Prince William Sound at its feet and the verdant Chugach Mountains rearing up around it like the Alps—as well as one of the more affluent cities in the state. For a place of only about 4,400 people, it's well served with such newer amenities as a civic center, a teen center, and a growing community college. Normal temperatures in high summer here are in the low 60s. In winter, the snow falls by the ice bucket: an average of 25 feet a year compared to Anchorage's 6; in January 1990, a record 47.5 inches landed in a single day. In early March, motorists park in the world's most unusual drive-in theater to watch movies projected on an immense snowbank. And not unexpectedly, this is home to the World Extreme Skiing Championship.

Port Valdez, on which the city's busy SMALL-BOAT HARBOR fronts, was named in 1790 by Spanish explorer Don Salvador Fidalgo for Spain's marine minister, Antonio Valdes y Basan. (Alaskans unaccountably pronounce the civic name Val-*deez*) The most northerly ice-free port in the western hemisphere, it's the southern end of the Trans-Alaska Pipeline, which descends Thompson Pass behind Valdez to deliver oil to the $50-million container terminal. Supertank-

Valdez has the most northerly ice-free harbor in the western hemisphere.

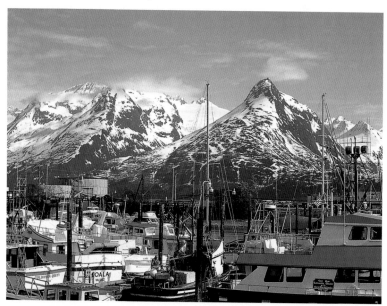

ers berth at the 800-foot-deep anchorage and, on their way to the Lower 48, ply tricky Valdez Arm, the estuary leading to Prince William Sound. There's also a land link to the Alaska Highway system and Fairbanks via the old gold-rush trail and wagon road, which became the Richardson Highway.

During the Klondike gold stampede of 1897–98, about 3,500 people, along with their horses and dogs, landed at the port to carve an all-American route to the Yukon Territory. They had to cross the virtually impassable, mile-high Valdez glacier to the Klutina, Copper, and Yukon Rivers. Their foes were fog and wind-whipped snow and rain, crevasses and avalanches, and sunburn and snow blindness from light bouncing off the ice. Once over the glacier, only about 200 stampeders managed to survive the Klutina's fearsome rapids. Most who didn't die turned back, heading south for the safety of home below the 49th Parallel. By the winter of '99, those still left in the tent town at Port Valdez were dying horribly of scurvy. After spending a total of $3.7 million, the gold seekers had failed to establish an alternative U.S. passage to the Klondike.

But the relatively few who did surmount the glacier found copper in the Wrangell Mountains during the early 1900s. The notorious Alaska Syndicate of American financier J.P. Morgan and the Guggenheim mining family purchased rights to the copper lode and planned to use Valdez as the terminus of a railroad from the mines. When it switched to another site, promoter Henry Reynolds created the Alaska Home Railroad of Valdez to compete with the Syndicate's line through KEYSTONE CANYON. The Syndicate disliked rivals; its guards met Reynold's men in the canyon and shot five of them, killing one. (Today, you can take a WHITEWATER RAFT TRIP on the glacial Lowe River through the steep-walled canyon, or a SCENIC MOTORCOACH TOUR through this gorge where Bridal Veil Falls tumbles nine stories.) Lacking funds, Reynold's railroad soon failed. Another, launched by British-backed Michael Heney—who had pushed the White Pass & Yukon line between Skagway and Whitehorse—was bought out by the Syndicate, which retained Heney to complete the track from the copper mountains to the port of Cordova, south and slightly east of Valdez.

In the 1920s, the Richardson Highway was paved, and for the next four decades Valdez survived only as the major cargo route to the Interior. Then, on Good Friday 1964, the hard-pressed town of 1,100 was shattered by an earthquake and battered by a giant wave that rolled 30 miles up the inlet, crashed onto the land, and knocked down power lines that ignited fuel tanks and sent flames spilling across the port. Thirty-one people died, 225 homes were leveled or damaged. In its wake, residents decided to re-create Valdez on a new site four miles west along the port.

Little more than a decade later, it finally came into its own as the TRANS-ALASKA PIPELINE TERMINUS. A tour of the 1,000-acre Alyeska Marine Terminal across the bay reveals the sophisticated complex demanded to store up to 9.18 million barrels of crude oil from Prudhoe Bay and load it from four berths onto the mega-tankers that take it around the globe. The statistics of the place are astonishing. It took $1.4 billion and a peak workforce of 4,300 to build the terminal (but it needs only about 380 people to operate it). There are three fixed berths, each of which can load a ship with 100,000 barrels an hour, and a single floating berth, loading four-fifths that fast, which weighs 6.5 million pounds. The capacity of each of the 18 holding tanks is 510,000 barrels, enough fuel to fly a 727 jet around the world 376 times.

By 1989, the property taxes on the tank farms and loading docks were accounting for 94 percent of the city's revenues, and oil salaries were a major contribution to the local economy, with income from fishing a far second. That was the year the dark side of this dependence on petroleum surfaced. On the twenty-fifth Good Friday since the great quake, the supertanker *Exxon Valdez* went aground 25 miles from the port, on Bligh Reef, known until then for the state's finest silver-salmon fishing. Three hours before, a city council committee had been warned that it was just a question of when—not if—a major oil spill would pollute Prince William Sound. In the worst such spill in American history, the ruptured ship spewed at least 10.1 million gallons into the fish- and mammal-rich waters along 1,100 miles of coastline. Although the port itself was spared, 9,000 workers valiantly cleaned up the beaches of the sound; Valdez's summer population leapt to 12,000. Today, though environmentalists remain watchful, government biologists agree with Exxon that the remaining oil seems not to pose any lingering threat, and a chief government scientist has reported that the eco-system of the sound and the adjacent Gulf of Alaska have emerged from the spill largely intact.

You can see how untroubled the waters now are in a HISTORICAL CRUISE in a motor vessel that navigates the sound, often hugging the shoreline for better views of waterfalls and the Shoup Glacier; on a HARBOR AND NATURE KAYAKING TOUR through sheltered Duck Flats to spot nesting birds on small islands and mammals such as sea lions and seals; or SPORTFISHING from a boat using light tackle to catch coho (or silver) salmon. And if you want to see hordes of salmon during the fall spawning season, a BICYCLE ADVENTURE— on cruiser mountain or tandem bikes—will stop at the right creeks along a few miles of easy terrain with guides knowledgeable about fishing, wildlife, local history, and the unavoidable topic of the pipeline.

The VALDEZ VISITOR CENTER (200 Fairbanks Drive) offers, along with city maps, a cross-section of the pipeline and the first barrel of oil that flowed from it. VALDEZ MUSEUM (217 Egan Drive) is a good place to comprehend not only the construction of the line and the marine terminal (revealed in an illuminated model) but also the aftermath of the city's two disasters: the earthquake and the oil spill. Diverse displays feature a "pig," an instrument-toting cylinder that travels through the pipeline; the bar from a nineteenth-century saloon; and "please touch" sea otter pelts and Columbia Glacier ice. Tours from Valdez let you see glaciers up close on a THOMPSON PASS AND WORTHINGTON GLACIER DRIVE and COLUMBIA GLACIER FLIGHT-SEEING by helicopter.

And if you take a tour of the ice fields, remember to salute those argonauts who tried to scale Valdez Glacier during the gold rush, sunburned, snow-blind, blanketed by fog, and sometimes buried by avalanche.

THE ALASKA INTERIOR

The state's second-largest city, Fairbanks, is the hub of the Interior, where Mount McKinley—the Great One—looms within one of the biggest wildlife sanctuaries on the planet, Denali National Park. And for something completely different, a side trip to Tok offers revealing looks at Native crafts and the musher's art in Alaska's sled-dog capital.

Fairbanks: The Golden Heart

Fairbanks, near the geographical heart of the state, is a place of hope, of golden dreams realized and dashed only to be dreamt of again. A place of optimists. The 85,000 inhabitants of the city and the neighboring North Star Borough *must* be, given the location of their community less than 150 miles south of the Arctic Circle, which spawns their long, laborious winters. In December the sun may appear for less than four hours, seasonal temperatures regularly plummet below 40 degrees below Fahrenheit, and the strongest air inversions in the world (three times worse than those in Los Angeles) can create ice fog and winter pollution for weeks at a time. That combination of factors means that the smog you breathe is frozen. Yet during the summer—and the warm, dry summer always comes—Fairbanks lives in perpetual, moonless light and welcomes the visitors who now fuel its feast-or-famine economy.

Outsiders do appreciate its frontier charms, its waning and waxing legacy of gold and oil, and its hopeful, if often cantankerous people. A city of extremes, locals say with pride. Where for three

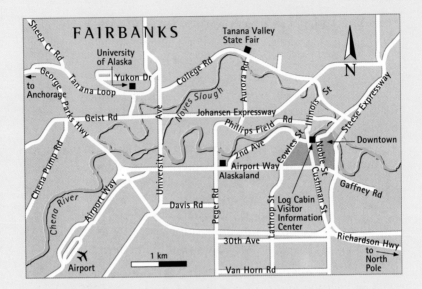

Walkabout

Log Cabin Visitor Information Center, 550 1st Avenue, close to a monument marking where the city was born, offers self-guided walking tours of historic downtown Fairbanks. Stroll 2nd Avenue—Two Street in local parlance—for a hint of the grittiness the city suffered during the pipeline invasion. And on the block between 3rd and 4th Avenues and Noble and Lacey Streets looms the Northward, the Interior's original steel-girder skyscraper, which inspired Edna Ferber's Alaska novel, *The Ice Palace*.

Alaskaland, Airport Way and Peger Road, with bus service from downtown, is an interesting pioneer theme park with old structures from Fairbanks, entertainment, and a popular salmon bake. Noteworthy are the gold-rush and mining towns, the Alaska Native Village, and the sternwheeler *Nenana*.

years in a row, voters rejected an official bond issue to finance a much-needed new hospital, then spontaneously launched a citizens' campaign to raise more than enough funds privately. As a former Alaska governor, Jay Hammond, once described it, this is a place "where ideas flourish, where debate, sometimes strident, searches for truth, regardless of how many sacred cows are milked dry or barbecued in the process."

The Interior encompasses one-third of Alaska, between the southern Alaska Range and the northern Brooks Range. Fairbanks, lying amid the spacious Tanana River valley, is the Interior's service and supply center, its hub, spreading north into the summer-green hills from the downtown floodplain of the Chena River, where sternwheelers take you on riverboat tours. The past and present commingle here. Big-city concrete office towers hulk over small-town wooden buildings and western bars. Not far from the core, you can visit the ghosts of gold dredges that were still producing half a century ago, and the very-much-alive Trans-Alaska Pipeline that continues to create wealth for the state. And nearby is the University of Alaska's research range, Poker Flat, where scientists take advantage of the isolation—the immense, natural geophysical laboratory—and launch rockets to plumb the secrets of earth's atmosphere. Fairbanksans are still looking up at the stars and dreaming optimistically.

Felix Pedro was one of the first dreamers here. In 1900, after mining coal in the U.S. Midwest and hunting gold in British Columbia and the Klondike, the hard-luck Italian-American arrived in Tanana River country. It had been prospected for years with little success. Pedro plugged on in the valley, encouraged by traces of yellow, joined by sourdoughs who worked at a nearby trading post on the Chena River above its junction with the Tanana. Finally, in July 1902, Pedro hit pay dirt and discreetly shared his find with a few friends—and the unscrupulous trading-post proprietor, Elbridge Truman Barnette, who let the whole world know.

In a rush that would repeat itself throughout Fairbanks history, thousands flocked to what was Alaska's biggest gold field—a field of broken dreams for many who wanted a quick payback and weren't

prepared to work for the mining companies that had to dredge the gold from deep below the permafrost. One of them was Otto Nilsson, who half a century later talked about how he, Felix Pedro, and others met to organize a mining district: "After the meeting I went out to stake my claim. I passed up creeks worth $130,000 a season. I staked on Little Eldorado and worked the creek thirty-four years, but I never found a pay streak." Legendary Alaska judge James Wickersham asked the first mayor to name the townsite that boomed around the trading post for Senator Charles Fairbanks of Indiana, who later became vice-president under Theodore Roosevelt. The mayor was Elbridge Barnette, who grew wealthy enough to open a bank before being charged with embezzling $317,000 worth of deposits in 1911; he was found guilty of only one misdemeanor before fleeing south.

By then, despite devastating flood and fire, Fairbanks was a boom town with electric lights, steam heat, and sewers. Because of long-term jobs with the large mining companies, it had a settled populace that was remarkably law-abiding for Alaska—a characteristic unchanged over the next six decades. After the gold was gone, the massive military spending of World War II and then the Cold War kept the city stable. Eielson Air Force Base still numbers several thousand people, who build on the city's aviation heritage—it was here that Alaska's first bush-pilot mail service began. In 1967, Fairbanks was flattened when the usually mild Chena River flooded, wreaking $200 million in damage. But just a few years later, construction began on the pipeline from Prudhoe Bay, and the population of Fairbanks went from 40,000 to 65,000. Governor Hammond had to send in an emergency force of legal specialists to control the surging crime wave. It ended in 1977 as quickly as it began, the prostitutes and muggers one step behind the departing construction workers.

Now the university (the most northern in North America) and tourism are among the city's mainstays. A must-see is the UNIVERSITY

Denali can be austerely beautiful or,
in the brief summer, lush and welcoming.

OF ALASKA MUSEUM (907 Yukon Drive), which features a superb
art collection and sophisticated natural-history and gold-mining
exhibits, including a 36,000-year-old steppe bison mummy and
more nuggets than you've ever seen. The university's renowned
Geophysical Institute studies earthquakes, the atmosphere, and the
aurora borealis—the "dawn of the north." The colorful, magical
northern lights are created when the sun's rarified gases erupt and
send their electrically charged particles into space to be picked up by
solar winds. Approaching earth's upper atmosphere, they're caught
by the magnetic field lines in the polar regions; electrons emit green
light when striking an oxygen molecule in the ionosphere, red light
when colliding with a nitrogen molecule. A university geophysicist
describes the lights as a "gigantic neon sign with a high-volume
electrical discharge." Eskimos thought they sounded like whispering
spirits; scientists now acknowledge that they can make a noise like
an electrical transformer's. Fairbanks witnesses them an average of

**Tour buses taking visitors through Denali
(then McKinley) park in the 1930s.**

240 nights a year, most brilliantly in the spring and fall. Some Japanese couples honeymoon here because folklore suggests that a marriage consummated under the aurora's lights will be a happy one.

RIVERBOAT CRUISES take you back in time as the sternwheeler *Discovery* navigates the Chena and less-ladylike Tanana Rivers where the two-story paddlewheel boats once carried freight and passengers to the gold fields. Some tours offer a stopover to see a prominent musher and sled dogs and to visit a replica of a camp of the local Athabascan Natives.

Outside town, GOLD-RUSH TOURS can include a visit to a five-story-high old dredge that dug up gold-filled gravel, and to a working gold mine with a narrow-gauge railway, tent city, permafrost drift tunnel, and mining relics. At both destinations, you can pan for the yellow flakes. Running near the city is the TRANS-ALASKA PIPELINE, and motorcoach excursions provide good views of the unique construction of this ongoing reminder of Fairbanks's boom-and-bust, dream-and-endure history.

Denali National Park: The Compleat Wilderness

You are on the open tundra of Sable Pass 3,900 feet high, and the astonishing land around you belongs to no one but the grizzly bear. Whole families of this most compelling emblem of the wilderness live here in Denali National Park and Preserve, fully protected from their only enemy: humans. You are not allowed to step outside the shuttle bus that brought you to the pass (nor would you want to, given the grizzly's mercurial reputation), but from its windows you can watch patient sows with their cavorting cubs, often twins or triplets who have little fear of the people staring at them, round-eyed with wonder. Perhaps only 300 grizzly bears exist in the Lower 48. Alaska has as many as 43,000—and the 5 miles along Sable Pass are the finest place in the world to observe them.

Elsewhere in Denali, where people are allowed to roam and the grizzlies are almost as likely to appear, the park staff have tried to ensure that direct contact between bear and human is slight. After placing radio collars on some grizzlies that had pillaged backpackers' food supplies, the biologists would later check up on them by concocting a meal that might attract a hungry bear. If a problem grizzly showed up in their camp, they'd shoot it with painful but harmless plastic shotgun slugs—a process repeated until the bruin lost all taste for domestic dining. But since 1955, the bears have not had to deal with any humans hiking around the off-limits Sable Pass area, which is why it remains such a superb setting to see the animals in all their wild dignity.

Yet there is so much more to the natural drama of Denali than the grizzly. This sub-Arctic park is reputed to be the largest protected ecosystem in the world, 9,420 square miles of mountain and forest, river and valley—bigger than the state of Massachusetts. Straddling a 160-mile stretch of the Alaska Range, it encircles Mount McKinley, at 20,306 feet North America's highest peak, which also soars above its base farther than any other mountain in the world (7,000 feet more than Mount Everest does from its foot). Until 1989, when a University of Alaska team remeasured it with satellite equipment, McKinley was thought to be 14 feet taller. No matter: it deserves its

The aurora borealis colors the sky around Fairbanks an average of 240 nights a year.

Athabascan designation as the High One, Denali—which gave the park its newest name. Every year about a thousand mountaineers test their skills on McKinley, half of them achieving the summit, but at least seventy have died on its steep slopes in storms or from falls or cerebral and pulmonary edema.

Denali is second only to Portage Glacier as the most-visited tourist attraction in Alaska. Not surprisingly: among Denali's 37 species of mammals, 155 of birds, and 450-plus of plants there are more big animals to be seen more easily than in any other U.S. park. Caribou mingle with Dall sheep on the mountains while moose stroll through the parking area at the Eielson Visitor Center. Trumpeter swans, ptarmigan, and golden eagles abound; golden plover visit from Hawaii, arctic terns from South America. The tundra and taiga are swathed in electric-colored blankets of short-lived summer vegetation, such as the lavender of mountain saxifrage and the golden waves of tufted cotton grass. No wonder Denali has been selected as a United Nations International Biosphere Reserve.

Tourist operators in the area outside the park offer RIVER RAFT-ING, LAKE KAYAKING, HORSEBACK RIDING, WAGON RIDES, and a HELICOPTER FLIGHT-SEEING TRIP over park, mountain, and glacier. Walkers might prefer a BOTANICAL NATURE WALK or a BACKCOUN-TRY HIKE. But although the park itself has fine natural hiking routes, there are only a few signs, marked trails, and designated campgrounds. There's a quota system for hiking the backcountry. Private vehicles are limited to local landowners and registered campers traveling only to their camps. Otherwise, the U.S. Park Service strictly controls the single 87-mile road, mostly gravel, on which the shuttle buses run regularly. (Your first glimpse of Mount McKinley on a clear day is Mile 9, looking to the southwest.) To minimize disruption of wildlife and to avoid traffic hazards along the twisty roads, park officials regulate the number of bus trips each summer.

Cruise-ship passengers on land excursions may take either a NATURAL-HISTORY or TUNDRA WILDLIFE TOUR by bus. The many pairs of passengers' eyes on a bus can spot animals more reliably than a couple of people in a private vehicle will. You might catch sight of foxes, coyotes, lynx, martens, and beavers. Or wolves wandering the banks of the Toklat River, golden eagles and gyrfalcons launching from Polychrome Pass, and early in the season, within the first hour of the tour, perhaps a grizzly stalking calving moose.

Since its birth in 1917, Denali has been a natural laboratory. It was here in 1939 that pioneering wildlife biologist Adolf Murie began to record the reality of wolves, chronicling their kills of the weak, young, and old among their prey, and changing the common attitude that they threatened herds of domestic and wild stock by hunting down animals in their prime. Today, park rangers and visiting biologists continue the field work—for example, discovering the biggest breeding ground of golden eagles in Alaska. And they continue to respect Denali's wolves. One ranger traveling by dog sled in winter had to endure a night of wolf howls outside his cabin. They meant no harm, he told his companion. They'd simply picked up the scent of the female huskies and wanted to be with them. Still using dogs to get around (and giving dog-sled demonstrations behind the Park Service headquarters in summer), the park staff have a lab so large that even some veteran rangers have never visited some of the more remote areas.

The park keeps getting larger. Created only a year after the National Park System, and designated from the start as wilderness, it was then named Mount McKinley. In 1922, the year the first official tourist visited, it was enlarged to the Nenana River on the east, and ten years later embraced Wonder Lake on the west—which is the reflecting pool for the mountain in so many photographs that you might feel you've seen it before. (Other good photo viewpoints: Eielson Visitor Center and Stony Hill.) It wasn't until 1972 that a new all-weather paved road between Anchorage and Fairbanks skirted the park's eastern border, generating twice the number of visitors. And eight years later, when the park was renamed Denali, 2.5 million acres were added to provide areas for Native people's subsistence hunting and trapping as well as snowmobiling. Today the total acreage is 6,028,924, including 1.3 million adjacent acres that were declared a national preserve, where sport hunting and aircraft landings are permitted. Next door lies Denali State Park, whose 324,000 acres yield similar wildlife experiences and striking vistas of the Alaska Range.

Those lofty mountains have always intrigued explorers and climbers. McKinley and its mates are so high that they latch on to the moisture from the Gulf of Alaska and cool it, creating snow at about the 14,000-foot level that sustains plentiful glaciers, including a half-dozen around McKinley. Southwest of it stands Mount Foraker, at 17,400 feet. Captain Vancouver, writing in 1794 from Knik Arm, said he could view on the far northwest horizon "distant stupendous mountains covered with snow, and apparently detached from one another." Natives in the Interior had already named the grandest one Denali, while other tribes knew it as Dolyeka and Traleyka. The Russians called it Bulshaia Gora (Great Mountain) and on their maps labeled it Tenada. Its first English name was the prosaic Densmore's Mountain, for Frank Densmore, an American gold prospector who saw it in 1889. Another prospector named William Dickey passed through the area seven years later, reporting: "We named our great peak Mount McKinley after William McKinley of Ohio, who had been nominated for the presidency, and that fact was the first news we received on our way out of that wonderful wilderness. We have no doubt that this peak is the highest in North America and estimate that it is over 20,000 feet high." (An alternative story says that, to spite prospectors who were trumpeting the cause of silver, he named it for the president who championed the gold standard.)

In 1902, federal geologists came here on foot and horseback, mapping the region so thoroughly that their work held up for half a century. And in 1903, much-loved U.S. district judge James Wickersham and four others attempted the first climb of McKinley. (*See The High One: A History, page 230.*) The most controversial ascent was the Sourdough Expedition seven years later, when two gold miners with basic gear and no specialized climbing experience surmounted the more difficult North Peak (19,470 feet)—scaling more than 8,000 vertical feet and returning to base camp in an extraordinary eighteen hours. They were among a quartet of miners who took a Fairbanks bartender's $500-per-person challenge that they

The High One: A History

1902: Alfred H. Brooks, leading a U.S. Geological Survey party, is the first white man to set foot on the slopes of Mount McKinley—and believes he may be the very first of any race because the Alaskan Native "has a superstitious horror of even approaching glacial ice."

1903: Judge James Wickersham and four others from Fairbanks make the first ascent, reaching the 8,100-foot level.

1910: William Taylor and Pete Anderson, two members of the Sourdough Expedition, climb on a bet and reach the summit of the North Peak.

1913: The Rev. Hudson Stuck and three others, including Walter Harper, Robert Tatum (Indian boys aged fourteen and fifteen), and Harry Karstens are the first to surmount McKinley's South Peak—and confirm the sourdoughs' success.

1947: Barbara Washburn is the first woman to reach the top.

1954: While making the first ascent by Ruth Glacier and the South Buttress, leader Elton Thayer is killed in the descent down Karstens Ridge.

1967: Ray Genet, Dave Johnston, and Art Davidson make the first winter ascent; Genet, who launched the mountain's first guiding service, is later lost on Everest.

1984: Japanese explorer Naomi Uemura makes the first winter solo ascent but dies in a storm during the descent.

1988: Vern Tejas makes the first full solo winter climb; on his next trip as a guide, a young woman collapses and dies while descending from the summit. Three Frenchmen with artificial legs reach the summit.

1991: In a sixteen-day expedition, twelve-year-old Taras Genet—Ray Genet's son—becomes the youngest mountaineer to conquer McKinley.

1995: Merrick Johnston, twelve, becomes the youngest female climber.

2001: Eleven-year-old Galen Johnston (no relation to Merrick) sets the new record as the youngest climber.

couldn't make the top of McKinley. Shod in insulated rubber boots and moccasins and wearing bib overalls and long underwear under their parkas, they carried snowshoes, home-built crampons, and primitive ice axes. After reaching their final camp at about 11,000 feet on March 17, three of them toting hot chocolate and doughnuts started for the summit on April 1. In 30-degree-below Fahrenheit weather, Billy Taylor and Peter Anderson crested the peak and, in a pyramid of rocks below it, planted a pole with the American flag. But when one of their party later claimed that all seven had climbed both the North and South Peaks, most people doubted the whole story of the successful ascent—especially when a climbing party two years later reported no sign of the sourdoughs' flagpole. In 1913, however, Taylor and Anderson were vindicated when an expedition under Episcopalian missionary Hudson Stuck became the first to ascend the South Peak and sighted the pole still standing on the North Peak.

It was the Reverend Stuck who, after his climb, summed up the magnificence of Mount McKinley so eloquently: "There was no pride of conquest, no trace of that exultation of victory some enjoy upon the first ascent of a lofty peak, no gloating over good fortune that had hoisted us a few hundred feet higher than others who had struggled and been discomfited. Rather…that a privileged communion with the high places of the earth had been granted…secret and solitary since the world began. All the way down, unconscious of weariness in the descent, my thoughts were occupied with the glorious scene my eyes gazed upon, and should gaze upon never again."

What he saw, and what visitors to Denali National Park and Preserve can still enjoy more than eight decades later, is a compleat wilderness in harmony with itself, one of the few such parks left in the world where the rawness of nature can be experienced without much interference from humankind.

Tok: The Sled-Dog Capital

Alaska's Eskimos may have been using dogs to pull sleds as long ago as the late Middle Ages, archeologists suggest. Certainly, when Bering came through in 1741, sled dogs were crucial to Natives' winter survival, the huskies hauling freight and hunters through the wilderness of snow and ice. They continued their key role until the 1970s when snowmobiles, the so-called iron dogs, threatened their position. What saved the animals was the resurgence of competitive mushing as a sport. At the turn of the century, gold miners in Nome raced teams of dogs for large sums of cash; soon after World War II, Anchorage's Fur Rendezvous and Fairbanks's North American Championships provided decent purses for sprint-like competitions. But it wasn't until Joe Redington, Sr., of Knik mortgaged his homestead and put up a $25,000 purse for the first long-haul Iditarod Trail race in 1967 that the state's official sport became legitimate. Full-time professionals now win prizes totaling hundreds of thousands of dollars a year and even attract annual coverage on TV. And today, when the dogs are more numerous than they were in 1900, the Alaska Highway community of Tok is the acknowledged Sled-Dog Capital. One estimate suggests a third of its 1,400 residents are somehow involved with breeding and training the animals.

Tok (rhyming with *spoke*) is also known as the gateway to Alaska from Canada: 125 miles northwest of the border, it's a key junction between the Alcan route to Fairbanks and the Tok Cutoff of the Glenn Highway to Anchorage. The unincorporated town began as an Alcan construction base in 1942, and the official story is that it was called Tokyo Camp for its proximity to the Tokyo River, until wartime feelings abbreviated the name. Another tale is that it comes from the Athabascan for "peace crossing" because the area was, and remains, a trading center for tribes in the Upper Tanana valley.

Women from nearby villages still create NATIVE CRAFTS: beaded necklaces, moccasins of tanned moose hide cured in the smoke of rotted spruce, and baskets of birch bark stitched together with spruce root and dyed with everything from food coloring to berry juice. They sell these and other Athabascan crafts in Tok's gift shops, which also offer soapstone carvings and fur hats and earmuffs.

THE ALASKA PUBLIC LANDS INFORMATION CENTER, near the junction, is an entertaining stop, with its interpretive exhibit of a fire that swept the Tok River in 1990; an impressive floor map and a room devoted entirely to a historical time line; and a wildlife museum featuring walrus, wolves, and an 8-foot grizzly.

Predictably, the town's many mushers offer visitors SLED-DOG DEMONSTRATIONS, including training sessions and rides. The animals might be blue-eyed, snowshoe-footed Siberian huskies, the most common of competitors, or the bigger Alaska malamutes bred to pull large loads—or a cross of such breeds as wolf, Labrador, and even Irish setter. Tok's trail (20½ miles) is the site of the Race of Champions, a contest that originated in 1954 as a bet between two roadhouse owners and now ranks as the third leg of the sport's Triple Crown after the Anchorage and Fairbanks races. With the largest field of any sprint race in the state, it features as many as 100 teams or more in two heats over two days during late March. Championship racers might have anywhere from six to sixteen dogs on their teams and, because they can't replace them during a heat, often end up with fewer than they began with—losing animals to aching muscles and sore feet. Most nights in summer, a local inn shows *Spirit of the Wind*, an Alaska-produced film documenting the state's best-known dog racers.

Dog mushing has become big business in Alaska. Competitors attract corporate support, professionals rent their dogs to amateur racers (for $10,000 and more a team), and breeders sell pups for $500 and veteran animals for twice that. Although they may spend as much as $30,000 maintaining their teams, the few top racers—such as Susan Butcher and Rick Swenson—have made a good living. Butcher, born in Cambridge, Massachusetts, not only won the Iditarod consistently, she and Joe Redington, Sr., were the first to gain the summit of Mount McKinley by dog team.

ARCTIC AND
WESTERN ALASKA

They are Alaska ports that never see cruise ships. On the Arctic Ocean at Prudhoe Bay, amid the caribou-rich tundra of the North Slope, American petroleum companies wrest black gold from the continent's largest oil field. Across the Arctic Circle, on the edge of the Chukchi Sea, Kotzebue is a vital Eskimo community whose inhabitants herd reindeer and still hunt walrus and other sea mammals for subsistence. And southwest of there, on the Bering Sea, Nome retains its flavor as the most riotous of pioneer gold-rush towns. They're all accessible in land adventures offered as post-cruise extensions by the major cruise lines.

Prudhoe Bay: Where Oil Meets Mammal

At twenty-one places along its route, the Trans-Alaska Pipeline dips underground for about 60 feet and then resurfaces to continue its zigzag course across the tundra. There are no "walk" or "don't walk" signals at these spots, but they are pedestrian crossings of a sort.

Freedom of movement for Alaska's mammals was one of the many environmental issues raised by the building of the pipeline. As a result, more than 500 animal crossings were provided. But the caribou herds created a difficult problem. The herds had to be free to migrate to their calving grounds. Biologists had experimented with various mammals' reactions to a pipeline. They found that moose would scramble on their knees under low pipes, but caribou wouldn't enter the enclosed space under a raised pipe nor use a ramp to get over it. Even a mother separated from a bawling calf would stay on her side of the line. Buried pipeline under level crossings was the only answer for the herds, and engineering them created one of the wonderful peculiarities in the 800-mile pipeline from North America's largest oil field, at Prudhoe Bay on the North Slope, to the port of Valdez on Prince William Sound.

The caribou are still plentiful along the DALTON HIGHWAY to Prudhoe Bay (*see* Driving the Dalton, *page 237*), and a trip to the source of the oil shows how humans and mammals are cohabiting around a community that exists for a single purpose: to extract from the Sadlerochit Formation about a quarter of the petroleum produced in the U.S. Fronting the ARCTIC OCEAN on Alaska's northeastern coast, 9-mile-wide Prudhoe Bay (usually pronounced *Prude*-oh) was named by Sir John Franklin for a fellow British explorer-scientist, the Baron of Prudhoe, during an expedition that took Franklin down Canada's Mackenzie River to the sea.

The population center is the private company town of DEAD-HORSE, the Dalton's northern limit. A few miles from the ocean (whose bone-numbing waters you can dip fingers or toes into), it is operated by several multinational oil corporations who bring workers here for a few weeks at a time to labor intensively for stratospheric rates of pay and then fly Outside as fast as they can for rest and recreation. Aside from mountains of food and the latest videos, there are few of the amenities you'd expect in a town equipped for up to 8,000 people, and workers seldom have time to consider the starkly magnificent tundra and the plenitude of wildlife—whales, polar bears, and caribou—surrounding them. Jonah Goldberg, writing in the *National Review*, says, "Deadhorse chauvinists are quick to brag that this sprawling, gravel-lined lot of airplane hangars, cargo dumps, and corrugated trailers has a ZIP code; once this postal luxury has been mentioned, the frills drop off dramatically."

Thanks largely to Prudhoe Bay, Alaska vies with Texas year by year as America's leader in oil production. The North Slope spreads over 89,000 square miles, about the size of Minnesota. The vast fields here have estimated recoverable reserves of at least 16 billion barrels of oil and 26 trillion cubic feet of natural gas. It was in 1968 that Atlantic Richfield announced a wildcat well, Prudhoe Bay State

No. 1, creating a stampede of the world's oilmen, many of whom came to Anchorage with cash in hand to bid for leases the following year—quadrupling the state's revenues overnight. Within two decades, half the estimated oil reserve had been pumped south. To make the most of the remainder, a $2-billion waterflood project has been forcing extra oil out of the rock. Meanwhile, a Central Gas Facility—the world's biggest gas plant—produces tens of thousands of barrels of natural gas each day. And though the known petroleum reserves are in decline, in recent years there has been a revival of exploratory drilling on the North Slope.

While security prevents visitors from wandering the docks or local roads, guided tours show you the most relevant areas of the oil-drilling activity and the environmental measures the petroleum companies take as they pump the black gold to Valdez. The oil that comes out of the ground at Prudhoe Bay is hot—about 180 degrees Fahrenheit. Inside the 48-inch pipeline, it cools to about 145 degrees. Slightly more than half the line is above ground, supported between 78,000 pairs of upright piping (for which four million feet of hole had to be drilled). Above ground, the pipeline wears an insulated jacket to protect it and keep the oil warm enough to flow after an interruption. When it goes under the tundra, the pipe is buried in stable ground to protect the permafrost. To keep the ground frozen at the caribou crossings, the excavated ditch around the pipe has been surrounded with sheets of Styrofoam and filled with gravel. But in some cases the engineers had to go one step further and lay underground pipes through which brine is pumped to keep the frozen ground of Alaska frozen.

Alaska presented unique challenges for the pipeline engineers: temperatures that range from 80 below to 95 degrees Fahrenheit; three mountain ranges; earthquake and avalanche zones; and 800 river and stream crossings. Their solutions were inventive and sometimes novel. The line's zigzag pattern is intended to give flexibility in controlling movement from earthquakes or thermal expansion and contraction. Zinc anodes placed beside buried sections of pipe attract electrical currents in the earth's surface (the same currents that generate the northern lights), returning the

Driving the Dalton

It's a two-day trip on the damnedest highway you've ever driven along. Gravel for all but 39 of its 414 miles, the Dalton Highway takes you through the taiga forest and treeless tundra of the Alaska wilds north of Fairbanks, over the Brooks Range and the Yukon River, across the Arctic Circle and the Continental Divide, through the GATES OF THE ARCTIC NATIONAL PARK AND PRESERVE and the ARCTIC NATIONAL WILDLIFE REFUGE, across Alaska's highest mountain pass, into the summering habitat of hundreds of thousands of caribou in the Porcupine and Central Arctic herds—and on the whole trip you won't pass through a single population center unless you count WISEMAN (population 21) and America's northernmost truck stop, COLDFOOT (population 13).

The Dalton began life in 1974 as the North Slope Haul Road to truck supplies for the Prudhoe Bay oil fields and the northern section of the Trans-Alaska Pipeline, whose route it generally parallels. Named for James Dalton, a pioneering Arctic engineer involved in exploring the North Slope for oil after World War II, the 28-foot-wide highway took only five months to build—at a cost of three million man-hours and $125 million, with $30 million of that for the 2,290-foot-long, wood-decked Yukon River Bridge (at Mile 55.6 on the way up, Mile 358.4 on the way down). The Yukon is Alaska's longest river, meandering 1,400 miles.

Ownership of the highway—still called the Haul Road—has reverted to the state, which now allows limited public access with permits as far as Deadhorse. Heading north in the air-cushioned comfort of a luxury tour bus, you'll see the sign marking the Arctic Circle—latitude 66°33'—at Mile 115.

You're in the BROOKS RANGE, one of the world's most northern mountain networks, which sweeps across the top of Alaska from the Mackenzie River in Canada's Northwest to Kotzebue on the Bering Sea. At Mile 244, you reach the summit of 4,752-foot ATIGUN PASS, the highest on the continent, where avalanches are common in winter. Driving down from the Continental Divide, you can often spot Dall sheep and caribou, grizzlies and wolves, as you approach the North Slope and the pipes and rigs of Prudhoe Bay.

currents to the earth and reducing the risk of damage to the pipe-line. In earthquake zones, where the pipe is raised, it is free to slide from side to side on its vertical supports. At Atigun Pass through the Brooks Range, the highest point on the line, the pipe is buried to protect it from avalanches and swathed in 21 inches of insulation inside an 8-foot-wide concrete sarcophagus to protect it from cor-rosion.

In the late 1960s, before construction had begun, estimates were that the line would cost $900 million. By the time the final design was finished in 1974, Alyeska Pipeline Service Company—the con-sortium of seven oil companies that built and still operates it—had revised its estimate to $8 billion, which was what the line cost when it was finished in June 1977.

In recent years the average volume of oil pumped through the line has declined to about half the peak of two million barrels a day. Moving at 6 miles an hour, it takes a little over five days for the oil to reach Valdez, where it is stored before being pumped into ocean-going tankers. By the end of the twentieth century, more than thir-teen billion barrels had been taken from the North Slope fields.

Safety features have been incorporated with Alaska's delicate envi-ronment in mind. Pump stations along the route monitor the flow, and computers at Valdez can indicate a drop in pressure, signaling an operator to close valves at the pump stations. Inside the line itself, valves will close if the oil flow stops or reverses. These measures are supposed to limit the size of a spill. In February 1978, when the line was sabotaged, 16,000 barrels escaped east of Fairbanks.

Each year, the interior of the pipe is examined with a "pig," a cylindrical device carrying sophisticated measuring instruments. Some pigs clean the inside of the pipe; some check changes in shape or look for corrosion. The newest ultrasonic pig takes twenty-seven million readings in a mile, detecting and recording changes in the thickness of the pipe wall. When, in 1989, it revealed small spots of corrosion at points along the line, Alyeska handled the problem by increasing the amount of drag-reducing agent it normally injects to reduce turbulence in the oil and make it easier to pump. This temporary increase lowered the pressure in the pipe and allowed repairs to be made. In 1991, 8½ miles of pipe were replaced in the Atigun Pass floodplain. This was the largest construction project on the pipeline since startup in 1977.

While the oil continues to flow, so do the caribou. The Nelchina herd, which had decreased to 10,000 before the pipeline was built, grew to 45,000 animals in 1992. Scientists, watching the animals' behavior over a period of three years, observed that 99 percent of the caribou successfully cross the pipeline.

Nome: No Place Like It

"It is the liveliest, speediest, swiftest mining camp ever seen in Alaska. All sorts of sharks are making fortunes," wrote a pioneering prospector in 1899, when Nome was briefly the gold-rush capital of the world. A century later, the city continues to be a modest gold-mining center and—though short of sharks—one of the zaniest, zestiest of Alaska communities. It's the kind of place where locals golf with an orange ball and an iced tee on the frozen Bering Sea in March; swim between ice floes in its numbing 35-degree waters just after breakup on Memorial Day; play baseball in the midnight sunlight in June; in summer build homemade rafts of any materials to run the Nome River and win a fur-lined honey bucket; and on Labor Day celebrate the end of the season with a bathtub race.

At the turn of the twentieth century, one hopeful American prospector came to town on a bike he'd ridden down the frozen Yukon River and across the tundra, while a Norwegian attempted the trip on ice skates. Ever since, Nome has had a history of attracting characters. These days, most everyone flies in on the ninety-minute hop from Anchorage, and perhaps 60 percent of its 3,500 people are Eskimos, a fiercely independent group who finally abandoned the spartan life on nearby King Island in 1959. Yet the western Arctic city lures adventurous visitors and has a decidedly mixed bag of residents. Because Nome sits only 190 miles from Siberia, the tourist traffic along the sea on Front Street might include Russians, although cab drivers and shopkeepers no longer accept their

devalued rubles as they once did. Meanwhile, trade across the Bering Strait (and the International Date Line) is slowly growing since the border reopened in 1988: one Nome entrepreneur installed meat processors on Siberian farms to make sausages from reindeer—in return for the animals' antlers, which he exported to South Korea for use as aphrodisiacs.

Nome, 102 miles south of the Arctic Circle, lies exposed to the elements on the southern verge of the Seward Peninsula overlooking Norton Sound, an extension of the Bering Sea. It may take its name from an Eskimo phrase, *Kn-no-me*, meaning "I don't know" (supposedly the answer to "What's the name of this place?"). But more likely it comes from nearby Cape Nome, itself a misinterpretation of the markings on a nineteenth-century British map of the area when ? *Name* was misread as C (for Cape) Nome.

In the westernmost time zone in the U.S., on about the same latitude as Fairbanks, Nome is milder than its coastal neighbor Kotzebue—which in summer means average lows of 40 degrees Fahrenheit and highs in the 50s, with an occasional heat wave of 75. The surrounding permafrost terrain is classically treeless. (In December, convoys head down to the tree line east of the city to cut scrubby-looking spruce for the whole community's Christmas.) Summer briefly brings a riot of wildflowers, sedges, and grasses reaching ankle height in the encircling hills. Off the three dirt roads leading out of town, the Arctic tundra supports moose, musk oxen, and reindeer. (Local reindeer herds played the part of caribou stampeding during the 1983 Disney film *Never Cry Wolf*.) Nearby lakes and streams run thick with salmon, arctic char, and grayling. The Seward Peninsula attracts 180 kinds of birds, many of them Asiatic species seldom seen in North America. And in the sea there are seals, whales, and the plentiful walrus.

Only Alaska Natives are legally allowed to possess ivory from the tusks and teeth of walrus, which they carve into works of art and offer for sale locally. Some of the ivory is mineralized and fossilized,

In Nome of the early 1900s, legendary Wyatt Earp owned "the only second class saloon in Alaska."

the remnants of prehistoric mammoths and mastodons. Such artifacts of Eskimo culture are shown to effect in the CARRIE MCCLAIN
MEMORIAL MUSEUM (in the library building on Front Street), along
with an intriguing exhibit of gifts from Russia and the inevitable
gold-rush displays.

In 1898, the site where Nome now stands was an empty beach
of black sand. That autumn, two Swedish-born prospectors and
a Laplander—the legendary three Lucky Swedes—panned $1,800
worth of gold in a few days at Anvil Creek, three miles inland. By
the following summer the beach was a tent city of hopefuls from
the Klondike, the Lower 48, and the rest of Alaska. One day an
elderly gold panner decided to try the sand at his feet and found
grains of gold right there along the shore. By summer's end, while
prospectors extracted $1 million from the creeks, 2,000 elbow-to-
elbow miners along the beachfront had taken twice that much
more easily, using pans and the ingenious rockers that worked like
swinging sluice boxes. There was a third wave of discovery when
geologists realized that the water had once reached higher levels on
the land and that more gold was to be found below those ancient
beaches. Within a dozen years, the Seward Peninsula had given up
more than $60 million in gold.

By 1900, the fledgling town counted among its many businesses
20 saloons, 12 general stores, and a bookshop, and its population
included 11 doctors, 16 lawyers, and a masseur. It needed each of
those specialists to deal with the physical and legal conflicts that
erupted with the greed for gold. The new-money miners set the
partying standard for present-day Nome, importing troupes of
entertainers from Seattle and throwing lavish dinners catered by
their own Chinese chefs. Even Wyatt Earp ran a bar and promoted
local boxing matches, two decades after the gunfight at the O.K.
Corral. (However, John Wayne playing a Nome gold-rush miner in
The Spoilers never made it here; nary a foot of that classic 1942 film
was shot in Alaska.) In those early days, the recorded population
was 12,488, one-third of all whites living in Alaska. Nine thousand
of them had dug the sands on a single day in 1900. But fire, storms,
and outright thievery—some of it through the courts—reduced

those numbers, as did the decline in production six years later. And by 1915 only 1,000 people remained in Nome.

The allure of gold continues to keep the city lively. The Alaska Gold Company is the major operator in the area. Some gold dredges still run during the summer, and you can photograph the wooden hulks of several old ones within walking distance of town. GOLD PANNING on the beach remains a popular tourist pastime; all you need is a pan bought locally. Is there any precious metal left in that played-out sand? The local Convention and Visitors Bureau warns that "while panning for gold is most assuredly fascinating, and fun, don't count on it to pay for even a small part of your trip—let alone your subsistence." Of course, they don't mention that in 1964 a visitor found a 1.29-ounce nugget at the end of Nome's seawall.

The 3,350-foot seawall was built of tons of granite to stop the ocean from devouring the foreshore and Front Street along with it. Over the years, the city has survived many blows, including a storm that nearly knocked it flat in 1913 and a fire that caused $2 million worth of damage in 1934. It was during a diphtheria epidemic in 1925 that twenty mushers drove relays of dog teams to bring serum 674 miles from Nenana, near Fairbanks, over part of a mail route that had been carved fifteen years earlier. Today the IDITAROD TRAIL SLED DOG RACE—the so-called Last Great Race on Earth—starts at Anchorage and follows some of the same treacherous path, crossing two mountain ranges, snaking along the Yukon River, and arriving in Nome over the pack ice of Norton Sound. The actual distance now is more than 1,100 miles, and the run can take two to three weeks, although consistent winner Doug Swingley and others have done it in little more than ten days. High tech has overtaken the event: starting in 1993, vets implanted computer microchips in the dogs' necks to register them as entrants, rather than painting their fur, and officials at checkpoints used scanners to record their numbers as they ran by. Because the race takes place in March, summer visitors have to be content with viewing the arch of the finish line next to City Hall and perhaps get an unseasonal ride in a dog sled. There are usually sled dogs tethered along the east end of 6th Avenue to take pictures of but not to pet—they can be temperamental.

If you happen to be here in mid-June, the MIDNIGHT SUN FESTI-VAL will more than make up for missing the Iditarod celebrations. To commemorate the summer solstice, there's usually a parade, a mock bank holdup and trial, Eskimo dancing and blanket tossing, the overnight softball tournament, and the mad Nome River Raft Race. And as you might expect of a raunchy old mining camp, it's a day-and-night, week-long wingding.

Kotzebue: The Living Arctic

Shore Avenue, Kotzebue. About thirty miles above the Arctic Circle. Inupiat Eskimos repairing kayaks and umiaks sprinkled along the shore of Kotzebue Sound on the Chukchi Sea. The water illuminated with a strange summer light, not unlike the alpenglow of mountains. Beyond the flattened sea, silver-domed peaks on Cape Krusenstern National Monument melting into clouds. A sky as wide and high as the world. Salmon and walrus meat dry on racks under a sun that, from early June, won't set for thirty-six days. Telephone poles take the place of trees; the scrub brush promises more than it ever delivers. Along the gravel road of Shore Avenue, which locals also call Front Street, is the Native-owned Nullagvik Hotel, whose dining room serves reindeer stew, and a couple of blocks away the Arctic Dragon, which some visiting bush pilots believe serves the best Chinese food in Alaska.

Kotzebue perches on the tundra 550 miles north of Anchorage and 200 east of Siberia, linked to Outside by daily flights and, for three summer months, by sea-going deep-draft vessels bringing in fuel and food supplies for the year. (River sediment in the sound forces these ships to anchor many miles off shore.) The commercial and transportation center for northwestern Alaska, it's the state's largest community of Eskimos and one of its oldest. They represent three-quarters of the 3,100 population. For six centuries their ancestors made this a trading center, calling it Kikiktagruk—"almost a peninsula"—and *their* ancestors may have been living here, on the Baldwin Peninsula near the mouths of three rivers, since 8000 B.C.

The current name comes from—well, it's nicely explained in a mysterious movie called *Salmonberries*, starring singer k.d. lang, which was filmed here in 1990 and went on to win the major award at the 1991 World Film Festival in Montreal. The singer plays a young woman called Kotzebue; the local librarian tells her the city was named for Otto von Kotzebue, the third of seventeen children of the successful German playwright August von Kotzebue. She doesn't mention that Otto was sailing for the Russians, searching for the Northwest Passage, when he came upon the village in 1816.

Today's English-speaking Inupiat live in relatively easy coexistence between two worlds, herding reindeer and watching TV by satellite, hunting walrus and whale, and working even farther up north in the Teck Cominco Red Dog zinc-and-lead mine, which has major supply, servicing, and construction contracts with their Native corporation, the Northwest Alaska Native Association (NANA). But urban pressures intrude in the unlikeliest ways. With the immensity of the Arctic all around, the city is hemmed in on this narrow spit of land 3 miles long—and it's running out of room for housing. There's as much of a spartan quality to the unadorned wooden structures as there is to the landscape, in which minuscule willows may be 1 inch tall. Done in Polar Pre-fab, the commercial buildings and the dwellings—some of them with forty-one units—can be dun-colored or occasionally, to relieve the starkness, pastel. Besides the comfortable NANA-built hotel, Kotzebue has a small hospital, a bank, a recreation center, a library, video stores, a biweekly tabloid newspaper (the *Arctic Sounder*), radio station KOTZ, a University of Alaska campus, and schools for 700 students with a full-sized gym (basketball's the big sport).

Although the prime employer is the borough school district, the local success story is NANA, organized under the Native-claims legislation of 1971, with the parent company based in Kotzebue and a development arm in Anchorage. Its investment portfolio has included local seafood processing, reindeer harvesting, jade mining, tourism, and statewide oilfield services and mineral drilling—including well-paid work for the Red Dog Mine, the western world's largest zinc producer. With the cost of food here more than twice that in

Anchorage, residents need the money. They spend some of their discretionary cash on a popular pastime, bingo. Yup'ik storyteller John Active describes watching as a player in the bingo hall "raised his head up over the smoke, looked around quickly, then ducked down again. He looked like a seal. No, a ptarmigan."

On the Fourth of July, the people of Kotzebue celebrate with Native games, a whale-blubber-eating contest, and an awards presentation for the biggest beluga caught during the season. A week later, artisans from around the borough gather at the Northwest Native Trade Fair to show their handicrafts and perform traditional dances. Visitors throughout the summer can see dancers, meet with artists, and take part in blanket tosses at one of three not-to-be-missed attractions: the NANA MUSEUM OF THE ARCTIC. It has an ambitious multimedia program featuring ultra-realistic dioramas, which explain the local culture and wildlife, and offers a tour of a jade factory. At the CULTURAL CAMP, youngsters demonstrate traditional hunting and fishing, cooking, and sewing. LAVONNE'S FISH CAMP is well worth a stop, offering tour visitors and the seniors who take Elderhostel courses such programs as ivory-carving demonstrations, the use of medicinal plants, and storytelling with elders.

Above all, Kotzebue is a place for strolling through the dwarf fireweed and the cotton grass, for soaking up the accessible Arctic setting and its way of life. Summer is good walking weather, cool, seldom rising above 60 degrees Fahrenheit. As you wander, consider the winter climate, when the temperature can plummet to 52 *below*.

Visitors to Kotzebue can join the Inupiat in the high-flying blanket toss.

YUKON, CANADA

George Carmack was not interested in gold. He was a California-born white man who lived as an Indian, fishing and logging with his common-law wife, Kate, the daughter of a Tagish chief. Like most Indians, he considered prospecting a white man's game. Yet on Rabbit Creek in the Yukon one summer day in 1896, he was indeed searching for the stuff, prodded by his Indian friends Skookum Jim Mason and Tagish Charlie. Jim had detected traces of gold in the gravel of the creek; now he and Carmack were panning for more. They found a nugget as big as a thimble, then enough surface gold to pack a shotgun shell—enough to make them think this could be the richest stake in the whole territory. Carmack convinced Jim that no Indian would be acknowledged as the discoverer, so on August 17 he declared himself the first man on the site. That entitled him to a double claim—1,000 feet of the creek.

George Carmack had caught the gold fever. He would carry it, spread it, until it became an epidemic infecting thousands around the world. It would be the wildest, gaudiest gold rush in history, three years of astounding good fortune and much bad luck, of greed and hardship and starvation and lavish spending.

Another man shares the credit for the discovery. Robert Henderson, a Nova Scotian who had hunted gold around the world for a quarter-century, had directed Carmack into the promising area around Rabbit Creek. Henderson had been panning a nearby creek he called Gold Bottom. Like Rabbit, it ran into a river the Indians called Throndiuck (Hammer-Water), for the stakes they hammered in at its mouth to hold salmon nets. The guttural Indian word became "Klondike" on the tongues of whites.

Henderson invariably obeyed the prospector's code: if a man found gold, he informed others. The philosophy was less generous than practical. Having others around lessened the loneliness of working in the wild; competition was no consideration because even the discoverer of a site could stake no more than two 500-foot claims. So Henderson, happening upon Carmack and his friends earlier that month while going for supplies, had urged Carmack to make a claim on the Gold Bottom. But he offended Carmack by adding: "I don't want any damn Siwashes [Indians] staking on that creek." His slight would cost him a fortune.

Bonanza

When Carmack did stake his double claim as discoverer, the Indians each claimed 500 feet on the Rabbit—soon to be renamed BONANZA CREEK. Carmack and Tagish Charlie left Skookum Jim on guard and set off down the Yukon River to the community of Forty Mile to register their claims. At first nobody believed them, but within days prospectors descended on the creeks around the Klondike River. Robert Henderson wasn't among them: the slighted Carmack purposely neglected to tell him about hitting pay dirt. And a few weeks later, when Henderson did learn of the spectacular find, the best of Bonanza had already been staked.

Stampeders soon thronged into the territory, 186,000 square miles of wilderness, of mountains, forests, and tundra, of immense lakes and rapids-rich rivers. Bear and moose and caribou far outnumbered the inhabitants, most of whom were Indian tribes sharing dialects of the Athabascan language. As prospectors converged on the area where the Yukon and Klondike Rivers meet, trader Joe Ladue shrewdly guessed that land would become almost as valuable as gold. He staked out a townsite on swampy level ground on the Yukon's east bank and named it DAWSON, after a government geologist. The next summer, in 1897, as the population passed 1,500, his house lots sold for thousands of dollars apiece.

That first winter, when Dawson was still a chaos of tents, there

was virtual famine. "Food got scarcer and scarcer," A.T. Walden recalled in his autobiography, *A Dog Puncher on the Yukon*. "The sharing of food was remarkable. Food was priceless, but there was no price on it. This was the Starvation Camp that the people on the outside never heard of." By May 1897, the camp had no food but flour. More prospectors came in by boat when the Yukon River broke up that month, but not until early June did the sternwheeler *Alice* arrive with food—and with liquor that was served free the day the saloons reopened.

Scarcely a month later, the steamship *Excelsior* landed in San Francisco. Her cargo was Klondike prospectors and their embarrassment of gold. Their arrival jolted the continent—indeed, the world—and confirmed rumors that had been trickling out of the Yukon for months. The miners dragged ashore sacks and suitcases swollen with nuggets and dust. In Seattle another shipload of sourdoughs landed with more than two tons of gold. Together the two ships delivered $1.5 million worth.

The Klondike strike came at the end of an economic depression in North America, and men eagerly left behind homes and loved ones to follow the Trail of '98. The records teem with stories of gold-mad barbers deserting their shops, streetcar drivers abandoning their passengers, doctors forsaking their practices. The romantic name for such men was stampeders. In fact, most were tenderfeet—cheechakos in the Chinook jargon—and their inexperience would cause them incredible hardship.

A few could afford to go by ship to the Bering Sea port of St. Michael, in western Alaska, then by boat about 1,300 miles up the Yukon River to Dawson. But most trudged into the Yukon over the Coast Mountains, through the WHITE PASS or the CHILKOOT PASS. The White Pass trail began at the seaport of SKAGWAY, controlled by several hundred thugs and gamblers led by Soapy Smith. (*See* Skagway, the Lost Frontier, *page 182.*) In the fall of 1897, about 5,000 gold seekers, including some women, attempted the 45-mile trek

Whitehorse, the Yukon capital, lies amid the mountains and the historic Yukon River valley.

through the pass. The slippery trail was so narrow in places that competing pack teams could not squeeze by; traffic jams lasted for hours. The treacherous path became littered with discarded packs and the remains of most of the 3,000 horses that were forced up into the hills. Novelist Jack London, who took this Dead Horse Trail, reported that the animals died like mosquitoes in the first frost and were left to rot in heaps. It took only a few hours for a carcass to be mashed underfoot. In the White Pass, wrote Klondike chronicler Robert Service, "there is no mercy, no humanity, no fellowship. All is blasphemy, fury and ruthless determination." The climbers would pass a murdered man without pause.

"This Side of Hell"

Most cheechakos reached the Klondike in 1898 over the awesome Chilkoot Trail—which one of them, Martha Black, later a Canadian member of Parliament, called "the worst trail this side of hell." Raw

A gold-rush laundromat and fortune-telling parlor.

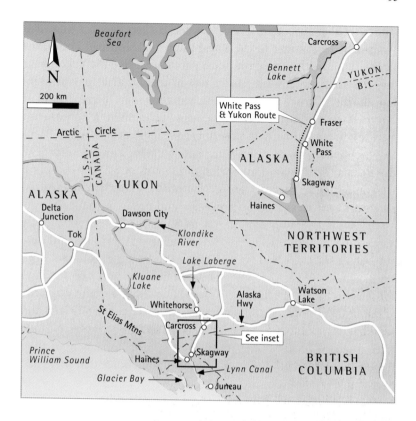

rock in summer, slick ice and snow in winter, the Chilkoot was 600 feet higher than the White Pass and all but impassable by animals—in some places the trail climbed at a 35-degree angle. Its base was Dyea (*Die-ee*), an Alaska town 4 miles north of Skagway. At the foot of the pass lay Sheep Camp, also in Alaska, its floating population of 1,500 living in tents, cabins, and the odd exotic dwelling such as a hut woven of branches by New Zealand Maoris. A lake of water behind a glacier burst into the Chilkoot Pass that fall, sweeping away scores of tents and drowning three men. In the spring an avalanche suffocated sixty people under 30 feet of snow.

Through the winter and into the summer of '98, about 22,000 men and women clambered up the pass in what seemed an endless string of humanity. It was 4 miles from Sheep Camp to the Chilkoot summit—and Canadian territory. Canada's North West Mounted Police (the forerunner of the Royal Canadian Mounted Police, the fabled Mounties) insisted that each person entering the Yukon have a year's food and equipment—a ton in weight. That meant making the climb thirty to forty times, sometimes in blizzards and at temperatures as low as 58 degrees below Fahrenheit. Much of each load was food, but luxuries went over the Chilkoot on men's backs and up rope and cable tramways: pianos, a grindstone, newspapers, 10,000 bottles of mosquito repellent.

The buffalo-coated NWMP arrived on the Canadian side of the passes in February 1898, bringing law and order to the stampede. Their commander was Supt. Sam (later Sir Samuel) Steele, a Mountie original with an impressive record of facing down rioters and outlaws. Steele's headquarters was at BENNETT LAKE, the bottom of both trails. There prospectors built or bought boats or rafts and at spring breakup set off for the Yukon River and Dawson. Near WHITEHORSE, at the boiling rapids of Miles Canyon, 150 vessels were wrecked and ten men drowned before Steele stepped in and enforced safety rules. In mid-1898—when he was responsible for law enforcement in all of the Yukon and British Columbia—Steele could boast that there had been only three murders in his territory.

Dawson, meanwhile, had endured a second starvation winter, with flour going from $6 a sack to $100. But after the supply boats arrived in the summer of 1898, the town boomed anew. The population reached more than 20,000, and the City of Gold was the biggest place west of Winnipeg, Manitoba, and north of Seattle with telephones, electricity, and running water. Yet it looked primitive: tents, shacks, and log buildings were set on permafrost, which became a bog in spring. And it *was* primitive: a man won a bet that he could cross Front Street by jumping from one dead horse or dog to another.

Nonetheless, Dawson was unlike such unruly settlements as Skagway. On Sundays the town slept, saloons and theaters were shut, and working men were required to rest from their labors. (Two were fined for merely examining their fish nets.) The worst offenders were given a "blue slip" ordering them out of Dawson on the next boat.

The town's fifty-one Mounties enforced laws that made carrying firearms and selling liquor to minors illegal.

But if Dawson wasn't lawless, it wasn't very nice either. In the dancehalls and saloons and gambling casinos, the motto was "never refuse a drink or kick a dog." The proprietors of these places prospered, as did many a female dancer-actress—some with such colorful names as Glass-Eyed Annie and Overflowing Flora. Behind the dancehalls, the prostitutes of Paradise Alley worked from seventy shacks called cribs, and most of their money went to pimps who had paid their way to the Yukon. The Dawson currency was gold dust, carried in sacks, and signs in the gambling dens warned: "Don't overplay your sack." Diamond Tooth Gertie, a dancehall girl, said it best: "The poor ginks have just got to spend it; they're that scared they'll die before they have it all out of the ground."

The Luckiest Cheechakos

Two fires levelled the core of Dawson in the winter of 1898–99. After the second, which destroyed 117 buildings, the town took on a different tone. Houses were built with finished lumber, sidewalks and roads were laid in macadam, schools were opened. The bubble of development would soon burst, but not before some latecomers, among the luckiest cheechakos, struck it rich—by disregarding the conventional wisdom that all gold was close to the creeks. Beginning in '98, new arrivals with no creeks to stake went into the hills and discovered broad veins with nuggets weighing half an ounce and more.

In the summer of '99, news of a gold strike at Nome lured Dawson people to Alaska—8,000 left in one week. The population continued to dwindle as mining by hand got harder. Most Yukon gold lay on bedrock, deep under muck and frozen gravel. The miners couldn't scoop it up in pans; they reached it in winter by burning wood—or later by driving steam through steel pipes—to thaw the ground. Then they tunneled laterally, setting aside the precious gravel until spring. During runoff, they used creek water to wash the gravel through sluice boxes where the heavier gold settled to the bottom. Eventually, big companies began to buy up small claims and work them with mechanized dredges. At the turn of the century, a year's hand-mining produced $22 million in gold; in 1907 the yield was about $3 million. That year the last of the dancehalls closed in Dawson.

The pioneers of the gold rush had long since left the Klondike. Joe Ladue, Dawson's founder, had come to earn enough to impress the parents of his girlfriend in Plattsburg, New York; he went home with $5 million, married her, and within a couple of years died of tuberculosis. George Carmack, Skookum Jim Mason, and Tagish Charlie all died wealthy. Carmack brought his Indian wife, Kate, back to the U.S. but left her for a prostitute. Kate sued him for abandonment, in one of the original palimony cases, but failed to have their common-law relationship recognized. And Robert Henderson, the unlucky man who learned about the Bonanza too late, left the Klondike to look for gold elsewhere in the Yukon and in B.C. When he died in 1933, he was still looking.

The Drama of Dawson City

Over the last several decades, the Canadian government has been maintaining and imaginatively restoring Dawson City as a national historic site. Parks Canada has done its work well: though a lot of rickety old wooden structures line Dawson's wide streets beside new buildings, this community of 1,800 no longer feels like the ghost town it verged on being for much of its life. Fishing, trapping, agriculture, and even some latter-day mining help stoke the economy. But it's tourism that has preserved and re-created a photogenic, self-assured little city brimming with boardwalks, clapboard storefronts, and houses with gingerbread detailing and floral gardens. The theme, of course, is the Klondike Trail of '98. Yet Dawson is neither theme park nor historic leftover.

Dawson City is Yukon's second-largest center, after Whitehorse, which has about two-thirds of the Territory's 30,000 people living in and around it (in a land 15 percent larger than California). The city is set against a mountain backdrop—the 2,900-foot MIDNIGHT

DOME, 5 miles distant, so-called because the sun shines on its peak at midnight on the summer solstice. The city sits low on a permafrost plain near the junction of the Yukon and Klondike Rivers, only 150 miles south of the Arctic Circle. The location prompts the local line: "This may not be the end of the world, but you can see it from here." Residents reveal their sense of humor about being in the boondocks by running the annual Great Klondike International Outhouse Race on Labor Day weekend in early September, placing outlandish-looking outdoor toilets on wheels and pulling them through the streets. The truth is that, like the rest of the Territory, this far-northern city is a pleasant place to be in summer. It's generally dry and warm, with the temperature rising as high as 85 degrees Fahrenheit in July and the sun shining nearly twenty-four hours a day in June and twenty in July.

Everywhere you wander in Dawson, there is drama—and melodrama. This is, after all, a city that claims both Robert Service and Jack London as chroniclers of the Klondike. But in the decade after they and most of the stampeders left town at the turn of the century, mining technology improved and reduced the Territory's dependence on its capital city as a supply and service center. Gold production

Not even avalanches could discourage the cheechakos who trudged up these trails.

ebbed throughout the Klondike during World War I and for a couple of decades afterward; just as mining began to recover, along came World War II. And with construction of the Alaska Highway, Whitehorse flourished and robbed Dawson of its status as capital. Another highway, the Klondike, which runs the 331 miles between the two cities, pensioned off Dawson's port. Finally, in the 1960s, the last gold dredge stopped operating in the Klondike River valley.

No wonder Dawson decided to resurrect its past. While fishing, farming, and trapping do contribute, tourism keeps the city healthy. Nostalgic visitors from the south come to see the gold diggings, where the occasional miner still works a claim. Seven miles north along Bonanza Road, you can do your own gold panning over a water trough at CLAIM #33 BELOW DISCOVERY (meaning thirty-three claims below the historic find on Bonanza Creek in 1896 that set off the great stampede), with a virtual guarantee of some flecks in every pan. Look for some of the original wooden claim stakes still standing here. Three miles farther north, you can see how the serious folk dug for gold on Bonanza. Here, GOLD DREDGE NO. 4— 76 feet tall, 140 feet long, and supposedly the largest wooden-hull dredge on the continent—now sits forlornly, no longer producing up to 800 ounces of gold a day from the river valley.

One of the last of the 250 steamboats to ply the Yukon River, the flat-bottomed, high-stacked s.s. KENO sits in drydock beside the river on Front Street, where you can tour the long white paddle wheeler, restored as a national historic site. A scaled-down sternwheeler, the YUKON LOU, offers trips on the Yukon, along with a salmon barbecue and a visit to the cemetery of steamboats on Pleasure Island. M.V. YUKON QUEEN II, a fast catamaran, features a riverboat cruise between Dawson City and the old trading post of Eagle, Alaska, along the Yukon where trappers' cabins and Athabascan villages are reminders of this river's richly storied past.

Through displays and old documentary movies, the DAWSON CITY MUSEUM, on 5th Avenue at Church Street, recounts tales of the gold rush and the effects it had on the city. (Look for the bones of camels that crossed the gold-rush passes.) History comes rollickingly alive at two local dancehalls. The original Palace Grand

Theatre dates back to 1899, when Arizona Charlie Meadows built it from salvaged sternwheelers to seat 2,200; the new one on King Street is a precise replica. Upstairs is a dressing room dedicated to singing, dancing Klondike Kate Rockwell, who wore a belt of $20 gold pieces and a tiara of illuminated candles (and who successfully sued theater tycoon Alexander Pantages, originally a Dawson waiter, for breach of promise). Now the Palace Grand is the setting for an "Olde Tyme" music-hall show called the GASLIGHT FOLLIES. At DIAMOND TOOTH GERTIES GAMBLING HALL, 4th and Queen—

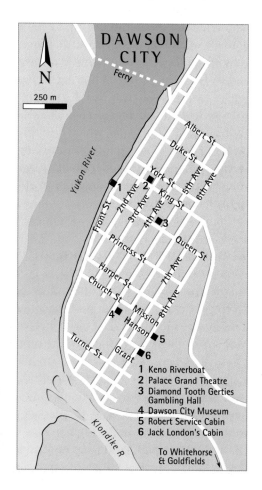

From riverboats to gambling halls, gold-rush bards to lively museums, the national historic site of Dawson City presents the past in an agreeable photogenic form.

1 Keno Riverboat
2 Palace Grand Theatre
3 Diamond Tooth Gerties Gambling Hall
4 Dawson City Museum
5 Robert Service Cabin
6 Jack London's Cabin

To Whitehorse & Goldfields

named for dancehall queen Gertie Lovejoy, who wore a sparkler between her two front teeth—there are can-can girls, honky-tonk piano music, and what for a long time was Canada's only legal casino, whose profits helped restore the city's heritage buildings.

Perhaps the most evocative places to visit in Dawson are the cabins that pay homage to the Klondike's bards. JACK LONDON'S CABIN AND INTERPRETATION CENTRE (8th Avenue and Grant Street) is the very basic lodging where the idealistic young writer and hapless gold seeker from Oakland, California, actually lived for a few weeks. By his bunk, he wrote his name and a punning self-description—"miner author"—that would belie his success as creator of *The Call of the Wild* and many other works. Close by, the two-room ROBERT SERVICE CABIN (8th Avenue and Hanson Street) reconstructs the life and work of the young bank teller who came to live in Whitehorse long after the gold rush had died, yet immortalized the Klondike with such books as *Songs of a Sourdough*, in which Dan McGrew got shot, and *The Trail of '98*, which he wrote in this log cabin. In both places, you can hear actors reading from the authors' verses and stories. And, as you wander along Dawson's broad thoroughfares, you might recall Service's description of "the midnight melancholy of the haunted streets."

The History of Whitehorse

Yukon's metropolis, Whitehorse suffers the sometime smog and traffic jams of many small but bustling cities down south. But, tucked between the mountains and lilting hills of the Yukon River valley at Mile 918 of the Alaska Highway, the capital city has a superb environment and advantageous suburban hiking and ski trails. This is a staging area for trips to such natural splendors as Kluane National Park and Reserve, only two hours west, where 19,550-foot Mount Logan stands second only to Alaska's Mount McKinley as the continent's highest. And Whitehorse, as a government town with a relatively stable population, has built an infrastructure of amenities that visitors appreciate, such as ethnically diverse restaurants and

To Alaska Hwy

DOWNTOWN
WHITEHORSE

N

250 m

1 MacBride Museum
2 Frantic Follies
3 Tourist Office
4 Old Log Church
5 S.S. *Klondike II*

a vital art and entertainment scene unexpected in a community nearly 100 miles north of Skagway, Alaska.

Boom and bust have been constants here, as in most northern centers, but Whitehorse seems to have risen above the cycles to endure with dignity. During the stampede of '98, it began as a temporary rest area after prospectors survived the two major obstacles of MILES CANYON and the Whitehorse Rapids on their way to the gold fields. In the canyon, the Yukon River's wickedest rapids capsized many boats, prompting the ingenious use of horse-drawn cars on a log tramway to circumvent the white water. (You can still see signs of the route.) Indeed, it was the manelike whitecaps that suggested the name Whitehorse. A hydro dam has since domesticated the canyon. The same company that created the WHITE PASS & YUKON ROUTE launched the British Yukon Navigation Company, which built and operated riverboats to Dawson until the 1950s. The stately s.s. *KLONDIKE II*, the very last working paddle wheeler to run the Yukon—powered by almost two logs on the boiler fire each minute—sits downtown at the foot of 2nd Avenue, landlocked but superbly restored as a national historic site.

With the railroad's arrival from Skagway in 1900, Whitehorse settled down as a community. Two decades later, after surfing the crests and troughs of a copper boom, the rail company began encouraging tourism and hunting using the city as a base, and in the mid-'30s set up an airline here for passengers, freight, and mail. World War II made the city a pivotal transportation center as North American military and civilian workers built a series of airfields across the north, the Alaska Highway, an oil pipeline from the Northwest Territories, and a refinery in Whitehorse.

By the time it became the territorial capital in 1953, the city was establishing itself as the hub of the highway system in the Canadian northwest: the Alcan to Fairbanks, which links with the Haines to the Panhandle, and the Klondike to Dawson, which links with the Dempster to Inuvik in the Northwest Territories. Other roads were constructed to service a boom in silver, copper, and lead-zinc mining in the Territory.

All of these arteries were soon throbbing with a fresh infusion of tourists, whose number has continued to increase. Some now ride the WP&Y from Skagway to Fraser, B.C., and then board a motor-coach to Whitehorse—or do the bus-and-train trip in reverse. However they arrive, visitors come here for the combination of history and handsome surroundings. On the western shore of the Yukon, the city hunkers under a 200-foot plateau while 4,900-foot Grey Mountain looms to the east.

You might book a GRAND CITY TOUR that winds through the newly landscaped streets of the downtown, whose architecture can still reflect the gold rush, and such distinctive suburbs as forested Porter Creek and hilly Riverdale; have a FLIGHT-SEEING TOUR of the magnificent area around the city; or take a RIVER CRUISE aboard the M.V. *SCHWATKA*. The OLD LOG CHURCH, 3rd Avenue and Elliott Street, is a century-old Anglican chapel, which chronicles, in artifacts and photographs, the church's extensive missionary work. MUSEUM TOURS include the Yukon Beringia Interpretive Centre (beside the Whitehorse International Airport), with fossils and artifacts of ancient peoples and recreations of woolly mammoths and scimitar cats that once roamed the north; and, next to it, the Transportation Museum, featuring relics of vehicles from the past and extraordinary model-railroad displays reflecting local rail history. Downtown at 1st Avenue and Wood Street, the sod-roofed Mac-Bride Museum, a treasure of Yukon memorabilia, has a group of log cabins, one of them a dwelling once occupied by the real-life inspiration of Robert Service's *The Cremation of Sam McGee*—whose fiery end came at a scenic spot not far from Whitehorse, "on the marge of LAKE LABARGE" (his spelling of Laberge).

An exciting destination outside the city offered in some cruise packages is the YUKON GAME FARM AND WILDLIFE PRESERVE. Danny Nowlan and his German wife, Uli, began stocking the 750-acre game and bird sanctuary three decades ago to protect and display Dall sheep, mountain goat, moose, mule deer, elk, woodland caribou, wood bison, and the far-northern musk oxen. Of the squat but powerful musk oxen, several of whom were born on the farm, Uli Nowlan says, "Their sense of play is to knock over trees. That's why we figure there are no trees in the Arctic."

A different kind of wildlife is on show back in town. FRANTIC FOLLIES, in the Westmark Whitehorse Hotel at 2nd Avenue and Wood Street, is a high-stepping vaudeville revue with a Gay '90s theme that has been running for more than two decades. There's magic, can-can dancing, and—inevitably, in a city that trades so well on its history—the whooping-it-up wit of Robert Service.

THE CANADIAN ROCKIES

Not far out of Calgary, Alberta, this morning, the sun was creeping above the fat shredded-wheat rolls in the fields and the beige-and-blonde cattle ruminating along the cliffs of the Bow River. "A deer! Wildlife!" somebody shouted. A little doe munched in the crease of a slope. Later a pair of large-antlered elk loped across a track paralleling ours. We were rollicking along the foothills in an air-conditioned observation car of the Rocky Mountaineer—the tourist train service that slices through the portentous peaks of southern Alberta and British Columbia and has become a popular option for cruise-ship passengers anxious to explore the grandeur of the Canadian Rockies. We were about to step down the spiral staircase to the rose-dotted dining car to breakfast on eggs Benedict, smoked salmon, and Alberta steak. There were about seventy of us in a deluxe dome car, relaxing in plush lounge chairs as we sipped on champagne and orange juice, gazed out the wall-and-ceiling windows, and listened to the occasional commentary from attendants in snazzy green vests and white shirts who patrolled the aisles, pampering us.

All at once, the Rockies reared up in the morning haze. The train was soon amid the ramparts and sculpted turrets that lent it their name. After a brief stop in the resort town of Banff to pick up the bulk of the passengers, some of us strolled to the back of the car to stand outdoors in the vestibule, open on three sides to the sweet air. "You can't do this on any other train in Canada," Roger, a former railroad employee on a sentimental journey, assured us. It was here, where we could reach out and almost touch the evergreen giants and mountain flanks, that the feeling of a rail adventure loomed largest. But outside or in, this was an intimate encounter with nature. We watched for grizzlies and mountain goats and spotted osprey families in their grand nests atop old telegraph poles—and the raven that, hearing the train whistle, routinely flies alongside the cars to the locomotive where one engineer will hold out a large cookie for the bird to snaffle up. The tight curves, bridges spanning turbulent rivers, tracks descending half a mile of grade, twisting tunnels (one twenty minutes long), all reminded us just how remarkable an exploit was the running of the original rail lines through this sometimes malevolent, always enthralling land.

This is the only all-daylight rail journey through the western mountains. The train makes an overnight stop at the halfway point in KAMLOOPS, a former fur-trading center, now the largest city in the British Columbia Interior (population 78,000), at the convergence of the North and South Thompson Rivers. We enjoyed a bountiful buffet dinner and an entertainingly historical music revue before bedding down in a hotel. Next morning, linking with rail coaches from Jasper, another grand Rockies resort, we returned to our dome car to journey through the surrealistic sagebrush- and pine-studded hills. A civilized lunch on white linen—wine, beer, and good lamb, beef striploin, salmon fillet, or cold Pacific seafood plate. Then we were between the Cascades and the Coast Mountains above roiling Hells Gate Canyon and, before long, dropping down into the Fraser River valley to Vancouver, where we pulled in on schedule in the late afternoon. A middle-aged woman, well-traveled, told us, "It was more than I thought it would be. There's nothing between you and nature. I got every dime's worth."

The North American Travel Journalists Association has called the Rocky Mountaineer the Best International Attraction, but a RAIL TOUR is only one way to experience the grandeur of these peaks and the sheer prettiness of the resorts among them. You can also take a MOTORCOACH EXCURSION that lets you explore the mountain communities on stopovers.

To most Canadians, CALGARY (population 845,000) is best-known as the nation's oil capital, the sophisticated business center of the province of Alberta's enormous reserves of petroleum, which satisfy much of North America's energy requirements. But to the rest of the world this is Stampede City, where every summer otherwise respectable residents take on the trappings of the Old West and kick up their heels while real cowhands and world rodeo champions compete at the Calgary Stampede. Even if you're not there for the Greatest Outdoor Show on Earth in early July, you'll see signs of the western influence in the offerings of shops and restaurants and in attractions such as the astonishing Glenbow Museum, Heritage Park Historical Village, and Fort Calgary. The latter is a replica of the fort that gave birth to the city in 1875 when the North West Mounted Police, the forerunner of the scarlet-garbed Mounties, put up a command post at the meeting of the Bow and Elbow Rivers to do battle with American whiskey traders selling their hooch to the Blackfoot Natives.

But if you're here for the wonders of the natural world, rather than rodeos and history, your tour bus or rail car will transport you to the three splendid resorts amid the Rockies. BANFF (population 8,500) is the hub of Canada's first and most popular national park, which bears the same name as the town. When laborers were punching the original Canadian Pacific Railway through the mountains to Vancouver, they took to bathing in local sulfur hot springs. In 1885, the Canadian government designated a small area around the springs as a reserve and two years later created the 260-square-mile Rocky Mountains Park. Today Banff National Park is ten times that size, a trove of lofty peaks; forests of pine, spruce, and fir; pure lakes and tall waterfalls; Canada's largest system of caves; the thirty or more glaciers of the Columbia Icefield—and a cornucopia of wildlife, from black and grizzly bears to moose, elk, and bighorn sheep. About 700 miles of hiking trails lead from the townsite, and alpine skiing runs and cross-country trails abound in the park and surrounding area. Routine stops for visitors include Bow Falls, Tunnel Mountain, and a gondola ride to the top of Sulphur Mountain, where there are several places to soak in the soothing, sulfurous waters of the hot springs that originally attracted tourists here.

From Sulphur's heights, you can see LAKE LOUISE, a 36-mile drive north of Banff along one of the world's grandest scenic routes, the 143-mile Icefields Parkway. And the lake itself is a diadem that must rank among the world's most gem-like mountain lakes, with its setting of indigo mountains and glistening snowfields reflected in the impossibly lovely glacial waters. The lake was created when the Victoria Glacier retreated, leaving an end moraine that trapped the meltwater from the shrinking ice. Today, perched atop the enormous moraine is the exquisite Chateau Lake Louise, one of the chain of castlelike hotels the Canadian Pacific Railway promoters built to lure tourists west in the late nineteenth century.

Farther north, adjoining Banff National Park at the Columbia Icefield, Jasper National Park is anchored by the community of JASPER (population 4,700), on the main Canadian National Railway line and the Yellowhead Highway. The park, which spreads northwest along the Continental Divide for 4,200 square miles, is the largest of four national parks and three British Columbia provincial parks that form a UNESCO World Heritage Site. It was established in 1907 to protect this historic region, which fur traders exploited and explorers crossed in their search for a route to the west coast. Here, there are mountains soaring to more than 11,000 feet; glacier-carved U-shaped valleys, alpine meadows, and subalpine forests; mighty rivers with names such as Sunwapta and Athabasca, inspired by the Native peoples who might have been on this land for ten centuries or more; and an abundance of wild critters equal to Banff's—among them big bears, mountain goats, and golden eagles.

After leaving Jasper, driving along the Yellowhead, you'll pass Mount Robson, the highest peak in the Canadian Rockies at 12,972 feet. Later on your trip southward through British Columbia you pass through the jaw-dropping Fraser Canyon, a jungle of cliffs that contain one of the wickedest rivers on the continent, the Fraser. But by the time the river reaches Hope, it has calmed down and flows peacefully through the Fraser Valley for the next 100 miles en route to your destination of Vancouver—where cruise ships to Alaska await.

INDEX